Praise For
Hand. Shadow. Roc

"*Hand, Shadow, Rod.* is a memoir that manages to be almost entirely "un-self-centered"—much like the author herself. Monica Leo is an artist who has always seen the value of collaboration, and in telling the story of her Eulenspiegel Puppet Theatre (still going strong some fifty years on). We learn as much about the people she worked with and for as we do about her. Anyone who loves puppets, whether from behind the booth or from out in the audience, will delight in the account of this plucky little troupe from the American Heartland. But there is so much more to it than that. This is an immigrant story, a story of love and loss, of deep friendships and grit and always finding ways to move forward and find the good in life. I've known Monica for fifty years. To my wife and me, she has been a colleague, a presenter, a collaborator, and a dear friend, but I learned new things about her in every single chapter, not least of which is that she is also a very fine writer. In *Hand. Shadow. Rod.* She has created a chronicle that will have an honored place on my bookshelf next to the finest examples of puppet memoir Forman Brown's *Punch's Progress* and Sergei Obraztsov's *My Profession*."

—Andrew Periale, editor of *Puppetry International* magazine

"To nurture and sustain Eulenspiegel Puppet Theatre for nearly fifty years there needs to be creativity, resilience, and optimism. Monica Leo has these qualities and more. This book is a unique and engaging chronicle of the twists and turns of running a puppet company and a puppet theatre, all intertwined with Leo's journey as a person and an artist and portraits of the many collaborators, partners, and friends she joyously worked with along the way."

—Steve Abrams, *Puppetry Journal*

"In *Hand, Shadow, Rod: The Story of Eulenspiegel Puppet Theatre*, Monica Leo shares with readers the richness of her long creative life; from her earliest days listening to her immigrant father's tales of his imaginary friend, to her travels with her puppet partner, Terry Jean Brietbach, and later, a cast of other puppeteers and musicians. This delightful memoir is packed with historical details, charming anecdotes, fascinating characters, and poignant memories. A perfect read for puppet fans, Iowa history buffs, artists, and those who love a good story."

—Michelle Edwards, artist and Charlotte Zolotow Award-winning author of *Me And The Boss*

"What a thrill to see Monica Leo's story *Hand, Shadow, Rod* between the covers of this memoir! Like one of the characters in her fairy tales, Leo takes the reader on an enchanting world tour of Eulenspiegel Puppet Theatre Company performances. With beautifully written prose and masterfully crafted block prints, Leo is the trickster in this narrative. A highly recognized puppeteer, partner, teacher, and mentor, Leo models not only artistry but entrepreneurship. You will delight in her story, how she founded her troupe and has kept it flourishing for fifty years. A book every aspiring artist should read."

—Mary Swander, author of *Squatters on Red Earth*

Hand, Shadow, Rod.

The Story of Eulenspiegel Puppet Theatre

Monica Leo

with Head Puppet Alfred Schulz

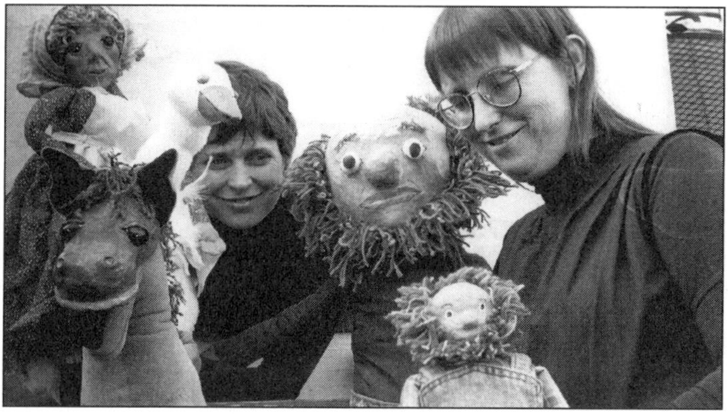

ice cube press, llc
north liberty ia 52317 usa

Hand, Shadow, Rod. — The Story of Eulenspiegel Puppet Theatre

Isbn 9781948509466

Library of Congress Control Number: 2023944870

Ice Cube Press, LLC (Est. 1991)
1180 Hauer Drive North Liberty, Iowa 52317
www.icecubepress.com steve@icecubepress.com

The paper used in this publication meets the minimum requirements of the American National Standard for Information Sciences—Permanence of Paper for Printed Library Materials, ANSI Z39.48-1992.

Made with recycled paper.

Manufactured in Canada.

All illustrations and artwork by Monica Leo.

Page 27: Drawn by a 2nd grader somewhere in Iowa, ca 1978.

Cover & author photos are all by Michael Kreiser.

Photo on title page: Monica and Teri Jean with a selection of puppets (including Schulz) from different shows-early 1990s.

Lovingly dedicated to my partners now on the other side:

John Jenks

Teri Jean Breitbach

Eli Portugal

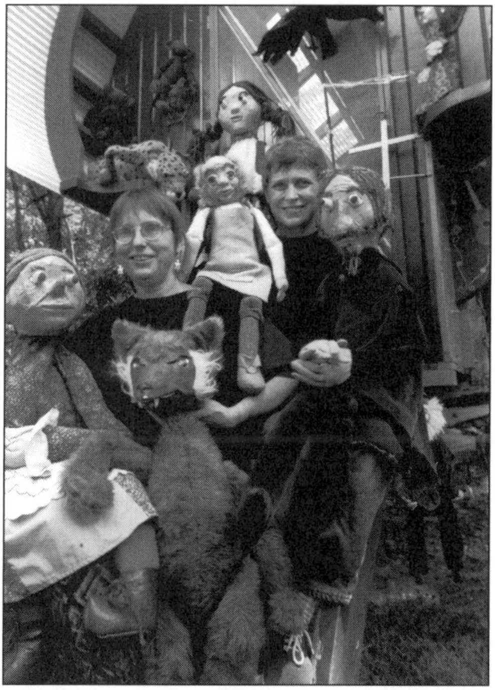

Monica and Teri Jean with a selection of puppets from different shows-early 1990s.

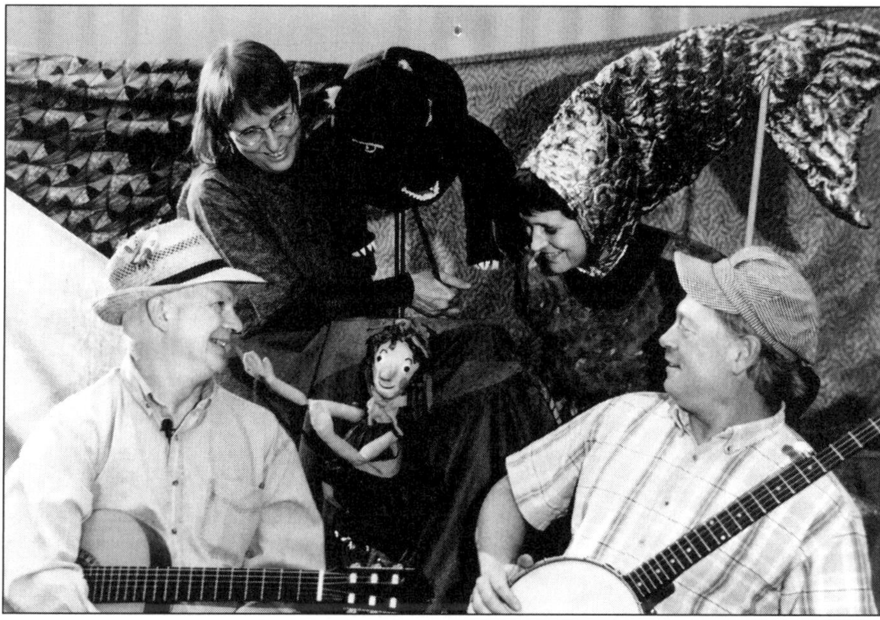

Sal Fink the Mississippi Screamer, 2000, Monica and Teri Jean with musicians Ron Hillis and Guy Drollinger.

Contents:

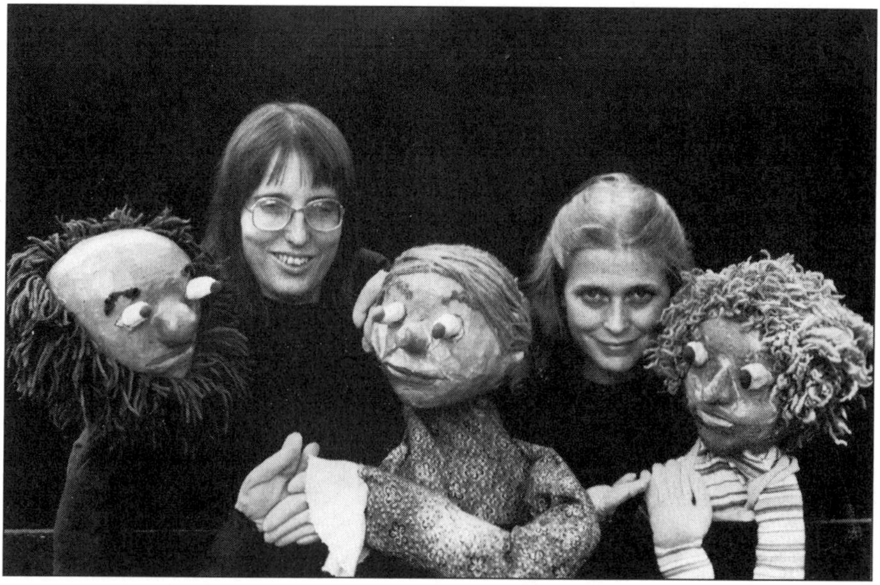

Monica and Teri Jean with puppets Schulz, Moms, and Michael, ca 1980.

Prologue

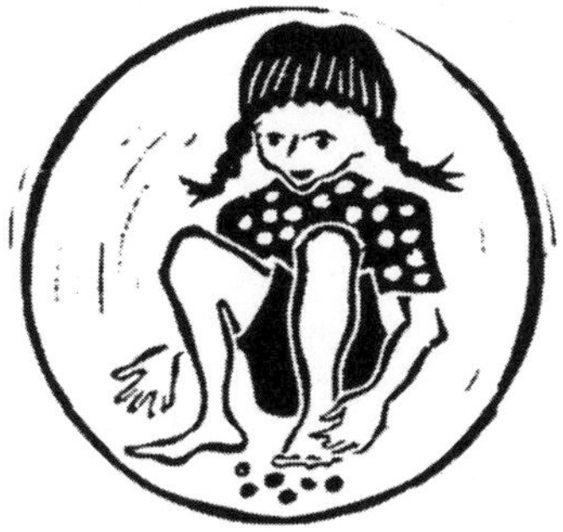

I opened the door to Vati's—Daddy's—empty study and tiptoed inside. The room was bathed in golden light from the ocher curtains covering the large window. The walls were lined with ceiling-height bookshelves. Vati's large, dark brown, wooden desk stood in the middle of the room. I approached the desk.

I was fascinated by a round box, small and ornately painted, on his desk. I stretched as tall as my five-year-old body would allow and reached for the box. What could be special enough to belong in this magical receptacle?

I lifted the lid and looked at the contents in confusion. A handful of dirt, no different from the dirt in Mutti's—Mommy's—garden. I sifted it through my fingers, feeling its grainy texture. I held it to my nose and breathed in, absorbing the earthy aroma. Oh no! I dropped it! All over the carpet! The door opened, and Vati stepped in.

"Oh, Liebchen! That soil is from my garden in Germany!"

Mutti entered briskly, wielding the vacuum cleaner. Vati looked devastated as the hose sucked up his last tangible connection to his cherished garden.

He didn't leave his beloved homeland willingly. The Gestapo arrested him during Kristallnacht and sent him to Buchenwald Concentration Camp, perhaps for his Jewish bloodlines or perhaps for his occupation as a pastor in the Confessional Church that opposed Hitler. Vati was a sizable man, bald on top with a curly black fringe of hair, a comfortable paunch, and a twinkle in his blue eyes that showed even through his coke-bottle thick glasses.

At Gestapo headquarters, a Storm Trooper searched his pockets. He took his wallet, keys, and watch, but let him keep his glasses and, surprisingly, his little leather-bound Bible. Vati considered this "an exceptional act of clemency; an example of how some spark of life can remain in a broken conscience," as he wrote in his journal.

He also let him keep Paulfen. He didn't have the imagination to see him. Paulfen was Vati's imaginary friend who lived in his jacket pocket and weighed in on family issues. He made the important announcements in our family.

Good news—

"Children! Listen! We're going on a trip! To the lake!"

And bad news—

"Oh, children. Vati tells me the report cards weren't so good this time."

We always knew when Paulfen was about to speak by the goofy expression on Vati's face and the silly voice that emerged.

I'm pretty sure that Paulfen was born in 1931 to keep Vati's baby daughter, Anne—my big sister—company after her mother died in childbirth. Anne has often told me how she regarded Paulfen as a brother and how his imaginary existence comforted her during those troubled times in her home and in her country.

Paulfen was five years old.

"Children, Paulfen has decided that five is the perfect age! He has no plans to grow older."

Mutti was a little spooked by Paulfen. She was a practical sort—both feet on the floor—and she wasn't sure she liked the idea of her husband having an imaginary friend. She was afraid the church members would find out and think that Vati was unhinged.

"Paul, what will the parishioners think? It's time to stop this foolishness!"

"But how will they know?"

"You know they'll find out. Really, Liebchen, is this so important?"

"Very well, Eva. If it means that much to you, I will send Paulfen to Quaker Boarding School."

"Mutti, how come Christopher and I go to Bryant School but Paulfen goes to Quaker boarding school?"

"Hmmpf!" She realized she'd lost the battle for our hearts and she may as well make her peace with Paulfen. Paulfen started coming home every weekend and of course for holidays.

I'm sure the imagination that led Vati to create Paulfen also helped him survive the concentration camp without bitterness and with his optimism intact. He was released several months later with an order to settle his affairs and leave Germany in a month.

In 1958, a month before Vati died, we celebrated Paulfen's 27th fifth birthday and Vati's 65th birthday. I missed Paulfen when he died, right along with Vati, when I was 13 years old.

Mutti was a passionate artist, the first woman to be accepted into the German Metalworkers' Guild as a Master Craftsman. She was tiny—"little but oh my," as Vati used to say—but she had a personality to match the biceps she had gained from hammering metal. She had finely chiseled features. Her salt-and-pepper hair had turned snow white by the time I finished high school, and she set it off with a wardrobe of colorful scarves she wore as headbands. She usually wore shades of aqua and blue.

She had gained a reputation for creating stark, stunning, beautifully hammered metal art for churches. She made Communion services, baptismal fonts, crucifixes, and altars embellished with reliefs of scenes from the Bible. In my travels in Germany, I occasionally see something that I immediately recognize as her work, though many of the churches she supplied were bombed out during World War Two.

When she and Vati fled the Nazis, shortly before the war started, she had to leave her tools behind. There was no way she could leave her artistry behind. She turned to drawing and water coloring the scenes around her: landscapes, our home and animals, and portraits of us. Even when there was little money, she kept me supplied with sketchbooks, good pencils, and watercolors. When I reached puberty, I lost my childish ability to simply draw imaginary scenes, but not my desire to draw.

"Mutti, what can I draw?"

"Draw your hands and feet. It will be good practice."

"My hands and feet?"

"And your face! Look in the mirror! You always have a model by your side!"

She was right. Those drawings were the best possible way to build my observational skills.

When Vati died, Mutti fell apart. She got up every morning and went to work, supporting us with the greatest efficiency, but her spirit was gone. She spent her free time weeping.

My brother and I had always been proud of her strength. We'd bring the neighbor kids in and say, "Mutti, roll up your sleeves and show off your muscles!" Mutti would flex obligingly. She'd never been afraid of work of any kind, but Vati's death, leaving her alone in this strange land with her American children, found her unprepared.

And then one day a package arrived—from Germany. Her metal sculpting tools! One of her nieces had squirreled them away when Mutti fled Germany and had forgotten about them. Hammers, chisels, saws, a drill, and more. It gave her an idea! Vati's grave was unmarked. Mutti had been too overwhelmed to even think about a grave marker. But now she got to work. She built a workbench in our basement. She went to the quarry and selected a large chunk of Mississippi River limestone. She went to the roofing supply store and bought a sheet of copper. She bought a blowtorch that weighed more than she did to soften the metal. Now, when I came home from school, the sound of hammering and the smell of the flaming torch replaced the sound of weeping.

She made a beautiful copper relief of a risen Christ and had it embedded into the limestone. Vati had his grave marker and Mutti had a new life.

She inspired me to discover my medium, and I made my first puppet, a papier mâché witch. We were on our way!

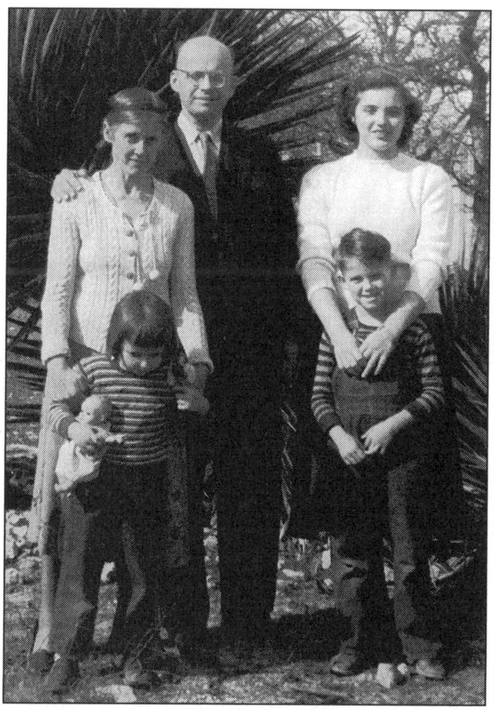

Leo family: Vati, Mutti, Anne, Christopher, Monica, 1949.

1. School Days

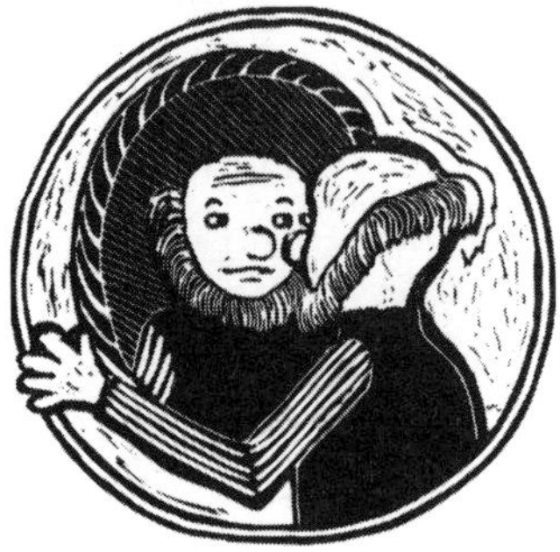

The old red pickup truck rolled through Mason City and Clear Lake, past Garner and Britt. I drove as Teri Jean studied the map, flicking cigarette ashes out of the window, blond hair flying in the breeze. It was 1978, long before cell phones or GPS. In the truck bed, under the metal topper, rode Schulz and his gang of near life-size hand-and-rod puppets with papier mâché heads and protruding, soulful, movable eyes. Schulz was the head puppet. He called the shots. He wore a purple shirt, tan pants, and brown boots and sported a red beard with a bald pate. He'd started life as a king, but he soon shed his crown and became a sort of "every-puppet", doling out sage advice to the other puppets and even to us, his human manipulators. He and his pals shared the space with the stage, four plywood panels, each designed to look like a house, with a pitched roof silhouette and a window cut-out.

"Turn left!" The truck screeched around the corner and headed into Corwith, the site of our first-ever school residency. A couple of weeks earlier Teri Jean and I had been sitting at the round table in the kitchen, nursing our coffee, when we got a call from the Iowa Arts Council. Would we like to try doing some 5-day school residencies through the newly minted Artists in the Schools program? Of course we would!

And here we were, driving past the bank, the café, the hardware store, and pulling into the elementary school parking lot. Our tiny 2nd-grade teacher-sponsor was there to meet us and help us unload our pick-up truck. All five feet of her picked up a six-foot wooden panel and started across the parking lot. She was accosted by a strong wind and looked as if she was about to take to the sky like Mary Poppins.

We all conquered the wind and set up in the gym under the basketball hoop. The kids filed in grade by grade, the kindergartners following their teacher like baby ducks, sitting "criss-cross applesauce" on the floor in the front row. The 6th graders sat in the back. Schulz's big moment was about to start:

Schulz here: Whoa, look at all those kids! Boy, I hope they like me! But why wouldn't they? Don't worry, Schulz, just act out the story, Monkeys and Owls! I get to play a baker, and I have to bake a 30-layer cake with a miniature castle and a waterfall on top, made out of frosting. But I feel awful because I just ate six—count 'em—six chickens, and I need a nap! Well, the story goes on and I get Till Eulenspiegel to do the work for me. Only, instead of baking the cake, he bakes monkeys and owls! Don't ask me how he got that mixed up, but it was hilarious, and the kids thought so, too. WHEW!

After the show, we headed into the classrooms, one by one, and started making puppets with the kids. We began to develop ideas, schedules, and teaching techniques that would stand us in good stead for the next twenty years. After that first trip to northern Iowa, the word got out, and soon we were doing an average of two 5-day residencies a month, sometimes more, in all of Iowa's ninety-nine counties. We stayed with families, which meant we were "on" all day and all evening. Our host family one week had kids who were super excited to have the guest puppeteers staying with them. It was getting to be a little much.

"Hey, how about this?" I said to Teri Jean. "We tell them we need to get into school in the evening so we can work on a new show."

"But we're not working on a new show, are we?"

"So??"

"Oh! I'll bring my Jane Fonda tape!"

Teri Jean figured out how the VCR in the school library worked and, before we knew it, we were doing aerobics with Jane and her crew. We loved the conviviality of this tape. It showed Jane with her class, which included her mother-in-law, Betty, a few women of assorted ages, and one man, Frank. We felt like class members, greeting the group and exercising right along with them.

"Hi, Jane!"

"Hi, Betty!"

"Hi, Frank!"

"Hi, Teri Jean!"

"Hi, Monica!"

And away we went! One-two-three-four-again! One-two-three-four-again! And again, in the next town. And the next town. Sometimes we actually worked on a new show, but only after we'd worked out with Jane!

A residency in the mid-'80s took us to Cascade, a little town near our hometown, Dubuque. I stayed with my mom, Teri Jean stayed with her sister, and we commuted to Cascade to work with Mrs. Smits, a gold star first-grade teacher. She had 31 students, mostly "slow learners." We started by passing out sheets of newspaper and taping strips of masking tape to their desks.

"The newspaper is your puppet's brains. Look at the brains and see what your puppet is thinking about today. Now crumple the brains, fitting them over your finger. Your finger is the brain stem."

Furious crumpling ensued.

"Take your longest strip of tape and wrap it around the brains. Wrap the other pieces over the top and under the bottom and you have your puppet's skull!"

Next, we passed out the clay-like papier mâché and watched as 31 heads bowed over desks and worked intently forming the features of their chosen characters, then carefully brought them to the front of the room and lined them up to dry. The next day, after the puppet heads had dried, we passed out paints and watched the explosion of six-year-old joy. Our main problem was making sure they stopped painting!

Next came bodies and hair. This was a little more tedious and involved standing in line at the hot glue gun, which had to be operated by an adult. To make the waiting easier, Teri Jean assigned the kids to bring a silly joke, and we regaled each other while the puppets got their outfits and hair-dos. *Why was 6 afraid of 7? Because 7 8 9! What did the nose say to the finger? Quit picking on me! What do elves learn in school? The elf-abet!* Gales of laughter!

Sonny was a sweet little boy with a big smile and no self-control. He loved the hand puppet he made, especially when he realized its hands—his fingers—could be used as pinchers. Little girls all over the room squealed as Sonny's puppet pinched them. Mrs. Smits brought order with a withering glare. She had eyes like a fly: in the back of her head and on all sides.

After the puppets were done, we taught them some movements: walking, running, going up and down imaginary stairs, sleeping, sneezing, what have you. We were getting them ready to perform for the second graders, whom Mrs. Smits had invited to watch. There was a problem. The kids had their movements down, but they simply didn't comprehend that they had to hold their puppets up over the curtain if anyone was to see the clever movements. No amount of "hold your puppet up!" sunk in. Teri Jean had an idea. "OK, kids, I'm going to show you some more moves! Sit down in front of the curtain!" She stepped behind the curtain and held her puppet low.

"Look! Somersaults! What do you think of that?"

"We can't see anything."

"Why not?" You could almost hear the penny drop.

"You're not holding your puppet up!"

Whew! Just in time. The second graders arrived, and Mrs. Smits's first graders did just fine!

Hey, Schulz here again; my turn to talk! Remember the first time we had breakfast in a café? I think it was the café in Wesley. We thought we could just waltz in there and eat breakfast like anybody else. Ha! Every head in the place turned when we walked in. You could hear 'em thinking, what are those gals and that puppet doing in OUR cafe! Sure enough, not a single gal anywhere! A whole row of old farts all dressed in overalls, seed caps, and shitkickers. We sat down, ordered our breakfast, and little by little, the good ol' boys started talking again. Don't know why they were so worried about us hearing. It was mostly weather talk and the like! Too much rain, not enough rain, is it gonna freeze tonight, can I get into the fields, no good help, kids today, on and on. Boy, those eggs and hash browns were tasty, though! You could tell by the taste and the color of the yolks…those eggs came from backyard chickens!

In the early years, we spent many weeks in a classic little river town on the Mississippi. During one of these weeks, we performed in ten schools, two each day. Our show was *The World's Greatest Fisherman,* a Norwegian folktale about a placid fisherman and a trickster fox. The fox sees that the fisherman has a string of fish in his wagon. He decides to play dead, hoping the fisherman will pick him up and throw him in the wagon for his fur pelt. He does, and hilarity erupts.

Teri Jean played the part of the fox in an overhead mask and vest, which she donned in the teachers' lounge, leaving the black tunic she usually wore over black tights and leotard in the lounge. The fox entered through the audience. In the end, the fox exited through the audience to the teachers' lounge, where Teri Jean removed her fox costume, put on her tunic, and came back to the stage.

I worked the fisherman—played by Schulz—and wore my tunic over tights and leotard during the whole show. It was Friday morning, the last day and the second last show of the week. The kindergarten teacher walked in, followed by her charges who sat on the gym floor, forming the first row.

"These two shouldn't be sitting together," she told me with a hint of malicious glee as she seated them next to each other. The rest of the audience came in, the principal introduced us, and the fox came in through the back of the audience, startling and delighting the kids. When the fox reached the front row, the two little rascals who should have been separated, let loose. One of them stood up, reached through the fox's open mouth, and poked Teri Jean in the face. The other grabbed her legs. The teacher sat impassively by with a vindictive little smile on her face. This continued. Other kids joined in the harassment. Teri Jean tried to stay out of their way and finally resorted to "accidentally" stepping on a finger or two. It was all we could do to get through the story. As soon as it was over, Teri Jean came backstage, ripped off the fox costume, and hissed.

"Gimme your tunic!"

Obediently, I took off the tunic and handed it to her. She put it on, stalked out, and faced the audience.

"You kids should be ashamed of yourselves!" she yelled. "Harassing someone who's just trying to put on a good show for you! Who taught you to behave like that? Your parents would be horrified! And you teachers," she screamed, pointing straight at the offending teacher. "Shame on you! What kind of example are you setting for your kids?" Dead silence in the audience!

She marched through the audience to the teachers' lounge, wearing my tunic and leaving me in my tights and leotard, fat rolls—real and imagined—bulging out. I couldn't show myself like that, but I couldn't just do nothing!

That's when I saved the day! I poked my head through the stage window and talked to the kids. "Hey, kids, I think Teri Jean's feelings are kind of hurt. Why don't we apologize? OK now, all together, "We're sorry Teri Jean!"

"That was genius, Schulz!"

It worked. 300 voices chanted, "We're sorry, Teri Jean!" Teri Jean heard, came back, graciously accepted the apology, and returned my tunic. Whew!

Most of our residencies were in grade schools, but we did summer camps, halfway houses, facilities for the developmentally delayed, county homes, senior centers, and even high schools, especially of the alternative variety.

For a few years in the 1980s, The Iowa Arts Council sponsored residencies in county homes, care facilities for less affluent and disabled people. These homes were always in the country with sizable grounds. At one time they all had large gardens and livestock, and the residents had been responsible for their care. The homes were usually large, brick, three-story houses. Each resident had a bedroom; living and dining areas were shared. Their quality varied, to say the least.

We were asked to do a residency at one of the better homes, the Cedar County Home outside of Tipton, Iowa. We agreed to seven meetings, twice a week for three and a half weeks. We made hand puppets and built a wooden puppet stage in their wood shop.

Everyone sat around the large dining room table to work on the puppet heads. They were soft-sculpted out of discarded nylon stockings. The toes were stuffed with pillow stuffing to form the shape of the head. Then features were pinched off and secured with stitches to form noses, lips, eyelids, and ears.

Ruby, a middle-aged woman with dishwater blonde hair, had obsessive-compulsive disorder and had trouble stopping.

"Ruby," I said. "Your puppet's nose is long enough! Time to stop and move on to a different feature."

Ruby couldn't stop, and soon the nose went over the top of the head and down the back.

Eldon loved painting, but before he could paint, the stage had to be built. He took us to the wood shop and we breathed deep, relishing the aroma of freshly sawed wood. He and another resident were building a classic hand puppet stage. When they finished, they put it out in the gravel driveway to paint, and Eldon chose a color and found a paintbrush. We didn't think it was necessary to supervise him; what could go wrong with such a simple task?

"Eldon!" said Teri Jean, checking on him. "Pick up your brush! Don't drag it in the gravel!!"

Too late! Every brush stroke started at the top of the stage, made its way down, and ended up collecting gravel which was then deposited on the stage with the next brushstroke. When Eldon had finished, we had a stage with a unique textured surface!

Then it was time to practice working the puppets and to rehearse the show. Some of the residents designed a program and invitations, which were sent to the neighbors and to a Tipton preschool.

The big day arrived, the last day of our residency. Excitement ran high as the audience assembled. I narrated as the residents worked the puppets and Teri Jean supervised the backstage, making sure everyone had what they needed to pull off a good show. The neighbors and the preschoolers sat enthralled and rewarded the performers with loud applause. I think we felt at least as good as our puppeteers did!

One summer we spent a week in western Iowa at a halfway house for teen girls. My 15-year-old niece, Deborah, came along to help and serve as a bridge to the other teens.

"Puppets! Puppets are for babies!" This was going to take some convincing! But crafts are a universal language, and once the girls got their hands dirty making puppet heads, everything came into focus.

We had a plan. We were making characters for a favorite Grimm's fairy tale, *The Fisherman and His Wife*. At the end of the week, we would perform the show. You've heard it: a poor fisherman catches a magic fish who grants wishes. His greedy wife keeps wishing for more and more, including a castle and a cathedral, but when she wishes to rule the universe, he puts them back in the shack they started in. We liked the story because it was about greed and lust for power and what happens when you let those desires take control of your life. We also liked it for the practical reason that there were lots of things to make. Since the wife changes clothes every time a wish is granted, four different girls made puppets of this character, each in a different, fancier outfit: one in rags, one in a pretty dress, one in a robe and crown, and one dressed as the Pope! We made all of the different dwellings as well as a fancy, whimsical fish.

There was one problem: the story as told by the Grimm Brothers presents the wife as a nasty shrew who orders her husband around. To me, that was incidental, not really what the story was about, but Deborah reported that the girls were outraged!

"You guys have been talking to them about girl power and how they can do anything, and the role model you give them is a bullying shrew!"

Hmmm. We hadn't thought of it that way! It was an easy fix: we had the husband and wife in cahoots with each other and made it into an equal opportunity greed-and-lust-for-power tale.

That story has followed me all of my life. I recently created yet another version of it and, as I wrote the equal opportunity script, I thought about those long-ago girls who are, I suppose, middle-aged women by now. I wonder how their lives turned out. Did they outgrow their problems and become middle-class citizens? Mothers, perhaps, of girls like them? I wonder if they ever think about their puppets.

2. Beginnings

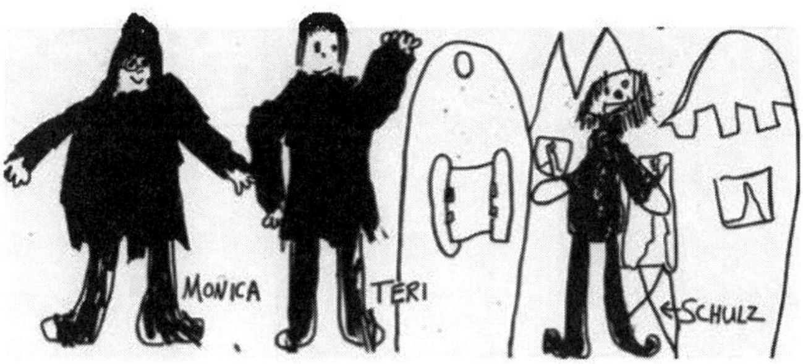

By the time I started performing, I had already built quite a business selling puppets and dolls at art fairs and Renaissance Faires. In 1972 toymaker friends had taken my seven-year-old son, Little John, and me to our first Renaissance Faire. We both loved the fantasy, the costumes, the music and strolling performers, and the after-hours campfires. We were hooked and added another fair. Soon we were making 600-mile round trips, to the Chicago area and the Twin Cities, twelve weekends during each summer.

Spring three years later, I was preparing for a busy summer when John brought a co-worker—a young woman who had been helping out on his construction site—home for dinner. Average height with a quick, wiry body, a quick wit, and a quicker tongue, her eyes were sparkly blue, her hair wavy blonde. It turned out to be Teri Jean Breitbach! She described the invitation:

"Hey, Breitbach, you wanna come home and meet the old lady?" asked John.

"Someone's *married* to you? This I gotta see!"

And so, my life partner introduced me to my artistic partner, and Teri

Jean became a permanent fixture, first as an assistant puppet maker and soon after as a puppeteer. She blamed my meatloaf; she was convinced I had laced it with something that mesmerized her!

The puppet troupe started by accident. I'd studied art and saw myself as a toymaker—making puppets and dolls—not a puppeteer. Puppets were a large part of my childhood.

Mutti had a network of German artist friends. From one of them, she ordered a set of papier mâché puppets: a traditional German Kasperle, the equivalent of the British/American Punch, and his crew—his wife Gretel, his crabby mother-in-law, his friend Seppel, a devil, a skeleton, and a butler. The butler, dressed in black with a white collar, became a pastor in our family, and Vati put on little plays for us that featured dialogues between the devil and the pastor.

I was one of those oddball girls who stayed in Girl Scouts all the way through high school. Our leader had the bright idea of having us hire out to cater birthday parties, each with a theme.

Mutti poo-pooed the idea: "Who would pay somebody else to put on a birthday party?" she asked with German can-do contempt.

The joke was on her. Our troop's party business was a raging success. We sent letters to all of the local women's clubs—numerous in the 1950s and early 60s—soliciting business. We promised to provide everything from the cake to the party favors to the games and entertainment. We were amazed by the trepidation! Mothers were terrified of planning and hosting birthday parties, and they loved the idea of turning the chore over to us. My friend and I took charge of the puppet show party. Story ideas were easy. We had the stock characters we needed for a plethora of fairy tales, and if we didn't, I simply made new puppets. Rehearsals? Nope! We jumped straight from idea to performance. My friend was in charge of baking the birthday cake, and I made sure we had everything we needed for the show. I guess that planted the seed.

When it came time to go to college, I followed my big brother Chris to

Wartburg, a small liberal arts college connected to the Lutheran Church. I declared a history major, but I spent more time in the art building, even though I wasn't taking art, than I did on history. The college was well known for its music department, but visual arts were granted only a single studio and one part-time instructor. Miss Green was a fussy little middle-aged lady who knew little or nothing about the equipment in her domain. She found me useful.

"Monica, do you know what this is for? I found it in one of the cupboards."

"That's a silk screen frame, Miss Green. Do you want me to show you how to use it?"

"Please do!"

"Good! I've been wanting to make a silkscreen!"

One day my advisor, Dr. Ottersberg, the head of the History Department, called me into his office.

"Monica, every time I see you, you're either going into or coming out of the art building. I saw the illustrations you made for the campus literary magazine. They were quite good. Might I ask you why you're majoring in history?"

"Well, I'm interested in history."

"Actions speak louder than words. Have you considered majoring in art?"

"But Wartburg doesn't offer an art major."

"I guess you'll have to transfer, won't you?"

I asked Mutti what she would think if I went to art school in California.

"California! Never! That's much too far away!"

"How about Germany?" We'd recently made a trip there and I had bonded with a group of cousins my age.

To Mutti, Germany felt much closer than California.

I researched art academies and found one in Düsseldorf, the home of my favorite cousins. I assembled a portfolio of drawings and prints I'd made and sent it off to the State Art Academy. I was accepted! They assigned me to the class of Joseph Beuys, a famous avant-garde conceptual artist. I had never heard of him. I had never heard of conceptual art. I have no idea how I landed in his class, but I suspect he missed the faculty meeting at which they decided to accept me.

"We have an applicant from the U.S. I don't want to reject her."

"I don't have room in my class."

"I don't want her in my class."

"Let's give her to Beuys. He's not here."

My first day: I entered the formidable fortress-like 18th-century building and made my way down the long, echoey, arched-ceilinged hall to the very end. Studio 19, where I had been assigned, was the second to last room. Tentatively I opened the door and saw a large space with a concrete floor, a huge window, and white walls. The room held a handful of cool but scruffy-looking students working on various projects. They ignored me. There was no professor in sight. Finally, one student—who looked downright respectable in his tidy clothes and was busily painting in a corner— took pity on me. He told me Beuys was in the hospital where his wife was giving birth. No one knew when to expect him, but that—according to Ted, the kind student—was nothing unusual. Beuys came and went as he pleased, turning up now and then to check on his students and give critiques, spending the rest of the time in his own studio. I gathered he was intimidating.

"I've been here three years, and I still jump when the door opens, thinking it might be Beuys come to give me one of his scathing critiques."

"What should I do?"

"Just do some drawings. He'll show up once his child is born."

I settled in as best I could and on the third day, Beuys appeared. He was a wiry middle-aged man wearing orthopedic work boots and a hat—always. Ted told me Beuys had been a prisoner of war in Siberia during WWII—like all German young men, he was drafted into the Nazi army—

and had walked home to Germany in the dead of the winter of 1945. His feet had frozen, and the special boots enabled his walking.

"Who are you?"

"I'm the American girl."

"I don't know how you ended up in this class, but you may as well stay. Who knows if you'll pass the trial semester."

Trial semester! No one had told me about a trial semester!

Apart from Ted, everyone in Studio 19 was the caricature of the disreputable artist. I felt vastly out of place. It seemed others also saw me as out of place. The custodian and the lunch lady both asked in slightly different ways:

"What's it like for a nice girl like you in that Beuys class?"

One day during the second week the door opened and two vibrant young women breezed in.

"Where's the American girl?"

"That's me."

"Come on! We're taking you to lunch!"

Marion and Annette had been in the Beuys class the semester before. They could only imagine what I was going through. They decided to befriend me. Fifty-five years later, Marion and I are still friends.

In addition to Studio 19, Beuys had a group of students next door in Studio 20. One day two of them showed up.

"Pack your things and come to Studio 20 with us. You don't belong here."

They were so right! Studio 20 looked much like Studio 19, but the atmosphere was completely different. In the middle of the room was a pedestal for the nude model, who came every day for two or three hours. The students in each class chose their model from a group approved by the Academy. We had Irmgard, a young single mom, not because she was the best model, but because the students knew she needed the job. We arranged our drawing chairs—chairs that you sat on backwards and rested your drawing board on the extra-long back—around the pedestal and drew. The more experienced students helped the newbies with suggestions. Now and then we took a break, Irmgard donned her robe, and we looked at pictures of her little girl.

In the afternoon we all worked on separate projects in different parts of the large studio. My classmates included two quiet, hard-working sculptors making portrait busts; a religious artist; a part-time student whose other job was as a policeman traveling to schools and giving puppet shows explaining traffic rules; and a young Iranian woman who planned to go back home and teach. We were a cozy group, working hard but breaking every afternoon for aromatic tea with a shot of rum. I'd found my place.

The cop was named Anatol. Stocky and middle-aged, he had a strawberry blond handlebar mustache and a booming voice. No matter how often I told him my father was a German academic, he imagined me as an American farm girl. One day he came into class brandishing a bottle of grain alcohol. He offered his classmates a drink. They all turned him down, so he turned to me.

"Come on, old American farmer's daughter! Surely you know how to drink! These lame-asses, they don't want to drink with me, but you will!"

Apparently, flattery will get you somewhere. I had no idea what I was sipping, but my spinning head soon made it clear. I composed myself and carefully walked to the cafeteria, not wanting to shock my lunch lady friend.

I was beginning to feel as if I belonged, but that trial semester still hung over my head. The semester's end coincided with Karneval, the Rhineland version of Mardi Gras celebrated big-time in Düsseldorf and neighboring Cologne. My friends, my cousins, and I went to parties every night. One night we saw Beuys.

"Ask him!" hissed Marion.

I sidled up to Beuys: "Herr Professor, did I pass the trial semester?"

He laughed. "Of course! If you weren't going to pass, I would have told you!"

Whew!

Beuys was intimidating, but I was stubborn and persistent, and though his critiques could be cruel, they were perceptive. In my fourth and last semester, I made a wood sculpture, a portrait bust of one of my cousins.

"You should paint that," Beuys said.

"Paint it! And cover up that beautiful wood grain?"

"You should be doing folk art," he replied in an offhand manner.

I shrugged it off, but years later, as I found my niche in puppetry, I remembered that remark and realized he'd seen something in my work that I wasn't ready to see or acknowledge.

After four semesters in the Beuys class, I decided it was time to go home. I had seriously considered staying in Germany. I felt quite at home and loved being surrounded by relatives, something immigrant families crave. But I started feeling hemmed in and missing the wide-open landscape I'd grown up in. If I wanted an American BA, I would have to enroll in college, but where? I considered Madison, but when I compared the cost of out-of-state tuition in Wisconsin with in-state tuition in Iowa, the choice was easy. Iowa City it was!

I declared an art major and went about transferring my credits. I knew this would be tricky because the art academy gave evaluations instead of grades. I had explained the problem to Beuys, who cooperated by using words like "excellent", "good", and "fair" and specifying how many hours I had spent on drawing, painting, and sculpture.

I went to the foreign students' office; they claimed they couldn't help me. "We'll see about that", I thought, and appeared in their office every morning at 8:00 AM till they got tired of seeing me and passed the buck to a German professor in the art department. He perused my portfolio, looking bored. "There go my credits," I thought.

"Who was your professor?"

"Joseph Beuys." His ears perked up.

"Herr Professor Beuys? What did he say about your work?"

I pulled the evaluation out of my back pocket and handed it off. The professor read it and took another look at my portfolio.

"Oh! Such sensitive line quality! This is quite good!"

Whew! My credits were transferred. Next, to address my major. I wanted an art major with an English minor and a certificate to teach both in secondary schools. Just in case. Iowa didn't offer that option. If you wanted to teach art, you had to have an Art Ed major. I decided to try the technique I'd used on my credits, and I appeared in my advisor's office at 8:00 AM

"Mr. Stumbo, I'd like to major in art, minor in English, and have a secondary teaching certificate for both."

"Iowa doesn't offer that option."

The scene repeated the next day. And the next. And the next. Finally, two weeks later:

"Mr. Stumbo, I'd like to major in art, minor in English, and have a secondary teaching certificate for both."

"I'll sign anything you want if you promise not to be here tomorrow morning!"

I was on my way to graduation and life as a puppeteer in Iowa City, married to an Iowa City native, with a sweet Iowa City son, and Iowa City relatives!

But first, the summer between my two years at Iowa, I spent three months with my beloved big sister, Anne, her husband Bill, and their two little boys, four-year-old Paul and two-year-old Jonathan. Anne was 5'8", almost my height. She had inherited Vati's classic features, curly dark hair, and gentle sense of humor. Bill was a 6'2" African American. He looked more Arab than African, with his café au lait-colored skin and narrow features. He radiated calm. Four-year-old Paul was like his father, serene and responsible, while two-year-old Jonathan gave new meaning to the term "terrible twos." His explosive temper tantrums included attempts to throw the car across the clearing.

He was so sweet and affectionate the rest of the time that you couldn't stay mad at him. I was helping out. They had bought a run-down farmhouse and seven acres of land in the Catskills, a weekend and summer retreat from their New York City apartment. The house reeked of urine—the old man living there had become incontinent years before his death—and needed paint and repairs. Anne scrubbed and painted while I chased kids.

I decided to sculpt a portrait of Paul, and he loved the idea. I set up a studio in an abandoned corn crib and got to work. Early every morning, Paul appeared at my bed, poked me, and said,

"Aunt Monica, it's time to get up and work on the portrait!"

When it was finished, I decided to cast it in plaster. I'd never made a plaster mold before, and I wasn't sure how. I called Mutti and got detailed instructions. The next time we went to town for groceries, I bought a big bag of plaster. I followed directions to a "T" and had what looked like a perfect mold. I smeared in Vaseline to serve as a mold release and poured my plaster. A few hours later, with bated breath, I opened the mold.

WHAT! The end of the nose was missing! I had a temper tantrum to match one of Jonathan's, grabbed the mold, and threw it into the trash. Bill quietly retrieved it. When I had calmed down a little, he presented it.

"Everyone is allowed a bit of artistic temperament. Now, I want you to call Mutti, find out what you did wrong, and try again."

"That's easy," Mutti said when I called. "You have to mix the plaster a little thinner so it flows into the end of the nose."

My second try was perfect. It still stands in Anne's apartment and brings back happy memories every time I see it. I still use the mold-making skills Mutti taught me over the phone.

After graduation, I decided to make puppets and dolls and sell them at art fairs, stores, and galleries. To supplement my income, I signed up as a substitute teacher in the Iowa City schools. The teaching certificate I fought so persistently for was coming in handy. Usually, I was called to sub for elementary art teachers, occasionally for high school art or English. When the phone rang at 5:00AM, I knew I'd be teaching that day.

One day I was called to finish out the semester for a junior high teacher who ran out of the classroom screaming, briefly stopping at the office.

"I quit!" she shrieked.

For the next few weeks, till the end of the school year, I spent every afternoon trying to bring order to the chaos of two 7th grade art classes. One was relatively easy to conquer—I rewarded them for good behavior by bringing puppets to class. The other class had organized their chaos so thoroughly that I was stumped. I knew one of the boys. He had come to my house for art classes when he was little. He was outrageously talented—and outrageously behaved. He thought I would treat him with kid gloves because of our history. One day I snapped and sent him to the office. He did not speak to me for the next 20 (!) years!

The class was as ill-behaved as ever. The chaos constructor seemed to be a girl I'll call Connie.

"Connie, if you don't behave, you'll have to come to the art room after school and help me clean up."

Every afternoon Connie and I cleaned the art room. The reason for her chaos finally dawned on me. Our after-school sessions may have been the only positive adult contact she had all day. The next day I changed my tune.

"Connie, if you don't behave, you can't come to the art room after school and help me clean up."

It was clear sailing for the rest of the year, and Connie helped me clean up every single afternoon.

Years later, after we'd opened the puppetry center in West Liberty, we hosted an event attended by a local middle school teacher. As I often did,

I told her the story of my middle school teaching adventure.

"What school was that?"

"Central Junior High."

"What year?"

"Must have been around 1978."

"I was in that class!"

What goes around comes around!

Making puppets to sell was satisfying, but there are only so many times you can make clones of the same character before you start to feel like a factory worker. I'd been making hand puppets and dolls, but I started making near-life-size hand and rod puppets with movable eyes. They were expressive and appealing, but difficult to impossible to sell, so they inhabited our living room. One day my friend Deanne Wortman stopped over.

"We should do shows with those puppets!" she said.

"I don't know; I'm not a performer."

"I can teach you! I'm a mime and a storyteller!"

So Eulenspiegel Puppet Theatre was born.

At first, we gave all of the kids—Deanne's three plus Little John— parts.

When we started getting calls for shows, and we felt the need to rehearse, we lost the kids. They had not signed on for rehearsals and responsibility.

Our first show was at an art fair in October 1974. People saw us and asked us to bring our show to other places. Our early stories were tales about Till Eulenspiegel, a 14th century jester whose tricks on the wealthy and the unscrupulous for the amusement of the poor filled a book with ninety-seven stories. Next, at nine-year-old Little John's suggestion, we added *The Fisherman and His Wife*, a fairytale I had told him many times.

Our first paid show was at the Iowa Braille and Sight Saving School. We set up in a multi-purpose room that looked like any other, and the kids came in, canes tapping. Some could see a little, enough to make out the bright colors we used, but some couldn't see anything. Some couldn't hear; the school catered to hearing impaired children, too. Had this been a good idea? Deanne and I wondered.

"We think it's perfect. The blind children can hear the story and the deaf kids will see the puppets!" their supervisor enthused when she hired us.

She was right. The kids were enthralled. They laughed in all of the right places. I didn't overthink it at the time, but in retrospect, it seems like an auspicious start.

After a few months, we decided to add a puppeteer, and we asked our friend Jenean Arnold, who was homebound with her first baby, to join us. Everywhere we went, we had an entourage of munchkins aged 6 months to 12 years.

That was Eulenspiegel when Teri Jean walked into my life. A few months later Deanne told us she had not planned for this to be any more than a hobby, so we were back to two puppeteers. It seemed natural to ask Teri Jean to join us.

"Now, Teri Jean," said Jenean, "this is a serious commitment, and I don't want you to say yes unless you mean to stay with it!"

A year later Jenean had to eat her words when she became pregnant with her second baby. There's a lot you can do with one baby in tow that you can't do with two! By now our shows were geared to three puppeteers, so we asked Marilyn Levin, cute as a bug and a born performer, to join. She stayed with us for two years till she was diagnosed with MS and needed a job with health insurance.

"Here we go again, Teri Jean. This is getting to be the story of my life."

"Listen, Monica, why don't we reorganize the shows so we can do them with just the two of us? I don't want to spend the rest of my life looking for third puppeteers!"

It was easier than we had imagined. It meant rewriting some scenes and moving a little faster.

In the early years, before puppetry became our livelihood, fun and play were the focus. In 1976, the brand-new Iowa Arts Council offered a bicentennial grant.

"Let's run our puppets for president! What could be more American than a presidential campaign?"

Much to our amazement, we got the grant and spent the money on bumper stickers and matchbooks with slogans: "Let's Run a Real Puppet!" We started with a slate of four different puppets with distinctly different platforms:

Schulz ("Vote for Every-Puppet!")

Schulz's wife, Pearl Miller Schulz aka Moms ("A Full Cookie Jar in Every Kitchen")

Bartholomew ("Divert the Military Budget to the Arts!")

Mehitabel, the law-and-order candidate (Mind Your P's and Q's!).

We held primary elections at each of our shows. Before or after the show, each candidate gave a short stump speech and solicited applause from the audience. The candidate with the most applause won the primary. Bartholomew won in Iowa City and other University towns; Mehitabel won in Missouri. When Schulz and Moms outstripped the other candidates, they decided to run as a presidential team, much as Bill and Hillary Clinton did fifteen years later. When we ran out of bumper stickers, they threw their support to Jimmy Carter (and he won the election!).

Before you guys got so darned serious about your work, we spent (wasted?) lots of time acting out stuff in our private lives. Remember when I put rods on Teri Jean and turned her into a puppet? People went nuts when I put her in the trunk and slammed down the lid! Oh, and the time Bartholomew went to the shrink because he had this delusion that he was a puppet. Ha! And maybe we shouldn't mention my little episode: when I figured if Henson could make money selling little Kermits maybe I could make a fortune selling "Little Schulzies." Didn't work. And there was that time you told the whole world about a little spat Moms and I had, as if it was anybody's business. Yep, we had a lot of fun playing, and then you guys turned it into a job!

3. Westward Ho!

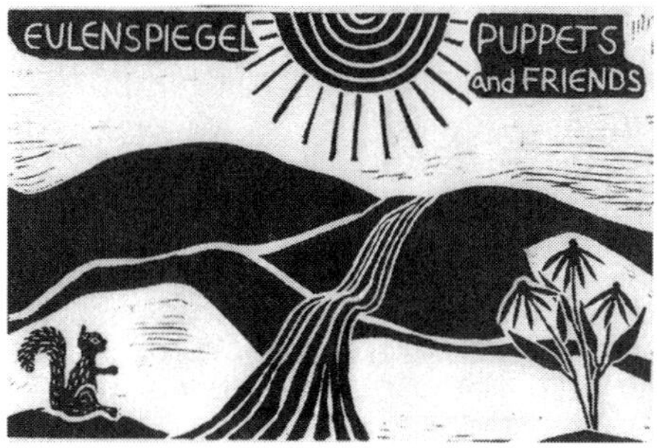

By 1984, puppetry was our full-time job. Teri Jean broke her foot on a falling table during one of our summer gigs. While she was laid up, she wrote to all of the other state arts councils to see if anyone wanted to add a puppet troupe to their roster. Wyoming nibbled, and for the next dozen years, we spent at least a month each year in the Rockies. Wyoming in those days had a population of 350,000, and everyone involved in the arts knew everyone else, so word of mouth brought us lots of residencies. We were yellow dog Democrats (the kind who'd rather vote for a yellow dog than a Republican), but we got along famously with the western Republicans who held to the "roll-up-your-sleeves-and-do-it-yourself" doctrine and saw us as "can-do gals".

In Mid-March of 1986, we took off from Iowa City in our blue Chevy pick-up truck with a topper full of puppets and supplies and made it as far as the Hershey, Nebraska rest area on Interstate 80. The truck stalled. It was late Saturday afternoon, but against all odds, we found an open service station in tiny Hershey and had the truck towed there. The timing chain had broken.

The mechanic shook his head.

"Sorry! We're about to close. And the parts stores are already closed. We can work on it first thing Monday morning, but you're stuck till then!"

"Crap! What are we going to do? We have to be in school in Star Valley first thing Tuesday morning, and that's on the Idaho border!" I moaned.

"We'll just have to call our teacher and explain," Teri Jean replied.

"Wait!" said Tom, the mechanic. You're going there to work? You're not on a ski vacation?"

"We have to do a puppet show at a grade school at 9:00 AM Tuesday!"

Tom made a quick phone call to a friend who owned a parts store in North Platte.

"You're in luck! He'll meet me at the store and sell me a timing chain. If all goes well, you can be out of here in two or three hours."

We waited at a neighboring café—feasting on our usual fish sandwiches and coleslaw—and sure enough, we were on the road before nightfall. For the rest of the trip, we sent Tom periodic postcards thanking him, again and again.

We arrived in Star Valley on schedule and appeared at our first school bright and early on Tuesday. We were scheduled to perform and do workshops in a different valley school each day, Tuesday through Friday. Schulz and Teri Jean did a little intro where they talked about meeting for coffee. It was our first encounter with a large population of Mormons, and we didn't realize their religion shunned coffee.

Friday, we found out.

"We had so much fun!" confided Mrs. B, a second-grade teacher, laughing heartily.

"I got a call Monday after school from one of the teachers in Afton; she told me about the coffee."

"Coffee?" I asked.

"Yes! They were calling each other all week and telling us not to let on to you!"

"Let on what?" I asked in confusion.

“Wait. Don’t you know that Mormons aren’t allowed to drink coffee? Your little intro gave us all a lot of giggles! Thanks!”

“You’re welcome...I guess. Thanks for letting us know. Better late than never.”

Saturday, we performed for the public. As we finished setting up, people poured into the auditorium, hordes of children and a moderate number of adults.

“I wish people wouldn’t just drop off their kids and leave!” complained Teri Jean.

“Who’s doing that?” asked Janet, our hostess.

“Well, look at all those kids! Where are their parents?”

“Well,” said Janet, ” those kids belong to the woman at the end of the row. And that woman is the mom of those next ten kids.”

We just kept learning, about the religion, families, and the weather.

Star Valley in March. There was only one way in and out of Star Valley, a mountain pass that was frequently snowed in. Was this a good idea? I wondered. Our contact person/teacher was confident.

“You’ll be just fine!” She assured me as we scheduled the residency.

Schulz here. I don’t think she was leveling with you, Monica. I overheard her on the phone while we were staying with her. She was yukking it up with her pal, bragging about how she talked those flatlanders into coming in March, of all months! Haha! She almost had to eat her words. We barely got out of there Saturday afternoon with a blizzard chasing us all the way to our next stop, Lander, and the Wind River Indian Reservation. She coulda had company for a looong time!

When we drove into Lander, through the iron-red mountains, I had an intense feeling of déja Vu. If past lives are a thing, I must have spent at least one of them in Lander. We were scheduled to spend two weeks on the Wind River Indian Reservation, home of the Arapaho and Shoshone nations, two that had traditionally been at war with one another. Weeks earlier I had called the school principal.

"Can we work on a schedule for our residency? Which grades would you like to target?"

"Don't worry about it. We can deal with that when you get here."

"We kind of need a schedule ahead of time if we're going to get anything done."

"It'll be fine. You've got two weeks!"

"I'd really like to make sure we have enough time and the right supplies."

"The first Monday you're here is a teacher planning day. We'll figure it out then."

Oh boy. Our midwestern punctuality, love of planning, and work ethic had just stumbled into culture shock!

Monday, we showed up for the planning day. We talked about our process and what we would do with the kids. Much to our relief, two second-grade teachers spoke right up. That still wasn't enough to fill up the day, so we asked the school librarian if she would like a set of puppets for the library. An enthusiastic "yes!" set us up. We spent half of each day the first week working with second graders and the other half sitting in the library making puppets, demonstrating for anyone who cared to watch. One by one, other teachers showed up and asked us to come to their classrooms the following week, until we had a full schedule. One day we did a show for the school. *The Puppet Showman* was a Hans Christian Andersen tale we adapted.

Yep, it starred me, Alfred Schulz, as an old puppeteer training an eager young apprentice. My backstory: I had wanted to be a real director with a real theater, and I settled for being a puppeteer. Louie, my apprentice, and I did a show with hand puppets, and after the show, I fell asleep and dreamed that my puppets came to life and became human actors. They were horrible! They insulted me, beat me up with a bandanna, abused me! I was so glad when I woke up and realized I could just pack them up in the trunk!

The part Schulz fails to mention is the hand puppet story we did in the middle. It was a time-honored European folk genre, a noodlehead story: one in which the leading character does everything wrong, and only because of that does everything come out right in the end. We thought it was hilarious. Nobody laughed. They were polite and quiet, but it was clear they didn't get it. As the days passed, the penny dropped for some of them.

"That was funny; that part with the hatchet."

"I liked the guy with the pumpkin on his head."

"That was silly, that they kept forgetting to count themselves."

For us, it was a lesson in humor and how closely it's tied to our cultural heritage.

We also learned a thing or two about a sense of time. We had made friends with a Tribal Elder who wanted to show us the Sinks, a geological formation outside of town.

"I'll meet you after school and drive you to the Sinks. You can buy me a steak dinner afterwards."

School was over at 3:00. We waited till 5:00 and decided he had been joking or something had come up. When he showed up at 6:00, we were long gone. The next day his granddaughter, the kindergarten teacher, told us how insulted he'd been. She swore us to secrecy, saying he would never forgive her if he found out she'd told. What to do? We had to do something to make it right! She told us his totem animal was an eagle, so we made him a beautiful eagle puppet, and he was mollified! Whew!

The next year we got a call from the Education Director of the Wyoming Arts Council.

"Have you heard from the Jeffrey City schools yet?"

"Yep. They want us to do a two-week residency in their elementary school."

"I thought I should call and warn you."

"Warn us? What do you mean?"

"They had a poet recently. She was in the elementary, but also in the high school. She antagonized a girl who's used to getting nothing but praise when she gave her a gentle critique."

"Oh?"

"That's not all. The kids had asked to see some of her poetry. She screened it through the teacher before letting the kids see it because it had some adult language. The prom queen who got the critique marched into the superintendent's office and complained about the 'foul' language."

"Wow!"

"That's still not all. The superintendent called her out of the class she was teaching and, without asking for her side of the story, told her she 'must leave Jeffrey City by sundown and never return!'"

"That sounds like the wild west!"

"I'm sure you two will be fine; just thought you should be forewarned."

Jeffrey City was a uranium boom/bust town at the beginning of its final "bust". The population of 5000 had diminished by well over half; the K-12 school population was 120, many of whom rode buses two hours a day to and from their ranch homes. When we arrived, I realized I had forgotten to pack one of the supplies we needed, clothesline rope. I figured I'd pick it up after school.

"Is there a hardware store in town?" I asked.

"Of course!"

"Where is it?"

"Which town do you mean? Lander or Rawlins?" Jeffrey City was halfway between—about sixty miles away from each city. Locals regularly drove that far for routine errands. We used it as an excuse to visit our favorite Lander family, friends from our residency there.

We moved into an abandoned mobile home that had belonged to one of the teachers recently laid off as the school population diminished. She must have been tiny; all of the furniture was diminutive. I felt like Snow White in the home of the seven dwarfs.

Our contact person was the art teacher, the wife of the superintendent who had threatened our poet colleague. She had taught home economics, but she tired of it and asked her husband if she could teach art instead. She loved puff paint and scented markers. She confided that she kept the television on all night, tuned to the shopping channel.

"That way, if I wake up at night, I can see if there's anything I want to buy."

Her focus was on keeping the art room clean. Luckily, Teri Jean had been raised by a clean-freak mom, and—unlike me—was very good at cleaning up and keeping things neat and tidy. She'd gotten plenty of practice in the carpeted classrooms we frequently worked in. We got along fine with the puff paint teacher, even if we did snicker behind her back. And the kids: they were like kids anywhere, ready to work, play, and use their imaginations!

I recently googled Jeffrey City and discovered there's not much left. The mobile homes have all been moved by cranes to new boomtowns. The uranium mine is played out. The school has six students and one teacher and is part of the Lander school system. I wonder what happened to our art teacher, but I suppose she's retired by now.

By 1988 we had abandoned the pick-up truck and graduated to a Suburban. We'd been performing in New England in August, and we stopped in Green Bay, Wisconsin on the way home to do a show. As we drove the blue Suburban down Main Street, the plug fell out of the oil pan and oil poured out on the street.

"Oops! That's not good!"

"There's a station on the corner. Think we can make it that far?"

"One way to find out!"

We limped into the station, they fixed us up, and we started home with crossed fingers. As we drove over the Iowa border, the engine started knocking, and we barely made it home. What now? We were supposed to leave for a residency in Worland, Wyoming, the next morning, and it would take a lot longer than that to repair or replace the engine. My husband, John, remembered the old pick-up truck that was parked in the woods by the log cabin he was building as our new home. He gathered some friends, pulled it out of the woods, and discovered it had become the home for a colony of mice who had devoured all of the wiring! He and his friends spent most of the night replacing all of the wires. There wasn't enough time to repair the transmission leak, so we left the next morning with the puppets, supplies, and a case of transmission fluid in the back.

"That was a close call!"

"Do you think we'll look respectable enough in this beat-up truck?"

"I think they'll be glad we didn't cancel!"

I'm guessing Petunia, our blue suburban was sad to be left at home if cars can be sad. On previous Wyoming trips her humongous, eight-cylinder, 454, gas-guzzling engine had charged up the mountains, sailing past semis, souped-up pickup trucks, and anything else in the other lane. Except for one time, when we came to a dead stop behind lines of vehicles in both lanes. We put the suburban in park and walked to the head of the line. There was a moose, relaxing, sprawled across both lanes of traffic, chewing its cud, oblivious to the inconvenience of the humans. We waited. And waited. And waited. Finally, a man in a Ford Explorer at the head of the line started his engine and slowly moved forward.

"Oh no! He's not planning to murder the moose, is he?" asked Teri Jean.

Slowly, slowly the explorer pulled up to the moose, nudged it gently, and nudged it again until it casually stood up and lumbered off the road.

As we drove over the Bighorn Mountains in the rattletrap pickup truck, we noticed a Native American woman stalled by the side of the road. We stopped.

"Can we help you?"

"I don't know what's wrong with my car. I can move in reverse, but it won't go forward."

"I think we can help you!"

I checked her transmission fluid and, sure enough, it was two quarts low. We filled her up, gave her a quart for the road, and said our goodbyes.

"Figures it would be the folks driving the junker who stopped to help! I can't count how many brand-new cars have whizzed by me!"

We arrived in Worland by the skin of our teeth, just in time to start our residency. We were staying with our contact person, who was married to a Republican State Rep. It just happened to be the week of the Democratic Presidential Convention, and we really wanted to watch. Fat chance! Then I overheard a conversation.

"Dear, I think it would be polite to let our guests watch the convention. They're Democrats."

"All right, as long as I don't have to watch!"

Turned out she was a closet Democrat, and we three had a ball hooting and hollering as Jesse Jackson gave the keynote address!

Just as I had suspected, our contact people, rather than being horrified by our junker pickup truck, were impressed and grateful that we had regrouped so quickly, driven the old heap over the mountains, and arrived in time. Our reputation as "can-do gals" was sealed!

4. Touring Arts Team

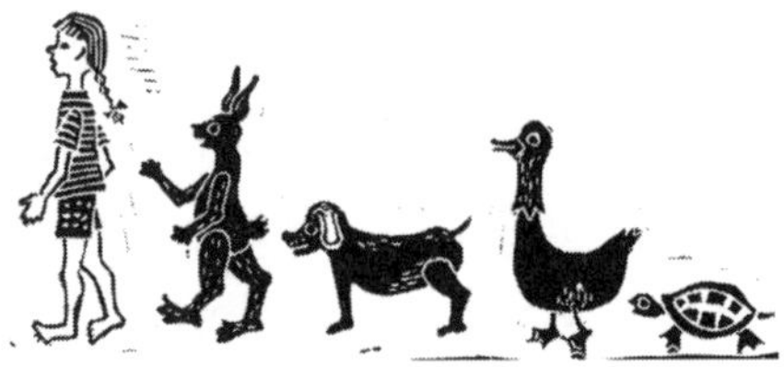

1981:"We've arrived!"

"How so?" asked Teri Jean.

"Just got a call from Carolyn at the Arts Council. They want us on the Touring Arts Team!"

"Cool beans!"

The Touring Arts Team was a group of six or seven artists in different disciplines, assembled by the Iowa Arts Council to do two-day residencies in towns with populations of under 1500. Each leg of the team lasted eleven days and went to five towns, with one paid day off in the middle, between June and August. Being a member of the team was a sought-after privilege. As I recall, there was no application process. The Arts Council staff reviewed their rosters of touring and teaching artists and, knowing their artists well, tried to assemble compatible teams. Teri Jean and I had done many successful school residencies before we were invited to join the team. The pay was relatively good (how often does a freelance artist get a paid day off?), and the collaboration and fellowship with other artists were heavenly.

Our first town was Klemme, where we met the rest of the team: musicians Shadric Smith and Dartanyan Brown, dancer Valerie Williams, and visual artist Diane Rockey. Klemme was a tidy little town. Rows of wood-frame houses mostly painted white, some with daring red or blue trim, lined the streets. The well-kept Main Street had a restaurant, a bank, a hardware store, a drugstore, and a grocery store, all well-maintained. We artists stayed with host families, each in a different home.

"In this town, everyone mows their lawn on Wednesday, so the grass is the perfect length on Sunday," my host mother told me.

"It's a good thing I don't live here!"

She chuckled. "We expect our artists to be a little different!"

Year after year, from 1981 to 1991, we arrived with each new team in each new town in time to have lunch with the hosts. After lunch, we all got ready for our workshops, setting up supplies in our assigned spaces, elementary school classrooms or church basements, or meeting rooms in the town hall. Teri Jean and I found our room and laid out newspapers, masking tape, plaster bandages, tempera paints, fabric, yarn, fake fur, lace and trims, and the ubiquitous hot glue gun. We'd turned to plaster bandages instead of papier mâché mash because it dried quickly. Kids could make the puppet heads and paint them in one 2-hour session.

At 2:00, we team members lined up and faced the assembled residents, children and adults alike, to "sell" our workshops.

"Come on, people! Shake a leg and come dance with me!" Various dancers in various teams uttered various versions of this line.

"We'll be playing with paint"—or wool or chalk or markers or ink, depending on the artist.

"Kids, let's make some puppets and put on a show!"

The locals chose their workshops, rolled up their sleeves, and got creative! Everyone in town, preschoolers to great grandparents, got involved. Fiddles and trombones that hadn't seen the light of day in decades jumped out of their cases, scattering dust, and came to life. Overweight teenagers shed their inhibitions and danced. Grandmothers switched from paring knives to carving knives and made linoleum block prints. Poems were written, puppets were made, and wacky collaborations came into being.

At 4:00, it was time to clean up and get ready for dinner, usually a huge potluck. Tables were laden with potato salad, three-bean salad, jello/kool whip/marshmallow salad, sweet corn, and—always! —ham loaf. Most of us ate light, knowing we still had to perform, but wiry little Valerie had whipped up an appetite dancing and heaped her plate—twice!

After dinner, we set up for the evening show. Each team member had 15 minutes to play music, show slides, demonstrate sculpture, read poetry, dance, or put on a puppet show. For the first few years, our show was *Clever Gretel*, a Brothers Grimm story about a clever cook whose voracious appetite leads her to eat both chickens that she is preparing for her boss and his guest. She tricks her boss into thinking that his guest has broken into her kitchen, taken both chickens, and run off with them. Mad chases and hilarity ensue!

You should be letting me tell this part! I got to play the part of the boss! Not that I liked being thought of as—well—a little dim, but I sure loved being part of that team, and sometimes you let me MC, or I got to do the bit where I turned Teri Jean into a puppet, or I got to help out at the workshops! Remember that town where the kids were so addicted to their TVs that we couldn't get 'em to focus? Ha! Teri Jean made a puppet stage that looked like a HUGE TV screen, got Shadric and Dart to play some theme music, and the kids did puppet parodies of their favorite programs! It was a hoot!

The next day, we had two workshops, morning and afternoon. In the evening, after another potluck, the workshop attendees performed and displayed their work. For the first few years, we ended the evening by passing out helium balloons, gathering in a big circle, and releasing the balloons on cue. We carried a helium tank in the state van and team members took turns filling balloons during the performance. This practice ended when someone explained the harm the balloons caused to wild birds and someone else expounded on the danger of traveling with a full tank of helium in an open van. We artists did not miss filling all of those balloons!

In some ways, the Touring Arts Team was like our school residencies. We did the same kinds of projects, making and performing with hand puppets and shadow puppets. There was one big difference: these kids brought their grandmas along.

In one town, we were working in a park shelter when our group arrived, with a dozen kids and almost as many grandmas. I started passing out materials—newspapers, tape, and plaster bandages for the heads.

"Here you go, Mandy! Would you like some, too, Mrs. Nelson?"

"Oh no, I'll just watch and help."

A few minutes later, in a whiny voice:

"Grandma, can I try?"

"Better get Mandy some more supplies," said Teri Jean.

As we team members got to know each other, private jokes made their way into public performances to be shared with our hosts. One year we were on the team with Carl Bleyle, a musicologist from Ames. He always began his first-night presentation the same way.

"I am a musicologist; no, that is not a disease, although it sometimes makes my students sick!"

He went on with a witty description of his obscure medieval instruments. By the third town, we had a plan. We made a plaster bandage hand puppet in Carl's likeness along with a set of tiny plaster instruments. On the second night, when everyone in town had heard the real Carl give his spiel, the hand puppet Carl danced around the stage in friendly parody.

Every town was different. In a tiny town, the tone is often set by a handful of people. If those people are positive, optimistic, can-do folks, that spirit infects the whole town. Of course, most of the towns that went to the trouble of applying for the Touring Arts Team were of that type, but there were notable exceptions.

In one town, all of the planning and preparation had been done by a single person, a banker's wife. We never figured out whether she had failed to spread the news or whether she was just unpopular, but the result was that nobody showed up!

The next town, Volga, was the polar opposite. The town had a population of 200, and 300 people showed up for the first evening's performance! It was held in the old opera house, which was in the process of being renovated, but luckily no one had painted over Jenny Lind's signature, which we found in one of the dressing rooms. Volga had achieved its huge participation by involving as many people as possible in the project. Each artist stayed with a different family; each artist was assigned an assistant for each workshop, whether or not they wanted one; families not involved in housing were enlisted to bring food to the potlucks. Consequently, everyone in town was involved in one way or another and wouldn't have dared to stay away!

These were the years of the farm crisis, and, from one year to the next, we watched as local businesses shriveled and big box stores appeared to suck whatever life remained out of the downtowns we passed through.

One of the women we met told me a story that describes perfectly what we've lost. She was a teacher, and she was reminiscing about the clothing store that had succumbed. Her husband was a lawyer; he'd called her at school one day and told her that they had to attend a dress-up event that evening. She had nothing to wear, so she called the local clothing store and asked the owner (who knew her taste and size) to select three outfits and deliver them to her house. She tried them on after school, picked one out, and returned the other two the following day.

"Try getting Wal-Mart to do that for you!" she said.

As the years went by, the shoe and clothing stores were replaced with thrift shops, which we team members eagerly patronized. One year I found a sock monkey with a black velvet vest and embroidered eyelashes. I named him Terrence Eugene after Teri Jean. He looked just as cheeky as she was! He still hangs out at our puppetry center.

My favorite year was 1986. Our team that year included Preston Love, a 65-year-old black jazz musician from Omaha who'd toured the Midwest his entire life and knew just how to work an audience. You could tell he'd spent his life performing for white folks: he knew exactly how far he could go in ribbing his audiences without quite insulting them.

Preston loved fishing. As soon as we arrived in Oxford Junction, he enlisted some old-timers who took him to the best fishing hole around. Within the hour, he caught the 40-pound catfish they'd been trying to catch all summer. That, and a giant carp he caught right after, was dinner that evening for a crowd, gathered around a makeshift—plywood on sawhorses—table in the church basement.

"Where's the cornmeal?" Preston asked the church ladies who graciously allowed him to use the church kitchen and agreed to make the side dishes for the feast he planned.

"Yellow cornmeal? No! I need white!"

Preston sent the old-timers to the next town for white cornmeal while he gutted and filleted the fish. Cornmeal, Crisco, and cayenne, along with Preston's cooking skills and the church ladies' side dishes, made the best dinner we had that summer!

Preston bonded with the old-timers in more ways than one. It turned out they were all members of a local polka band. By the second evening, the polka band had become a Dixieland Jazz Band under Preston's direction! After the show that night, we all gathered at the mayor's house for a party. We heard loud music pulling into the driveway. It was Preston and his band, driving up in a boat of a Cadillac convertible, top-down, old men and instruments spilling out, a recording of their performance in the tape player, the sound turned up as loud as it would go.

Vernon Windsor was the dancer on our team that year. A tall, elegantly built African American, he'd grown up in southern Iowa, close to the Missouri border, and had started adult life as a rodeo bull rider. Growing up in the 1950s, he had a finely tuned sense of what was considered "acceptable" for a man of his complexion. When Teri Jean wanted to cut across a private yard to get to our destination, Vernon declined.

"You won't catch someone who looks like me cutting across a private yard in this part of Iowa."

When one of the older women in that little town expressed shock that the Arts Council would allow single and married people of different races to travel in the same vehicles, all of us except Vernon and Preston were horrified. We got an education that summer!

Vernon had a special way of making people feel comfortable. I noticed that he often had overweight, uncoordinated teenagers in his groups and that they always felt secure enough to join in the performance the second evening.

In Ossian, our last town that year, he even convinced reluctant team members to rehearse and perform a team dance that he had choreographed especially for that town. No one but Vernon could ever have talked klutzy me into dancing in front of an audience!

J Knight, our other musician, was steadfast and loyal. You knew he'd never desert you onstage, no matter how embarrassing the situation. In Oxford Junction, a town with Czech heritage, he and I got talked into singing a song in Czech, a language neither of us knew. My little Iowa City band—the Honk and Bleat, Non-Marching, Mostly Polka Band—had played this song, so I thought I was prepared. At least I knew the tune. But the words—*Za naší vesnicí, na hlavní silnici, bosenský rostou švestky ba-jó*—who knew how to pronounce that! Luckily, most of the audience knew the words and how to pronounce them; we were drowned out!

J carried a suitcase full of harmonicas and organized harmonica ensembles in each town. Along with the instruments, his suitcase contained a large can of Lysol. He sprayed the mouthpieces between users. My nose remembers J in a cloud of Lysol.

Our visual artists that summer were Peter Coyle, a Scottish painter, and consummate storyteller, and Dana Schaeffer, a fiber artist who raised sheep and spun her own wool. Peter and Dana were both adept at leading group projects, so the towns were left with sizable pieces to display in their schools or libraries.

Peter's groups made collages, sometimes faces looking at fish in an aquarium, painted in pastels. Dana's made large felt hangings depicting rural scenes—usually the landscape surrounding the town we were visiting—felted from raw wool. These works were all created by groups of people who'd never thought of themselves as artists. Those pieces may still be hanging, reminders of creativity that we shed as we run around the hamster wheel of daily life.

Peter was quite the philosopher. No matter what happened, how embarrassing or grim it might be, he countered by saying "it's all part of life's rich tapestry," a line I repeat to this day.

Although all of the teams became fairly cohesive units, that 1986 team bonded more quickly and thoroughly than any other we were ever on. Every time we left a town in our State of Iowa van, we felt as if we were on the road to Canterbury. We echoed Preston as he repeated his standard farewell:

"They love us in Ossian" (or Oxford Junction or Ainsworth or Lisbon)!

We whiled away the hours traveling across the state by telling each other our personal histories and family stories. Afterwards, I felt as if I'd been on a different planet for eleven days.

One of the things we all loved about the summer tour was eating foods that we normally didn't allow ourselves. J was a notorious health nut, eating sensibly and exercising. On the third day, I saw him eating a chocolate brownie with ice cream and chocolate syrup. I knew it was all over, and that I might as well give in to the potato chips, mayonnaise, and Kool Whip. The Arts Council had advised the towns that the artists preferred light lunches, perhaps a green salad. One town responded by serving us green Jell-O and brownies for lunch!

Mayonnaise flowed everywhere, so much so that we finally rewrote the words to Harry Belafonte's "Day-O". We amused ourselves in the last town by singing in multiple harmonies:

Mayo, mayo, mayo come and I wanna go home,
Mayo, mayo, mayo come and I wanna go home.
Mayo on potatoes, mayo on the beans,
Mayo on the apples, mayo on the greens.
Mayo on the noodles, mayo on the eggs,
Mayo on everything, running down my legs.

5. Summer Festivals

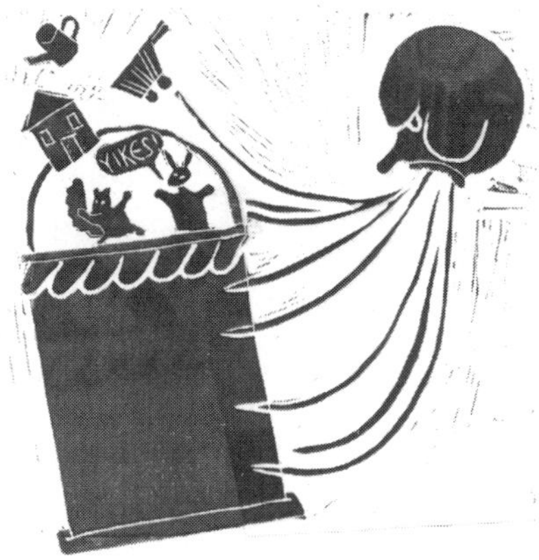

Another beloved summer activity was—and is—performing at outdoor arts festivals. Battling the prairie winds is a challenge many puppeteers categorically refuse, but a challenge energizes me and the payoff is big: when we're not performing, we listen to music, peruse craft booths, eat foods we never get at home, and hang out with other artists. And we get paid!

The time was the mid-1980s. Teri Jean and I were on our way to some show or some residency somewhere in Iowa. A dense fog rolled in, and we could only see a few feet in front of us. Just in time, we saw an exit and got off the interstate. We spent the next four hours sitting in a plastic upholstered booth, drinking coffee in the truck stop we found at that exit. We whiled away the time designing—on paper napkins— what we hoped would be an effective, wind-proof outdoor stage. When the fog lifted, we packed up the paper napkins and finished our trip.

Later, at home, I conferred with John, who used aluminum pipe to construct skeletons of two four-foot square tents. I made the tent walls and pitched roofs out of black corduroy to match the black costumes we wore. To connect the two tents, I made a panel which we attached to the trunks we packed our puppets in.

We initiated the stage at our favorite summer festival, the Smoky Hill River Festival in Salina, Kansas. The festival takes place in a large, tree-shaded city park bordered by the Smoky Hill River. In a town of under 50,000, Riverfest attracts an annual audience of over 65,000. It features four stages—three music stages and the Children's Stage, lots of roving performers, juried art and craft shows, food booths of all kinds, and lots of whimsical extras, like sand sculptures, interactive artworks, and decorated trees.

Our stage stood up to the Kansas winds!

I remember that stage! You made it for us big puppets! There were cool windows in the tents, with curtains! I could stick my head out and talk to the audience! And that panel in the middle: you put a meadow with wildflowers on that panel. It was gorgeous! Whatever happened to that stage? I suppose it's packed up in the basement with all of the other stuff we're not using anymore.

I had gotten what I thought was a bright idea. Instead of our regular black costumes, I got us black sweats, figuring they would absorb perspiration and keep us cooler. Boy, did that backfire! Teri Jean suffered a heat stroke during a noontime show! After that, for a while, we wore lightweight blacks. After every show, people would come up to us to talk. We were hoping for compliments!

"Are you all right? You gals look so hot in those black costumes!"

That did it! We packed up the black tents and designed a new stage, with beautiful light-colored batik fabrics, which had become readily available in good fabric shops. We dressed in the fabrics we used for the stage. Success! We never heard "you gals look so hot" again. Instead, we heard "I loved your show!"

In addition to the two shows we did every day on the children's stage, we were expected to rove the festival grounds with puppets. The first few years, eager to please, we brought full shows—small ones—to wander the grounds. Now and then we would stop, gather an audience, and do the show. We carried ten-pound packs on our backs holding a large battery, an amplifier, and speakers and attaching to headset microphones. One year it was a miniature marionette show, *The Cat, the Ram, and the Wolves.* Another year it was *Punch and Judy*, a hand puppet show based on the classic British model but with our original very American script. In addition to the sound pack, I wore the stage on my shoulders, working the puppets, while Teri Jean played the part of the proprietor, interacting with Mr. Punch, cheering him on, or scolding him. It started with a traditional song:

Mr. Punch is a jolly good fellow
Oh, his coat is all scarlet and yellow
And if now and then he gets mellow
It's only among his good friends.
Oh, his money most freely he spends.
Yes, to laugh and grow fat he intends
With the girls, he's a rogue and a rover
He lives while he can among clover
And when he is dead—it's all over
And so his comedy ends.

"Mr.Punch! Mr.Punch!" *(in a Cockney accent)* "The audience is waiting."

"I'm still in the shower!"

"I don't care! Get over here!"

"All right! You asked for it!" Enter Mr. Punch, just a head on my bare hand. Teri Jean covers her eyes.

"Mr. Punch! You're naked!" Giggles from the audience. "Get dressed!"

"Make up your mind!"

And so, the repartee started. The highlight of the show—in the minds of the kids watching—came when Judy handed the baby off to Punch, now dressed in a red and yellow outfit, while she went shopping. Mr. Punch notices that the baby has a wet diaper.

"PeeUuu!" Mr. Punch throws the baby out of the stage, Teri Jean picks baby up, smells his bottom, holds her nose, and wrings the baby's sponge body out over the front row of the audience. Gales of laughter! Kids approached us all weekend as Teri Jean and the stage wandered the festival grounds, saying shyly,

"I liked when Baby peed on the audience!

We did these shows as many as six times each day! Every evening, in our motel room, we'd massage each other's backs to prepare for the next day.

We started paying attention to what other performers did for their roving acts and realized we were working way too hard! We had been experimenting with giant parade puppets, so we made a sun and a moon puppet, each about ten feet tall, and walked them around the grounds. Easy-peasy compared to doing shows! People loved them; they were a great photo op. But even the sun and the moon got heavy, especially as we got older. Teri Jean saw roving with them as a tedious chore and sighed as she picked up the moon.

I decided to surprise her. Without consulting with her, I bought plastic irrigation pipe, easily acquired in farm country. I purchased bubble wrap and all sorts of shiny, lightweight fabrics. I wrapped the super lightweight pipe in layers of bubble wrap and covered it with a patchwork of fancy fabrics. I added a soft-sculpted head with an open mouth and glittery fabric flames. John embedded connectors for two thin rods into the irrigation pipe, and I loaded the dragon into the van. When we arrived at the festival, I unloaded the dragon and propped him against a tree. We finished our first show of the day.

"Teri Jean, I think we better do some roving now."

Teri Jean groaned. "All right."

Each of us picked up a rod and began hoisting the dragon into the air.

"Oh! This isn't heavy at all!"

Success! That tone of voice made all of the work I'd done worthwhile!

In 2001, Mallory Smith was our "Booking Angel". Mallory had a flexible brain and perceived unusual connections that brought us interesting bookings. She got a call from the Tumbleweed Festival in southwest Kansas, but they weren't willing to pay for our travel, so she had to find other bookings in Kansas to make our trip feasible. She'd read an article about the little town of Lucas, the home of the Grassroots Art Museum and the Garden of Eden. The people in Lucas had renovated their downtown movie theater and were presenting live performances there. We'd done something similar the year before. So she called them and said, "We did that! You should hire us!" They did.

The Tumbleweed Festival is held in a zoo on the outskirts of Garden City. You can take a break from listening to music or watching a magician and wander through the zoo, communing with uncaged—but fenced—critters. The festival has a relaxed feel; the layout spreads the visitors out so it never feels hectic or crowded. We loved hanging out with the other performers—jugglers, magicians, musicians, and even another puppeteer— between shows and going out to dinner with them afterwards. We became semi-regular performers at the Tumbleweed Festival.

After our last show that first year, we took off to Lucas. Neither one of us had ever heard of the town, but Teri Jean was not happy with the distance it took us out of our way.

"Doesn't Mallory ever look at a map?" she grumbled from the passenger seat.

We pulled into Lucas. Teri Jean was the first to notice the stone cabin surrounded by a giant sculptural installation representing the Garden of Eden. Adam and Eve, twelve-foot-tall concrete sculptures, guarded the entrance. The fence, made of concrete and reinforcing rod, looked like a giant grove of trees punctuated by a group of characters: Cain and Abel; the avenging Angel; and a series representing the chain of life. A man with a bow and arrow chased a large animal which chased a smaller animal which chased a smaller animal, and so forth. One sculpture reflected the creator's populist views: A huge crucifix with "Labor" inscribed under the corpus. The four corners each had a figure of a tormentor: Doctor, Lawyer, Banker, and Preacher.

Teri Jean gaped. "I think I know why Mallory sent us here!"

The Garden of Eden had been created by Samuel Perry Dinsmore, a retired teacher, Civil War veteran, and general character, between 1891 and 1920. In addition to the monumental sculptures, he had created a mausoleum where he was buried under a glass coffin lid. He had contacted a mortician who understood mummification and commissioned him to mummify his body when he died. His goal was to create a tourist attraction that he hoped would help support his very young wife after he died. He hadn't planned to die in the middle of a hot summer. When his widow contacted the mummifier, he declined, saying he couldn't get to Lucas fast enough to beat the decay caused by the heat. Undeterred, the widow talked a local mortician into trying his luck. The result was partially successful—the corpse is visible, but slightly decaying, under the glass. And of course, Dinsmore was very successful in creating a tourist attraction!

Not only that, but the presence of his work led to the establishment of the Grassroots Art Museum and several other installations in this tiny town. It also inspired artists from all over the world to relocate there. A porcelain artist who'd moved from New York City told us,

"I always wanted a city loft, but I couldn't afford it. Now I own a whole downtown building!"

Once we'd admired the Garden of Eden, we looked for our overnight accommodations, a boarding house—mostly used by hunters—on Main Street. No one was there. There was a sign on one of the inside doors: "Pick a room, put $5.00 in an envelope, and slide it under this door." We did.

The bathroom had a sign as well: "Please don't wash your dogs in the bathtub." We didn't. The refrigerator sported another sign: "Please don't put your birds on the ice maker." We didn't.

The next day we set up in their little downtown theater and performed *World Tales,* a collection of three folk tales—European, Latin American, and Chinese—for two audiences of school kids. It became the first of many trips to Lucas, with—I hope—many more to come!

Riverfest and Tumbleweed—and the Willow Tree Festival in Gordon, Nebraska—aren't the only festivals we've performed at.

In 2008, I got a big surprise when New Orleans puppeteer friend Karen Konnerth invited us to bring *Sal Fink, Catfish Wrangler* to Jazzfest, where she was in charge of booking the Children's Stage. We drove from our end of the river to the other end, bringing our river show with us. After Sal got done riding her catfish all over the children's tent, we wandered the many tents and stages, listening to a plethora of different styles of music. I stood in the rain for forty-five minutes to hear one of my favorites, John Prine. In the evenings, we prowled New Orleans neighborhoods, eating gumbo and PO-boys, and taking in music every bit as memorable as anything at the festival.

Since then, we've returned four times with different shows. I'm always overwhelmed by the music you can encounter anywhere in the city at any time of day!

And of course, we have our favorite Iowa festivals! Nordicfest in Decorah often features the comedy duo of Tina and Lena telling Norwegian jokes.

Tina: "Ole and Lena were driving north to Minneapolis on their honeymoon. Ole put his hand on Lena's knee."

Lena: "You can go further than that, Ole!"

Tina: So… he drove all the way to Duluth!"

Dancers from Norway don dark wool costumes and dance on the street in the heat of the day. We hope they won't drop over from heatstroke! And of course, we relish the church supper of Scandinavian food—lefse, rommegrot, lutefisk, Swedish meatballs—all white or beige.

Even the meatballs have a white sauce!

The Star-Spangled Spectacular in Storm Lake is held on the lakeshore. One year the wind off the lake was so strong that we tied our already windproof stage to a tree. It rattled and shook all the way through the show, but at least it didn't blow into the lake!

If you're a puppeteer in the Great Plains, and you perform outdoors, the prairie wind is your co-puppeteer, laughing at you as it snatches props and flings them into the audience. Over the years, we've designed a series of supposedly windproof stages. After we abandoned the black costumes and black corduroy stage, Teri Jean had an idea.

"If we screw pipes into boards, stretch fabric over the pipes, and put a playboard on top, we can sandbag the boards and also stand on them.

"Hmmm. Our combined weight plus the sandbags should be enough to withstand any wind," I mused.

We took our new stage to the Smoky Hill River Festival. Partway through the first show, I felt the wind lift the board I was standing on just a tiny bit, but we didn't blow away! Over the years, we expanded the design. We added a backdrop to display appliquéd scenery. Parallel playboards allow the puppets to leap from one level to another. In *Sal Fink, Catfish Wrangler*, our twelve-yard silk river can snake around the playboards looking like a winding waterway.

I designed this show shortly after Teri Jean quit performing. It was her idea, but the twelve-yard hand-painted silk river was distinctly not her idea!

"Are you planning on performing this outdoors?" she asked.

"Of course!"

"You can't have twelve yards of silk on stage! What about the wind? You'll go nuts; get rid of it!"

"Nope!" I said. "This is my show, and I want that river!"

I didn't exactly regret that decision, but it has given me pause. The wind-blown silk looks like a choppy river, and I enjoy the challenge of wrestling it into place, but sometimes it goes too far. In 2018 we took the show to the Tumbleweed Festival. Garden City, Kansas is always a windy place, but that year the winds were so strong that I simply couldn't control the river long enough to anchor it into place with the usual clamps. I gave up, and for forty-five minutes, twelve yards of silk blew straight out the right side of the stage. It looked like a river after the Corps of Engineers straightens it!

I could almost hear Teri Jean cackling, "I told you so!"

Nowadays, as climate change increases wind frequency and velocity, I often start outdoor shows with an announcement.

"Well, Ladies and Gentlemen, it looks like it's going to be a battle royal between the puppeteer and the wind! After the show, you can tell me who you think won the skirmish! So far, every audience has graciously named me the winner, but it was touch and go in Garden City in 2021. I had to pull two kids out of the audience to hold my props up when sandbags failed to deliver.

Every festival is different. Art museums and centers across the state—Mason City, Fort Dodge, Muscatine, Okoboji—hold summer arts festivals with craft sales and hands-on art activities for children and adults. We perform and sometimes make finger puppets or paper butterfly puppets with the kids after the shows.

I know I'm getting old, but I hope to perform at many more summer festivals before my curtains close.

Curtains! What do you mean, curtains?! We ARE going to do this forever! You should do what I do: just refuse to get older! I guess that's the advantage of being a puppet. You're born one age—I was born 49, and I was older than Monica by two decades—and you stay that age. Now Monica is decades older than me—haha!

6. Growing

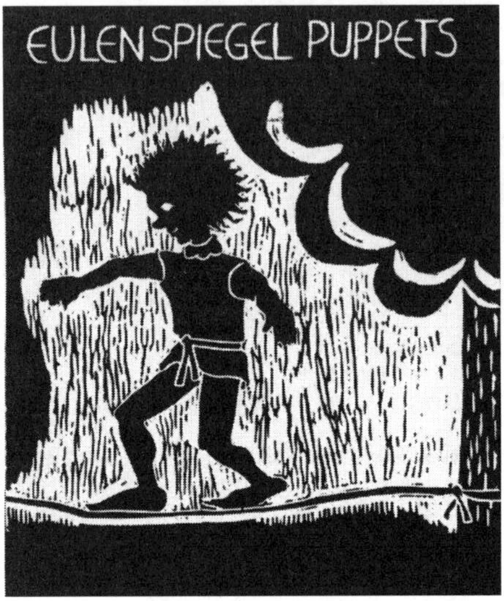

By the early 2000's I was beginning to feel as if I'd been doing this forever!

School residencies continued to be a major source of work and income till 2002 when the No Child Left Behind Act was passed by Congress. Known sarcastically as "No Child's Behind Left" or "No Arts Program Left," it required a level of testing that left little time for *frivolities* like puppet residencies. As teachers were put under more and more pressure to follow curriculum, we figured out how our shows connected to different areas they had to teach. We wrote study guides and developed activities. We condensed our residency offerings to three days to make them more feasible for schools. We applied to foundations for funding support to replace the Arts Council funding that had faded away. We made the transition.

But in the meantime, we still had lots of residencies even as we watched the numbers diminish and saw the handwriting on the wall.

In 1983, Little John was a senior in an Alternative High School. He was one of the kids who simply didn't fit into a traditional high school. His school let us take him out to help us at residencies as long as he kept up with his schoolwork and wrote about his experiences. He made us wildly popular, especially in 5th and 6th-grade classrooms where he was just enough older to be interesting! A cheerful, outgoing boy, he looked a little out of the ordinary in the small towns we visited. He kept his hair long and curly and wore clothes that were showier than the sports-themed T-shirts favored by the local boys. He was cool! He had no trouble connecting with the elementary kids. He was twenty years younger than me and ten years younger than Teri Jean, so Teri Jean regularly switched sides, sometimes acting as an ersatz prank-playing sibling and sometimes as a responsible auntie to Little John. They short-sheeted my bed. I found foreign objects in my purse. Some days it was like traveling with two teenagers.

I discovered how much teenage boys eat, something I had guessed at but not documented at home. In one town, the three of us stayed with our contact teacher and her husband. Every evening we joined them for dinner, but we had breakfast in the local café and lunch in the school cafeteria.

"OK, John. you can order anything you want for breakfast except meat. Meat is what runs the price up,"' I said.

"All right. I'd like two eggs, hash browns, toast, two pancakes, and a large orange juice."

After the first two periods, we moved to a different school.

"Can we stop at a Quick Trip? I'm starved!"

"All right. Get a granola bar or something."

After the next class, we went to the school cafeteria, redolent of the homemade bread the lunch ladies had baked that morning. The principal, a warm middle-aged woman, walked up to Little John.

"You're a growing boy. You go through the lunch line twice!" He did. And cleaned his plate. Twice.

After school he was starved again, so we stopped at the café where the smell of the pies for the dinner menu wafted through the door. Two slices of apple pie later—only coffee for Teri Jean and me—it was time to go to our home for the week. Our hostess had a roast in the oven, complete with potatoes and carrots. John made short work of two helpings.

In early 1988, Teri Jean and I were at my round kitchen table with our usual coffee when the phone rang with an invitation to do a seven-week fall residency in Evanston, Wyoming. Seven weeks! We'd never spent that much time in one town!

Evanston had six elementary schools and one middle school. Our contact, Charlotte Fry, had convinced each of these schools to sign on for a week-long residency and had enlisted the help of her husband, Bob, the director of the Lifelong Learning Center, in fundraising. Charlotte, the descendant of Pushcart Mormons—the settlers who had transported their households over the Rocky Mountains in pushcarts—was tall, slender, and dark-haired. She juggled the care of a large family—five children—with community outreach and using her amazing artistic talent. She made lovely, sensitive pencil drawings.

When we arrived in Evanston, she invited us to her home on Medicine Butte Road on the outskirts of town. We liked each other immediately. We sat in her spacious living room as the children filtered in from playing outside. Soon Teri Jean was on the floor, playing with them.

"What's this street you live on?" she asked. "Medicine Butt? Medicine has a butt?"

The kids giggled, and TJ became their instant friend.

"What made you decide to organize this residency as if you didn't have enough to do?" I asked.

"Well, I've always been interested in puppets, so when I saw there was a puppet troupe on the arts council's roster, I went to a show you did around here. I loved it!"

"Thanks!" I replied.

"Oh, I had ulterior motives. I figured if I got you here for an extended period, I could pick your brains. I want to learn as much about puppetry as I can."

Charlotte tried to find us an empty apartment to stay in. By the time we got there, the apartment had fallen through, and a local young couple agreed to house us. They had a family room in the basement that they designated as ours and two extra bedrooms. Since there was only one bathroom—with four adults getting ready for work—we joined the local YMCA. Teri Jean lifted weights and I swam laps every morning before taking our showers and heading for school.

"Didn't they promise us our own apartment?" asked Teri Jean

"Yeah, it looks like that fell through. Let's tell 'em we need a room in the school to work in."

"And this time it's true. We are working on a new show."

One of the schools had a temporary barracks classroom not currently in use, and that became our hangout. It had ugly red and black carpeting, a teacher's desk, and several tables. We set up our stage and our sewing machine We commandeered a table for papier mâché. After school, we'd relax and gossip for a while and then get to work. The Lifelong Learning Center was nearby, so sometimes Bob would stop in on his way home from work to chat. It was a presidential election year—George H.W. Bush was running against Michael Dukakis—and Teri Jean and I were both faithful Democrats. We assumed everyone around us was Republican, so we held our tongues. One day Bob brought up the subject. We exchanged glances.

"Last year Brother Jackson stopped in Evanston, and his speech was inspiring." Bob enthused.

Brother Jackson? Who's that? I wondered. Wait! He's talking about Jesse Jackson! He likes Jesse Jackson! Teri Jean and I had to revise our preconceived notions.

Seven weeks was long enough to make us feel like local residents. We'd see kids we recognized at the grocery store and we made friends at the Y. We traded gossip and dreams of the future with our hosts and collected jokes to tell Charlotte and Bob's kids.

Do you remember the cop who stopped us after about four weeks? He was very stern in admonishing you. "Ma'am," he said, "I've been watching you gals. When are you going to get your Wyoming plates?" Ha! Teri Jean got smart with him. "Sir," she said, "I don't think her husband in IOWA would approve of that! That showed him!

In early November we left Evanston and headed home. Teri Jean was driving when we crossed the Iowa border. I made her stop so I could get out and kiss the ground. Guess I was glad to be coming home! I loved the Wyoming mountains and big sky, but I missed Iowa's verdant green. Like many members of immigrant families, I valued the roots I'd put down.

We kept in touch with Charlotte even after our residency was over Five years later, when Charlotte heard about my plan to attend a festival in San Francisco, she invited me to stop in Evanston and teach a shadow puppet workshop on my way home. Twenty-some years later, my travels took me through Evanston again. Charlotte and Bob invited me to their now childless home for dinner.

"Monica, I want you to see what Charlotte's been doing," said Bob.

Proudly, he showed me a whole new cast of puppets.

John had been busy all seven weeks of our absence. He was building our dream house, a log cabin in the woods south of Iowa City. That year, 1988, was our busiest ever. In addition to lots of individual shows and our favorite Touring Arts Team, we did 23 five-day residencies in Iowa and Wyoming. The money I earned supported us and paid for building materials so that John could spend all of his time on our house. He'd been working on the interior.

"Oh! Look at those pretty green tiles on the counter! And the stairs: they're perfect! The floor!"

He'd salvaged the good parts of a water-damaged gym floor in a local high school. He hadn't sanded and finished it yet, so the rearranged stripes and circles looked like a Mondrian painting.

The house had an open floor plan, with the living room transitioning to a dining area—room for our round table—and a kitchen separated from the dining nook by the green-tiled counter and from the living room by a long, skinny bathroom. The front porch—the length of the house—was surrounded by a decorative iron railing designed and welded by John. We'd ordered as many logs as we could afford, and John stacked them up as high as they'd go. It made for a large loft—our bedroom—and a high ceiling which made the house appear more spacious than the size would indicate. John added many loving details: built-in shelves, nooks and crannies, and a bathroom exhaust fan embellished with a crescent moon.

When we moved in the following February, I felt wonderful about the contribution my residencies had made.

While we were gone, John had conducted a major battle against a group of feral hogs who had taken over our timber. He'd built a fence over the creek that joined our property to the property of the hogs' owner. The hogs were not happy. They liked the hickory nuts that fell from our trees.

One day a piglet got stuck in the fence. Its mother spotted John as the culprit and took off after him! John had spent his early youth working on a farm, taking care of the hogs, so he understood the danger and carried a pistol when he was in the woods. He barely escaped with his life, only because he shot the mama.

He dragged the carcass to his workshop, lifted it onto his workbench with his chain hoist, and called a friend to help him butcher it. We tried cooking the meat—smoking, slow-cooking, barbequing—but nothing we could do made it taste good. Maybe it was our bad feelings about having to kill the mama, but it was us or the hogs. I had nightmares about finding his picked-clean bones in the woods.

In the end, he won the battle and evicted the intruders.

The first new show we worked on after the Battle of the Hogs was a new adaptation of *The Bremen Town Musicians,* the Grimm's fairy tale about four aging farm animals—donkey, dog, cat, and rooster—who join forces and go to Bremen to become street musicians. They all realize they face impending death because they're too old to be useful on their respective farms. On the way, they encounter thieves living in a cabin in the woods with piles of stolen money. You can imagine what happens next, or you can read the story!

We located the tale in rural Iowa, and, instead of robbers, the villains of our story were two feral hogs with huge tusks. We named them Jowls and Hog Belly. They sang:

"We are nasty! We are nasty and mean!

We like making nasty villainous schemes!"

It was the first time we worked with a composer. Sven Hansell was a composer and musicologist married to my favorite cousin Marie. As a lark, he agreed to write music for the show. He wrote several delightful a capella songs that worked well for Teri Jean's tenor and my second soprano. Jack, the donkey; Howie (Ow-ow-owie), the dog; Marilyn (Meowrlyn), the cat; and Earl (Er-er-er-er-Earl), the rooster had a long successful run.

"Why don't we work on another show together?" I said to Sven. "Maybe I can get a grant from the Iowa Arts Council, and we can pay you!" Little did I know I had just planted the seed for disaster.

I got the grant, we picked a story—another Grimm's tale, *The Elves and the Shoemaker*—and began work on a script. We named the main characters, the shoemaker and his wife, after my favorite East Berlin cousins/surrogate parents. Inspired by their lovely urban garden, we created a puppet garden complete with flowers whose heads nodded when they were watered. The rabbits hopping around in the garden transformed into elves who spent the nights cobbling beautiful shoes for the shoemaker. The elf-created shoes were so desirable that they sold for large amounts of money and solved all of the shoemaker's problems.

Sven found the plot—based heavily on the original tale—a little too tame.

"We need a dramatic scene. Let's have vultures attack the shoemaker's wife while she's watering the garden!"

"You write the music; we'll write the script," Teri Jean replied.

"But the Iowa Arts Council. Will they think the story is important enough?" he whined.

"You let us worry about the Arts Council."

And so it went. The arts council funding, which I had thought would inspire and free us all, was more of a roadblock—for Sven, that is. He couldn't help but fiddle with the story and the text of the songs—trying to insert "weighty, serious" content into our light-hearted tale. When we demurred, he complained to Cousin Marie:

"These bossy feminists! I can't work with them!"

Teri Jean discovered that he was much more agreeable when he was well fed, so we started bringing orange juice and granola bars to rehearsals.

In the end—against all odds—we had a delightful production accompanied by two pianos—one played by Sven—and a lively percussionist with a sense of whimsy.

But Sven wasn't done with us. He was angry at us—especially me—for what he saw as a lack of cooperation. He tinkered with the tempo during the show so I was never completely sure how fast or slowly I was going to have to sing.

"Watch out!" TJ hissed at me backstage. "He's got that glint in his eye. He's going to mess with you!"

It kept me on my toes. It made us decide to record the music so we could perform it with an unflappable, unemotional CD.

I was terribly worried that my relationship with my favorite cousin would be marred. Luckily, Marie was aware of Sven's personality quirks—and mine, I suspect— and loved him—and me—all the same. After the premiere, Teri Jean proposed a female-bonding ritual: we would all get our ears pierced together and toast each other with margaritas. To this day, I think of Teri Jean, Marie, and the elves every time I wear earrings.

Sven wasn't our first collaborator. A few years earlier, we had run into our musician friend, Guy Drollinger, in a parking lot. On a sheer whim, we asked him to do a show with us. He wrote the melody for Mr. Punch's song and did the show with us a few times until we parted ways—for a few years.

In 1995 Macy Matarazzo joined us for eight months. Macy was short with dark hair, sparkly eyes, and an off-the-wall sense of style and humor. Her clothes were oversized and brightly patterned. She borrowed Teri Jean's bike and returned it, psychedelically painted with many colors of spray paint. We had met Macy a few years earlier when she was a student at Cornell College in Mt.Vernon, Iowa. She contacted us and asked to do an internship with us. She helped us create *Eulenspiegel's Circus,* a zany romp through the fantasy childhood of our namesake, Till Eulenspiegel. She loved the experience so much that she enrolled in a puppetry school in London for two years. When she returned, we offered her a job. She did residencies, alone and with the two of us. She helped us tour guest puppeteers around the state. She created and performed a quirky solo show, *The Matchmaker and the Mouse*, that was 100% madcap Macy.

Boy, that was a silly show! Macy wore this HUGE cape that transformed into all kinds of scenery, even a mountain! And the story: a mouse that almost marries the sun...and the wind...before she ends up marrying a mouse. What a letdown! Macy was fun; I missed her when she left!

As Iowa's 1996 sesquicentennial approached, the three of us decided to create a large production with a nod to Iowa history and folklore. *Sal Fink, The Mississippi Screamer* featured the folkloric daughter of Mike Fink, the keelboat man. Mike, called "king of the keelboaters", was an actual river boatman known for his strength and toughness as he pushed his boat up and down the Ohio and Mississippi Rivers. Sal may or may not have really lived, but legend held that she navigated the rivers on the back of a giant catfish named Nishnabotna (after the western Iowa river famous for leaving its banks and earning the "Naughty Nishnabotna" moniker). We asked Guy to be part of the show, and Guy suggested we also include his fellow musician, Ron Hillis. Ron turned out to be a gifted songwriter and wrote a lilting earworm as the theme song:

Swim around, up and down
There's a river most everywhere.
Iowa's the place to be
To ride a catfish if you dare!

Poet Mary Swander wrote an evocative monologue for a Mike Fink character and actor Rip Russell performed it. When we got stuck, we asked director Michael Sokoloff to step out of his world of "legitimate theater" and take on puppets. He saved our bacon and helped us create a show that was equally beloved by children and adults, our first show with live music! That is live music not created by our voices or our two-part harmony kazoo band.

Alas, by summer Macy realized that the life of a puppeteer was a little too uncertain for her. She stayed around and helped us create giant puppets for the summer parade and then she said her goodbyes.

But the seeds had been planted for future internships, community projects, and collaborations. We were getting a national reputation.

7. Hicks from the Midwest

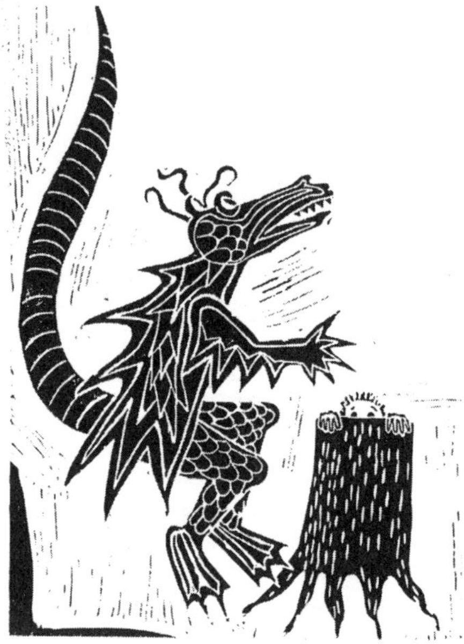

Our first exposure on the national stage came in 1983. Our Iowa/Nebraska puppetry guild had taken on the huge job of planning, promoting, and hosting a national festival for Puppeteers of America. If we had any hope of succeeding, everyone in our small group had to take on a job. The festival was to take place on the Iowa State University campus in Ames, 130 miles from us, so we couldn't be much help with on-site preparation. Veronika, our Guild President, had an idea.

"Let's send Teri and Monica to some regional festivals to drum up business! They're personable; they could talk people into coming to Ames!"

In addition to the national festival, each of Puppeteers of America's eight regions held regional festivals. We contacted the ones we could reach in a two-day or shorter drive and offered to perform or teach workshops. The Northeast/Mid-Atlantic festival agreed to let us do a performance workshop on adapting folk tales to puppetry. We would perform *The Devil's Three Golden Hairs*, our favorite show, and discuss the choices we made in adapting it to puppets. On the way back home, we would stop in Columbus, Ohio, and do our show at the Great Lakes festival.

We left Iowa City on a Wednesday morning and arrived in Glassboro, New Jersey, Thursday evening just as the festival started. Along with four hundred east coast puppeteers and puppet aficionados, we filed into the auditorium for the evening show. We'd been told it was a student production. We loved it! At the end of the show, Teri Jean jumped up to give it a standing ovation. It was good, but was it that good? When no one else stood up, I decided I couldn't leave her standing there alone, so I stood up, too. Four hundred heads, eyebrows raised, turned to look at us.

Later that evening everyone gathered in the student union for conversation and drinks. Teri Jean and I found a vacant table and settled in. A middle-aged man approached us and introduced himself as "Bud".

Bud had twinkly eyes in a round, friendly face, a round body, and a genial persona. We sat together and chatted. Bud came to the point.

"You girls aren't from around here. I need to fill you in on the politics of the region."

Apparently, our standing ovation had been frowned upon and had made us the subject of gossip and the butt of jokes about the ignorant hinterland. It was at least as much about regional puppetry politics as it was about the quality of the show. Who knew? Where we came from, puppeteers were few and far enough between that there was little occasion for rivalry or politics, just camaraderie.

Nonetheless, we had to face our scornful peers at 8:30 the next morning, the time slot for the first workshop. We were set up in a messy basement theater shop lit with fluorescent lights. Our backdrop stood amid table saws and paint buckets facing a few folding chairs. We expected a handful of people. After witnessing the drinking and socializing the night before, we figured most people would be sleeping in. And then they began to gather. All of the chairs were filled. More chairs were set up. The audience spilled over into the hall, standing room only. Everyone wanted to see what those hicks from the Midwest would do!

The Devil's Three Golden Hairs is a classic tale. It has folkloric, even Biblical elements: a wise crone living in the woods, an innocent young boy prophesied to become king, a devil as the instrument of justice, and the king seeking indirect ways to kill the boy. Our devil was a comic character who burst onto stage, sputtering.

"Darn it, darn it, darn it! I just came from the castle and I didn't pick up one single soul! I had three of 'em right on the line, and they all made last-minute conversions!"

Loud laughter from the third row of the audience. It was one of the most prominent puppeteers in the region, a trendsetter! She set the tone. Soon laughter punctuated the audience, loud applause at the end, and people lined up to talk to us and see whether we would agree to tour in New England.

After that we were free to enjoy the festival, watching other shows and attending workshops. Much to our surprise, one of the performers was a past nemesis of ours! He had briefly lived in Iowa and had tried, unsuccessfully, to discredit us and channel work in his direction. It gave us immense pleasure to sit in the darkened theater and watch his show. It was visually beautiful, but the script was so laborious that snores from the audience punctuated every line!

That evening there was a party for all of the guest performers. Everyone talked about our show, and no one even mentioned his!

Two months later, in August, we were back on the road to the east coast, this time to perform at Lincoln Center Out of Doors in New York City. As luck would have it, the organizer was my sister's neighbor, and he decided to take a chance on us.

What a deal that was! We were on a big stage in the middle of the plaza. We got to be the first group to use their brand-new sound system, mics mounted all the way around the stage. We looked fabulous! But why wasn't anyone laughing? The story was hilarious! Afterwards, all of these people came up and told us how great we looked. "Too bad we couldn't hear you," they said. Huh? What about that state-of-the-art sound system? Turns out they'd mounted the mics upside down. If we'd known that, we would've brought those ten-pound sound packs!

Two years later we were invited back, this time on a more intimate stage, with *Punch and Judy* and *Buttercup*, a Norwegian tale about a troll woman who tries to entice a little girl into her stew. Of course, the little girl wins the day! We thought we had won the day, too, when we saw a New York Times photographer snapping dozens of pictures.

"Is that the New York Times?" I whispered to Teri Jean.

"That's what his badge says! We're about to hit the big time!"

It was all I could do to keep my composure. Before we started our show, we heard mumbling and buzzing in the audience as people looked at their programs. I tiptoed close to eavesdrop.

"Iowa? Where's that?"

"Have you ever heard of Iowa?"

"Where in the world is Iowa?"

Yup! If the program said we were from China, nobody would've batted an eye. But Iowa.! Ha! That's exotic!

The next day we combed the paper in vain, looking for photos of our show. Much to our dismay, a major news story had squeezed everything else out of the paper. There went my dreams of "New York Times" as the photo credit in our next brochure!

In 1990, we were invited to perform at a storytelling festival—and a series of elementary schools—in Bakersfield, California. The festival director had seen us perform *Buttercup* in Laramie, Wyoming. She loved the big puppets, the masked character, and the folktale. We asked to bring *The Devil's Three Golden Hairs* instead. It used the same style of large puppets and a masked character. We thought it was a better show with a more complicated story, and—more importantly—we could pack it for flying.

We did not expect to be controversial.

"Some of the parents want to meet with you after school to ask you questions about the story," said our contact person after the first show.

"We'd love to!" I said. "Wow, Teri Jean! That's pretty cool that they're so interested in folklore."

"Why is there a devil in your story?" asked the first parent.

"Well, like most folktales, it's a story about the battle of good versus evil."

"And the devil represents evil?" asked another parent.

"Oddly enough, no. The king represents evil. The devil is the instrument of justice. He makes sure the king is punished for his crimes."

"Don't you think that's a little heavy for kids?" asked a third.

"Well, it's a super fun story with a lot of humor. It's very funny. And, you know, kids know there are bad people in the world. It's empowering to see evil punished."

A version of this scene was repeated every day that week. On Saturday, when we performed for the festival, a man ostentatiously walked out, slamming the door, when the devil entered. It came as a shock to me that a funky red devil mask could inspire such strong feelings!

It was a harbinger of things to come. Our storyteller friend had to stop telling stories about Baba Yaga, the Russian witch if she wanted to keep working. We had to put *Three Golden Hairs* away and abandon our plan of producing *The Devil's Gifts*, another favorite of mine. We chalked the changes up to the power of the right-wing Christian movement.

A decade later, I was listening to Morning Edition on NPR when they did a retrospective story about events in Bakersfield in the second half of the 1980s.

“Dozens of people, a group of children claimed, were members of a satanic cult that molested and then murdered 27 infants, dismembered them, and drained their blood,” said the commentator. The story went viral and versions of it popped up all over the country. I remembered the brouhaha but had never known the source.

I spilled my coffee, dropped the toast I was buttering and called Teri Jean. Finally, I understood what had transpired ten years earlier in Bakersfield.

In 1984, while Teri Jean was laid up with her broken foot, I took off to Germany to visit relatives and attend an international puppetry festival in Dresden, then part of the German Democratic Republic, aka East Germany. The breadth and quality of East German puppetry amazed and delighted me! I learned that the country boasted 17 permanent puppet theaters with sizable staffs of puppet makers, puppeteers, directors, playwrights, and administrators. They operated with significant state support.

Even so, many of the shows included veiled ridicule of the government, as puppetry always has. Since no one takes puppets seriously, they can get away with uttering the most subversive ideas!

Wandering the streets one day, I came upon a large crowd watching a young man with a tiny stage strapped around his waist. Miniature marionettes came to life, cavorting through a popular fairy tale. Entranced, I started dreaming of the miniature show Teri Jean and I would create when I got home. That show, *The Cat, the Ram, and the Wolves*, became the first—to date—of five Eulenspiegel miniature marionette shows.

The Rumanian tale starts:

“In a certain country, in a cottage in the woods, lives a little old lady who is neither rich nor poor. With her live her animals: a bird, a ram who’s grazing out back, and a kitty cat! Listen to the amazing tale of the cat, the ram, and the wolves.”

It goes on to tell how the cat talks the ram into running away from home with him. They encounter three wolves who want to eat them. Together, they outsmart the wolves and a bear and end up going back home to the little old lady. This story has always seemed to mirror my life: we first developed it shortly after Little John ran away to New York—with a friend who encouraged him. I worried about the "wolves" he might encounter. And now I'm an old lady living in a cottage in the woods with her kitty cat. Do I need to get a ram? And a bird?

When I got home from Dresden and reported to Teri Jean, we began scheming a way to see more. I wrote to the president of UNIMA-GDR, the East German branch of an international puppetry organization dedicated to the pursuit of peace through the art of puppetry. I asked him if there was a way for us to meet East German puppeteers and have a look at their shows and operations. He replied by inviting us to perform at their national puppetry festival. We had been recommended to him—wonder of wonders!—by the east coast puppeteer who had started the laughter going when we performed at the Northeast/Mid Atlantic Puppetry Festival! He knew her through her position in UNIMA-USA and had asked her if she'd ever heard of us.

In 1987, we packed up Schulz and *The Cat, the Ram, and the Wolves* and boarded a plane for Berlin. Cousin Hermann met us at the airport and escorted us to Checkpoint Charlie where we would cross the border to East Berlin.

We were like ROCK STARS! I'll never forget crossing that border! The man ahead of us had to empty his pockets and answer a bunch of questions. They even patted him down! Then us with suitcases and me in the trunk... nothing! Turns out the border guard loved puppets! She was impressed that we were performing at the National Festival. "That's quite an honor," she said as she waved us through. "I would love to have seen those puppets but to unpack them would be way too difficult!"

Everything looked different on the east side of the border. One side looked like other western cities, with high-rise buildings, neon lights, brightly lit store windows, billboards, and throngs of shoppers. Yards away, on the other side of the border, grey was the dominant color. Without the brilliant hues of commercialism, the subdued color of the streets, sidewalks, and buildings prevailed. Shoppers, like consumer goods, were few and far between. Warehouses—looking much like Walmart but with limited choices and without ads—were among the only places to spend money. Some small shops, bakeries, and grocery stores with scanty stock dotted the streets.

The warmth of our welcome contrasted with the dismal shade of our surroundings. My cousins were there with bells on to greet us! We walked the seven blocks to the family home on the Glinkastrasse. Cousin Hermann, who lived in West Berlin and crossed the border with us, carried Schulz in his trunk. Ami, my first cousin but old enough to be my mother, waited at home with coffee and cake.

After a convivial snack, Ami noticed Teri Jean yawning. She led her into her husband Peter's study and motioned to a day bed with a cozy blanket. She and Peter tucked TJ in.

"That's when I felt at home! Since then, East Berlin has always held warm memories for me," TJ told me years later.

The next morning, it was time to board the train to Magdeburg, the festival town. Peter and Hermann took us to the station. While we waited, Peter addressed Teri Jean.

"Monica is like one of our children. Hermann is, too, but he never visits."

Hermann and I looked at each other and rolled our eyes. We both knew that Hermann, with his busy schedule as a hospital doctor, visited as often as he could.

"I guess it's true that absence makes the heart grow fonder," I remarked.

We boarded the train for Magdeburg. It was a lovely medieval city that had been bombed out in WW II. A handful of beautiful buildings remained, but there were blocks and blocks of utilitarian Soviet-style apartment and office buildings, thrown up in a hurry.

Our train stopped at the main station. Two charming fellows with huge bouquets waited for us. One of them, Bernd, addressed us in German.

"Sind Sie die Amerikanischen Puppenspieler?"

The other one, André quickly translated.

"He said, *are you the American puppeteers*?"

André was disappointed when he realized I understood German. Luckily for him, Teri Jean's German skills were limited. He stayed by her side, driving her to distraction by translating every single word.

André and Bernd had been assigned to be our guides. Bernd was tall, slender, blonde, and laid back, married with a four-year-old son. André was quick and nervous, with dark hair and dark eyes. They were sweet and helpful, and they stuck to us like glue. They went to shows with us. They took us shopping to spend the money we'd made performing—money that was worthless at home. They even took us to see the Till Eulenspiegel fountain, a large fountain in the middle of town depicting our namesake, who, according to legend, had played some of his most famous tricks in Magdeburg.

Magdeburg was far enough from the border that it didn't get much in the way of Western television. Without TV, the puppet shows were mobbed. People stood in line for blocks to get tickets. After each show, our fellow puppeteers gathered around to ask us questions. They didn't want to talk about our puppets or how we chose our material or how we built our shows. They asked how on earth we could make a living as puppeteers in a market economy! After all, their theaters had the benefit of state support. Just three years later, after reunification with West Germany, they had to find out for themselves.

One day Bernd picked us up in his Trabant, the much-maligned car of East German manufacture. Nicknamed "Trabi", these tiny cars were made of plastic with two-stroke engines—like a lawnmower—spewing exhaust behind them.

"Where are we going?" I asked.

"I'm taking you to a little village that is celebrating its 1,050th birthday. They're having a festival!"

It looked so familiar! There was a fire engine, a beer tent, food booths, and even a petting zoo. Teri Jean had been feeling a little homesick.

"Wow! This reminds me of home! It looks just like an Iowa town festival."

"Plus 900 years!" I added.

At the end of the week, we bid goodbye to Bernd and André and got back on the train.

A few years later, when the Wall came down and we heard about the extent of Stasi—the secret police—surveillance, we understood that Bernd and Andre weren't just being nice guys; they were keeping an eye on us. At first, that realization made me feel bad, but the more I reflected on the experience, the more I made peace with it. Whatever Bernd and André had to do to work within their paradigm, we ended up being friends. We glimpsed the reality of each other's situations. They *were* nice guys!

8. Vehicles I Have Known

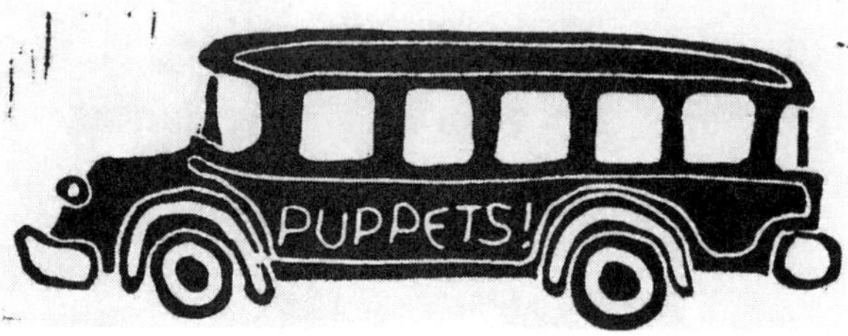

"You're getting way too heavy for the back of my bicycle!" I said to five-year-old Little John. "Guess I better learn to drive."

John found a 1950 Ford—not too rusty and most everything but the windshield wipers worked—for a mere $25.00. Sold! The brakes were a little sketchy, but they worked most of the time.

One driving lesson was enough for John. His nerves couldn't take teaching someone as un-mechanical as me to drive.

Our friend John Wright—JW—stepped up.

"I'll teach you. And the timing, January, is perfect. If you learn to drive on snow and ice you'll never fear driving in winter."

After a few lessons with JW, who sat in the passenger seat with a Buddha-like calm, another friend volunteered.

"I'll take you out for some practice sessions," said Mary Lea, Little John's sometime babysitter who had five young children of her own. I learned how to merge lanes on the highway, how to parallel park, how to manage four-way stop signs, and how to downshift when the brakes seemed iffy. I learned the pre-seatbelt mom-move: right arm straight out in front of child passenger at each application of the brake.

The Ford lasted until a friend borrowed it, ran the radiator dry, and fried the engine. Next came a formerly luxurious 1950 Hudson that made me feel like I was driving around in a hotel lobby. And—wonder of wonders—the brakes and wipers worked! I learned to change tires and identify numerous noises. Twenty-five-dollar cars specialized in strange sounds, bald tires, and short lives. A creaking Chevy Impala that cost the princely sum of fifty dollars could barely climb the slight rise on our street.

By the time we started performing, I had graduated to the first of a series of pick-up trucks with toppers, handy for hauling puppet shows—and children. I had also started naming my trucks, usually after the color of their bodies: Forest, Ruby, Scarlet, Bluebell. When Bluebell's topper was vandalized, apparently with a pocketknife or similar tool and seemingly out of sheer boredom—nothing was taken—we started thinking about a vehicle with a completely hard body.

Schulz weighing in here: Have you forgotten about the Toyota Corolla that crashed? How could you? That was a terrible scene! We puppets were scattered all over the road. People thought we were humans. For some reason, they didn't care as much when they found out we were JUST puppets. Just puppets indeed! As if puppets don't feel pain.

John found a blue Suburban that we could afford because it needed work. I named her Petunia. He and his friends restored her to good working order until the infamous oil dump in Green Bay, Wisconsin, that reduced us to pulling Bluebell out of the weeds and driving her across the mountains to Wyoming. By the time we returned, Petunia had a new engine and served us well for several more years, driving annually to New York to perform at the Puppet Playhouse and to Wyoming for school residencies.

When Petunia finally needed more repair than she was worth, we bought Dusty Miller, a shimmery grey Suburban I named after the silver-leaf ornamental plant. Dusty Miller had pretensions. Her former owners were way out of our income bracket, and she had all the extras of the day: fold-away captain chair seats, cup holders, a CD player, and electric doors and windows!

After Dusty Miller, we were back to basics: school-bus yellow Buttercup had been a City of Iowa City utility vehicle. She didn't even have air conditioning till we had it installed. No more captain chairs and cup holders. The radio sat on the seat between us instead of being built into the dash. No more electric windows either, which was fine with me since the mechanisms don't get along well with gravel dust.

As the price of gas went up, we eyed a neighbor's minivan and asked if we could measure the inside. It had the same amount of space—configured a little differently—as the Suburban and it got twice the gas mileage. By that time, we were both making more money and saving a decent amount.

"I want you to have a new car," insisted John. "A new minivan."

"A new car! Are you sure? Isn't that a terrible waste of money?"

"You've driven plenty of junk. You deserve something new."

Vanna Blue joined the company. She was a marvel. Squeaky clean with that unmistakable new car aroma. Basic in the best possible way: no electric doors and windows to get clogged with gravel dust!

After six years and 210,000 miles, she began to stall at intersections. No one could diagnose the reason. It was January. John had nightmares about a stall in the middle of nowhere and visions of me freezing to death. He always did have an overactive imagination. The fear in his eyes did me in, and I agreed to trade Vanna Blue in for Vanna White, a low mileage dealership service vehicle that had been used as a loaner for people getting their cars fixed.

After Vanna White made way for Vanna Scarlett, she—Vanna White—became Eli's vehicle. Vanna Scarlett, a former fleet vehicle, still serves well. By the time she goes on to the auto Elysian Fields, I hope to be able to afford her electric—or hybrid—cousin.

If you make a living as a puppeteer in the rural Midwest, touring is a way of life, and your vehicle is perhaps the most important member of your company. I make sure to stay on good terms with my wheels: calling them by name, praising them, patting them on the dashboard in encouragement. Ninety percent of the time they have rewarded me by getting all the way home before breaking down.

9. Moving East

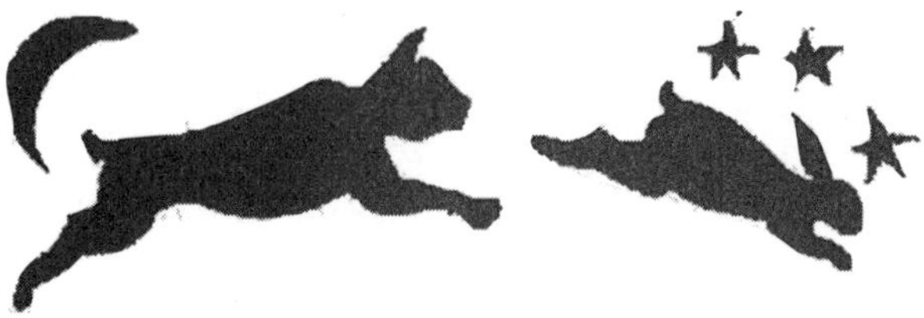

When Teri Jean got married, a Dixieland jazz band played at her reception. Lyle's trombone skipped up and down the scale. He and his bandmates swayed as TJ's friends gathered in Old Brick, a repurposed Presbyterian Church used as a performing and events center. Toes tapped and couples converged on the dance floor, the former church sanctuary. Everyone ignored the wedding cake on a side table. Everyone except six-year-old Buffy, who leaned her chin on the table and gazed at the cake, wishing the band would stop and someone would cut the delicate confection.

I shed all of my inhibitions and turned into a dancing fool, A fool with an edge of hysteria. I thrashed around the dance floor, alone or with any available partner, not caring how awkward I looked. I didn't know why, but I felt like I was dancing on my grave. A few years later, I understood the feeling as a premonition that my way of life would change.

"Charlie wants to move," TJ announced one day in 1986.

"I know." She had mentioned this before. "He knows that's a fantasy!"

"No! This time he's serious! "I can't hold him off any longer."

"But where to?"

"Pretty much anywhere but Iowa City. He doesn't like it here anymore now that he's out of the workshop. He says I can pick."

"That's easy. Move to Muscatine. Or Clinton. Or Washington." We'd done school residencies in all of those nearby towns. We liked them all.

"No. It's got to be outside of Iowa. As far away as possible, for Charlie."

Charlie was Teri Jean's husband. He'd been happy in Iowa City as long as he was a student in the highly regarded Iowa Writers' Workshop, but the town's appeal faded as his student days ended. It was a challenge to find a publisher, and he missed the adulation he got as a favored student.

For me, it was a gut punch! I didn't realize he wanted to move out of state. I saw years of work sprout wings and fly away.

"Do you still want to work with me?'

"Of course! But I don't want to fail at marriage!"

They had only been married for about three years. How could I argue with that? I didn't want to make her marriage fail. But I didn't want the puppet troupe to fail either. How could we possibly save both? There had to be a way!

"Well, where have we worked? Where could you find other puppeteers to hang out with? Even get involved..."

Since our successful appearance at the east coast puppetry festival in 1983, we had been making annual trips to Massachusetts to perform in the New England Puppetry Series. We'd made friends and found out about puppetry programs, including the Institute of Professional Puppetry Arts (IPPA) in Connecticut. We knew the program's director. We knew good puppeteers in the area. Teri Jean might be able to nurture more connections for us there. Maybe New England would serve both Charlie and Teri Jean. Charlie agreed, and they moved to Northampton, Massachusetts in 1987.

Schulz here: there you go again with your eternal optimism. Does it ever occur to you not to look at—or invent—the bright side? I felt like crawling into a hole when Teri Jean told us she was moving, but you, as always, had to try to find a silver lining! Well, as far as I'm concerned, it was a disaster. I'm just glad it didn't last forever.

It was up to me to organize our shows and residencies, to schedule them in blocks so that Teri Jean could be here for a month at a time and spend intervening months out east.

Teri Jean—outgoing and open-minded as she was—made connections. She volunteered to help with the New England Puppetry Series; she pursued and deepened a friendship with Bonnie and Andrew Periale, New Hampshire puppeteers we had spent time with at the puppetry festivals in 1983; she traveled to Connecticut to see if she could get involved in IPPA's events. She made the 1200-mile trip to Iowa, then back to Massachusetts, in a rickety boat of a 1970's car, camping or sleeping in her car to save money.

She'd leave Northampton or Iowa at the crack of dawn—"early thirty," as she said—and drive to western Pennsylvania or eastern Ohio. If she saw a campsite, she'd pull in. If it was early enough in the evening, she might even build a campfire. Otherwise, a rest area would have to do.

"It's a good thing this car is so big. I can stretch all the way out in the back seat. And open the windows to catch a breeze. 'Course the bugs come in, too," she mused as she scratched a mosquito bite.

"Don't you ever stay in a motel?" a friend asked.

"Nope. Charlie says we don't have enough money for motels. Rest areas are free."

Meanwhile, we tried to keep things in the puppet troupe as normal as possible. We worked on new shows, often after school during a residency. We built *The Three Aunts*, *The Lion in the Well*, *Jack the Cunning Thief*, and *The Adventures of Great Rabbit* during the four years of TJ's exile.

The Three Aunts was our attempt at a non-verbal show, non-verbal for Teri Jean, that is. On top of everything else, she developed nodes on her vocal cords—a response, in part, to stress—and had to go on voice rest for three months. I narrated and worked some of the puppets. Teri Jean worked the main character, a poignant girl who came to evocative life through TJ's sensitive manipulation skills, which she developed to compensate for her missing voice. When her voice rest ended, she and I harmonized on a lullaby sung by the aunts, and TJ voiced Auntie Ila, but her girl remained mostly silent, coming to sweet life through her movements.

The Lion in the Well, *Jack, the Cunning Thief*, and *The Adventures of Great Rabbit* are all trickster tales, African American, Irish, and Native American. I've always been fascinated by the universal humanity of folktales, and the way the same essential story appears in many different cultures. The flavor may be different, but the storyline is the same, and even the characters repeat. Rabbits, for example, are tricksters in African, Native American, Mexican, and African American tales. In Asian and Native American lore, they are sometimes elevated to the divine. Jack may be an Irish human, but his stories echo rabbit trickster tales.

To cement our often-long-distance partnership, Teri Jean I and started an Iowa City performing season, doing more or less regular shows in Old Brick.

One year we ran a twin performing season in Dubuque, where Teri Jean's sister helped out. Each time we did a show at Old Brick, we repeated it the following weekend in Dubuque. The Dubuque Arts Council had an art center in the old jail—"the oldest jail in the country still in use" was the dubious brag when I was growing up there. We got permission to do our shows in their gallery, surrounded by the rough limestone walls and tiny cells.

The first day we set up I asked the gallery attendant to lock me in one of the cells. I wanted to know how it felt to be closed in by those looming stone walls, looking out between the bars in the door. A feeling of dread overcame me, even though I knew the door would be unlocked in a moment. Do the emotions of past residents inhabit a space? Or did my fears for the future coalesce as the walls closed in?

Despite its dark history, the old jail was surprisingly intimate and comfortable as a performing space. We only abandoned it because we realized we lacked the promotional skills to advertise in both cities.

In the end, although she had no trouble keeping busy in Northampton, nothing satisfied Teri Jean the way performing did. As the months and years went by, she spent more and more time here and less out east. I would get a call for a residency. Before accepting, I would call Teri Jean.

"TJ, I got a call for a two-week residency in Clinton in October. I know that's supposed to be home time for you, but I told her I'd check."

"Wait a minute. Let me talk to Charlie." A few minutes later: "He said we need the money, so yes."

It seemed the money was more important to Charlie than Teri Jean's companionship. I felt glad—and a little guilty about my feelings.

Charlie convinced her they didn't have the money for two apartments—"Your home is here in Northampton, Teri"—so she stayed with John and me or another friend. When we moved out in the country, I put a bed in my workshop so she wouldn't have to sleep on the couch.

My workshop was forty feet long and eight feet wide—an old semi-trailer John had renovated with windows, shelves, and counters. We put my childhood bed along the back wall. Rocky—a cat who had already claimed the property we thought we owned—greeted us when we arrived, hoping for regular meals. He shared the workshop with Teri Jean. So did the country mice.

Late one night the front door flew open and Teri Jean jumped in, to use the bathroom, I assumed.

"Does she have to be that loud?" I grumbled to John as I noticed the clock dial pointing to 2:00 AM.

"Yikes! Rocky just jumped on my bed and caught a mouse!"

"Oh no, I'm sorry! Maybe you should sleep on the couch after all, TJ!"

The couch opened up into a double futon bed. I put a screen around the bed to give her some privacy, and Teri Jean settled in. She was a tidy person by nature, usually keeping her belongings well organized, much more than I ever did. You couldn't have guessed that from looking at her corner in the living room, a heap of clothes, books, and random belongings. It signaled how she suffered from her displacement and seemed to reflect the confusion in her emotions.

Shortly after we moved into our log cabin and added Rocky to our family, I walked down the porch steps with an open cat food can in my hand. I slipped on the ice, dropped the can, and smashed my hand into the gravel, breaking my left wrist. As if we weren't having enough problems! Now I had a heavy plaster cast on my arm. I couldn't keep my arm over my head for any significant length of time, so hand puppet shows were out of the question. Luckily *The Lion in the Well* and *Jack, the Cunning Thief* used tabletop marionettes. I worked them with my arms straight out in front, hovering over the tabletop stage. I could do that with a cast on my arm!

The doctor told me wrists heal slowly because there's not enough blood flow through that small joint. Not that, too! I called my friend—the licensed hypnotherapist—and asked her for suggestions that would make me heal faster. She got me started on a round of self-hypnosis. I visualized elves with power washers squirting blood through my wrist. After twenty minutes my cast was hot! I repeated the routine twice a day. The doctor was amazed at how quickly my wrist healed.

"I'll have to tell all of my patients to be puppeteers!" he exclaimed.

Since he was a bit of a macho M-Deity, I kept my secret to myself.

As the time dragged on into year three, Teri Jean finally rebelled and found an apartment she could share with two friends. I'm not sure she even told Charlie.

In Council Bluffs, where we were doing a two-week residency, she suddenly spoke up.

"I hardly have any stuff out there. If I never went back, Charlie could probably pack it all into one box and send it." A few months before she had reflected on her marriage.

"The average length of a marriage is seven years. I don't want to be a statistic."

"No matter what you do, you'll be a statistic," I replied. "We're all statistics."

One day in the summer of 1991, Teri Jean walked up our lane to the mailbox. She came back with steam pouring out of her ears and stalked to the phone.

"How dare you send me a bill?" She yelled and slammed down the phone. She showed me the itemized list in Charlie's letter. "Look at this! He says I should pay half of all of the expenses in Northampton, including groceries, because it's my home, even though I'm hardly there!"

Suddenly I understood why I had earned enough money to support John and me—and buy building materials—while he built the house, but Teri Jean never seemed to have any money. She felt guilty every time she bought anything new, like the denim skirt she admired and purchased in Wyoming. She had been supporting Charlie! He spent his days in a coffeehouse writing his novel and counted on her puppet earnings to keep him afloat.

"That does it! I'm done!" Finally. Whenever the conversation turned to divorce, Teri Jean's Catholic upbringing had stopped it short.

"I can't get divorced. I took vows. If I do, I know this big bag of shit will drop out of the sky and land on my head!"

It didn't. She filed for divorce and moved back to Iowa with her box of belongings. Before too long she met—and married—a man who had shared custody of his three boys. He lived exactly one mile away from John and me. Being the jokester she was, she couldn't resist a wisecrack.

“When I got back from Northampton, I got out a map. I made a one-mile circle around John and Monica’s house. I interviewed every single man in the circle and settled on Mickey!”

10. Across the Pond

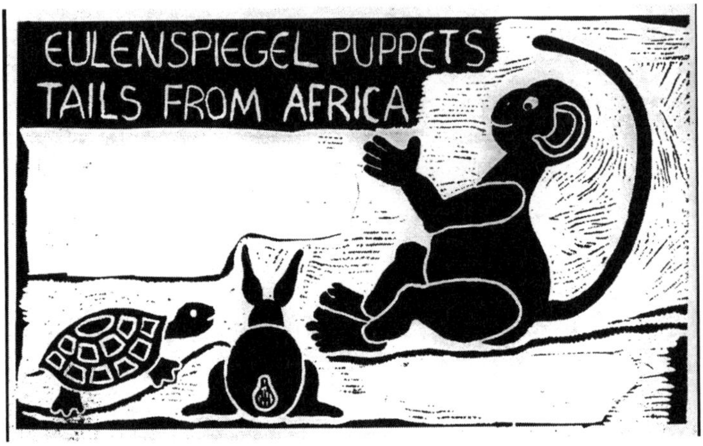

"I'm off!" said Teri Jean. "Wish me luck recognizing them!"

She steered the Suburban out of our driveway and off to the Cedar Rapids airport to pick up Olaf and Detlef, our guest puppeteers from Dresden, along with their wives, Sonja and Ilona. It was their first trip to the US, their first time in any West Block country apart from West Germany. In October 1993, Germany had been reunified for slightly less than three years.

In 1991 I had been elected to the Board of Directors of UNIMA-USA, the American branch of Union Internationale de la Marionette. With branches in ninety countries, UNIMA is dedicated to promoting peace and understanding through the art of puppetry. Allelu Kurten, the same woman who had facilitated our invitation to the East German festival, headed the American branch of the organization. She told all new Board members they should pick a project to develop and work on. She advised me to establish an informal exchange with a foreign company and use that exchange as a pilot project that would show others the way.

“This is a natural for you, Monica, with your fluent knowledge of German,” she said.

The idea intrigued me, so I turned once again to the director of UNIMA-DDR, even though that organization became defunct along with the country it represented.

Since reunification, there was only one UNIMA-Germany, not an east and a west, but I knew that he would have the contacts I sought. I sent him a letter, asking whether he knew of any small troupes—one to three people—who would be interested in an informal exchange. He passed the letter on to Olaf Bernstengel, the director of the puppet theater museum in Dresden, and Olaf, a performing puppeteer himself, seized the opportunity.

Teri Jean steered the Suburban through the tunnel of autumn-golden trees that lined my lane. She pulled up in front of my log cabin home.

“I spotted them right away!” she said. “They looked way too chic and European to be local!”

The car doors opened, and our guests stepped out. Olaf had perfectly styled and gelled dark hair and lively eyes. Sonja, his wife, tall, slim, and blonde, looked around in wonder. Was this bucolic scene–with honking geese and prancing goats–really the country she'd grown up to view as enemy territory? Detlef, blonde and stocky with twinkling eyes, crawled out of the back seat with his tiny, sweetly shy wife, Ilona.

They saw a log cabin surrounded with ten acres of woods, birdhouses fashioned out of discarded tea and coffee pots, a small garden plot surrounded by a fancy iron fence, even a gypsy wagon we'd taken to Renaissance Faires. Metal birds perched on tree stumps. Next to the house stood my workshop, a bright red repurposed semi-trailer. A few steps away stood John's workshop—yellow, red, and blue—flanked by two of his favorite finds: a railroad signal and a traffic light. He'd switched the light to green to welcome our guests. They stood agape, then relaxed and grinned.

Boy, do you remember their first rural Iowa experience? They put down their suitcases to shake hands, and Clover and Dandelion, our rascally pygmy goats, attacked their suitcases and ate the airline tags! We knew they were cool when they laughed instead of getting all bent out of shape!

In planning their visit, we intended to expose them, as much as possible, to the range of American puppetry. We represented the mainstream: family and school shows. We had put our own work on hold and become their roadies for the duration of their visit, but we scheduled a performance of *Hansel and Goosel*—our adaptation of Hansel and Gretel with goslings in the title roles and a fox in the role of the witch—so they could see us perform for a school audience. They loved hearing the giggles and squeals as much as we did.

Olaf and Detlef's production was a 19th-century marionette variety show using beautifully crafted copies of the original marionettes. The stars of the show were "trick marionettes," constructed and strung to do one specific thing—walk a tightrope, perform acrobatics, juggle. The piéce de résistance was the breakaway skeleton whose bones separate and seem to fly into the audience. Olaf and Detlef, in red satin vests and black bowler hats, acted as the 19th century proprietors, firing repartee at each other and the audience. The marionettes were beautifully crafted and manipulated and drew gasps from the audience, and the chemistry between the puppeteers kept the show moving.

We wanted our Dresden friends to see how this 19th-century German art was reinterpreted in 20th-century USA, so we rented a car and sent them off to St. Louis where we'd scheduled them to perform for the St. Louis Puppetry Guild. We made sure they'd meet Bob and Dug of the Kramer Marionettes. Their puppets were technically similar to Olaf's—acrobats, skaters, dancers—but the aesthetic was completely different. Olaf and Detlef's characters were hand-carved copies of the originals; Bob and Dug's looked distinctly American. Teri Jean prepared them.

"Just wait. You'll think you're watching a drag show. The costumes are fabulous! Satin, sequins, feather boas! Fantastic puppet hairstyles! Like watching the best ever fashion show!"

After seeing the show, they compared notes on construction and stringing and marveled at their similarities—and their differences.

To round out their experience, we wanted Olaf and company to see a politically charged show. Puppet theater, because it deals in metaphor and parable, can be an effective force for change. *In the Heart of the Beast Puppet and Mask Theater* in Minneapolis embodies this idea with strong stories and evocative visuals, specializing in giant parade sized puppets. Their work often centers on environmental problems and issues of hate and divisiveness. They had recently opened *Befriended by the Enemy*, the true story of a grand dragon in the Ku Klux Klan and the Jewish neighbors who responded to his messages of hate with compassion and offers of help, transforming all of their lives. The show opens with parade-size angels—long necks evoking Giacometti sculptures—coming through the audience. The story is mesmerizing and served as a perfect foil to the Kramer marionette show.

In between St. Louis and Minneapolis, we toured them and their show around Iowa during the most beautiful fall I can remember—endless sunny days, brilliant foliage, flocks of honking geese heading south, the aroma of burning leaves. Rural Iowa was not what television had led these German city children to expect from their American adventure! They imagined rampant consumerism, neon lights, and fast cars. Instead, they found sleepy small towns and occasional tractors and combines keeping traffic at a snail's pace.

"I love these little schools! They're like community centers!" enthused Sonja. "And the libraries! Even the tiniest towns have one!"

"Look! There's no one on the road but us!" added Detlef, accustomed to the city traffic in Dresden.

Led by chain restaurants, small town cafés had begun offering salad bars. Our guests loved them! Such an abundance of fresh food, and each one was different. Some focused on healthy green salads with raw vegetable toppings, and some were more like rural potlucks, with mayonnaise-rich macaroni salads, fruit-encrusted jello, and herring in cream sauce.

"Is your life always this relaxed?" asked Olaf. Little did he know how hectic the planning and finalizing of their tour had been—hundreds of phone calls, visits with our Senator's aide to check the legality of what we were doing, acquisition of the sound equipment they needed for their show.

Everyone loved their show! Olaf had gotten his Ph.D. in history, writing his thesis about traveling puppet theaters in Saxony in the 18th and 19th centuries. His knowledge of the puppetry of his homeland, the countryside around Dresden, was extensive. He was the director of a puppet theater museum that had received a donation of 19th-century variety marionettes, and he couldn't resist playing with them and demonstrating them for tour groups visiting the museum. He had them copied by a local marionette builder and enlisted Detlef, the grandson of their original owner, to join him in creating a show that was whimsical, funny, and engaging.

I remember one part of the show! They had a juggler with gold juggling balls, and Olaf introduced him as the man with the two golden balls. Howls of laughter from the grown-ups! You guys were mean—you never told him what was so funny till the end of the tour. Luckily, Olaf thought it was funny, too.

One day we took them to the elementary school in Jesup, Iowa. After the show, the art teacher asked if we wanted to join him as he made his weekly visit to the nearby Amish school, a one-room schoolhouse out in the country. We jumped at the chance! We were quite familiar with their culture, living so close to a large Amish settlement, but our German guests had never heard of contemporary groups living without electricity or motor vehicles and dressing in 19th-century garb. They were thrilled to be invited!

We entered the white clapboard one-room schoolhouse and were transported back to the era the puppets had inhabited. The children—twenty or so of various ages—looked as 19th century as the puppets did, with their long dresses, braids, suspenders, and bowl haircuts. They sat on rows of benches, eyes wide.

Olaf and Detlef got out a few of their favorite marionettes to show. These kids had never seen puppets of any kind, much less multi-string marionettes that could juggle, walk a tightrope, and perform acrobatics! Gasps and giggles filled the room. When question time came, Olaf, having heard them speak to each other in a German dialect, decided to talk to them in his native tongue.

"Guten Tag, Kinder! Die Marionetten sind schön, nicht wahr?" (Good day, children! The marionettes are beautiful, aren't they?")

No response.

"Hmm," said Olaf. "Maybe I should try my Saxon dialect."

"Güd'n Dag, Geender! Die Marionedd'n seend schane, neescht wahr?"

Excitement reigned, and all of the kids clamored to talk to Olaf in what sounded an awful lot like Saxon! The excitement only heightened as Olaf let a few kids try working the marionettes.

The first boy held the control gingerly, barely breathing, not sure what to do with it. Olaf stood next to him, guiding his hand to hold the puppet high enough that the legs straightened, and the feet caressed the floor. He showed him how to tip the control back and forth to make the puppet walk. Others clamored for a turn.

When we finally left, they all followed us outside and waved as we drove away.

On November 14, it was time to say goodbye. We awoke to a gray, drizzly day—the first since they had arrived that wasn't gloriously sunny—and packed the Suburban for the trip to the Cedar Rapids airport. Teri Jean brought a bottle of Champagne along. We sat in the airport, toasted each other as champagne fizzed on our tongues, and agreed to meet in a year in Germany. We bade our new friends goodbye and drove home in freezing rain. The magical interlude was over.

A year later, in September 1994, we found ourselves in an airport once again, this time the Chicago airport, to take Delta Airlines to Berlin. Teri Jean had quit smoking years earlier and, like many former smokers, had developed a severe allergy to cigarette smoke.

"I wish we could have found a smoke-free flight," she moaned. "This is torture! Non-smoking section, ha! The smoke doesn't know it's supposed to stay back there!"

Cousin Hermann met us at the Berlin airport and took us home for tea. Teri Jean promptly crashed and spent the rest of the day sleeping off the smoke hangover. We spent the next couple of days wandering around Berlin, east and west. It felt surreal to be able to go where we pleased with no checkpoints. The areas where the wall had been either looked like war zones, with remnants of the wall still standing or like construction sites, with scaffolding and cranes, very much in transition.

I thought back to my art school days, when I loved visiting my East Berlin cousins and once spent an entire month with them. I would arrive at Checkpoint Charlie where Americans crossed the border and submit to a search of my bags. I always carried forbidden items—a West German news magazine, a sought-after book—stashed away beneath dirty underwear. On the other side, I'd see my cousin's children waiting for me: Eva, just four years my junior, Benita, and the twins Friedemann and Sabine, ten years younger than me. When my visit ended, the kids walked with me back to the checkpoint, seven blocks from their home. Suddenly I could cross wherever I wanted, and Friedemann—whose baby daughter Johanne was my godchild—came along!

On the third day, Olaf and Detlef came from Dresden to drive us and the puppets to our first show. We arrived in Hohnstein, a lovely little village crowned by a medieval castle, facing the Elbe River. Hohnstein was the home of the Kaspar Kino, the resident puppet theater of the Hohnstein Kasperles, the most traditional of hand-carved hand puppets, the wooden cousins of the paper-mâché puppets I had grown up with.

The show we brought, *Tails From Africa,* was very different from the shows usually seen in the Kaspar Kino, time-honored fairy tales performed with hand puppets. Ours was a tabletop show, with handheld puppets and rod marionettes that resembled stuffed animals. The stories were African folktales, different in subject and structure from the German and eastern European fairy tales that the eastern German audiences were accustomed to.

We had created the show at the request of a Ghanaian fiber artist who lived in Iowa City. Teri Jean and I both admired her work and bought her batiked fabrics.

"Why don't you do a show of African folktales?" she asked us.

"I don't know if I feel comfortable going that far away from my own cultural heritage," I replied.

"If there were an African puppet troupe in Iowa, I would be asking them."

Unassailable logic! She said that she and her husband, a folklorist, would help us choose and interpret the tales. We ended up with a group of three stories: *Anansi and Tortoise, The Leopard and the Monkeys,* and *The Caterpillar and the Wild Animals,* all trickster tales. The folklorist told us that African storytellers add details relevant to their own lives. He advised us to do the same, keeping the spirit of African storytelling instead of trying to copy it.

"You're not African," he said. "Trying to create an 'African' show would be completely inauthentic. Keep the spirit by making the stories yours."

Tails From Africa became one of our most popular shows of all time. Although we last did the show in 2006, people still remember Cachinata the caterpillar's boast:

"I am Cachinata, warrior son of the long one. I crush wild animals to the earth and make cows' dung of their entrails. I am invincible!"

Or, translated to German: "Ich bin Cachinata, Krieger Sohn des Langen. Ich zermalme wilde Tiere und mache Kuhfladen aus ihren Eingeweiden. Ich bin unbesiegbar!" Translating that was one of my proudest moments!

We decided this was the show to take to Germany for purely practical reasons.

We could pack the puppets and props into two large suitcases, and Olaf could provide the right size tables. I could translate it so that I had most of the speaking parts, and I could teach Teri Jean how to pronounce hers in German. We did not anticipate how controversial it would be in a country that had, till recently, been part of an insular East Block that drew all of its cultural references from Germanic and Eastern European traditions.

The audiences were large, good, and receptive. The children, like children everywhere, got sucked into the stories and giggled at the silly monkeys, the greedy spider, and the self-important caterpillar. Just like American children, they left singing Anansi's song.

"Mine, mine, it's all mine, it's all mine
Everything I covet, when I eat, I love it!" became—
"Meins, meins, Alles meins, Alles meins
Alles gute Essen will ich gierig fressen"

Many of the adults saw things a little differently:

"It was a good show, but those aren't real fairy tales."

"I'm glad my children got to see this show. It's good for them to be exposed to other cultures!"

"I've never heard stories quite like these."

You'd think, having spent as much time in East Germany as I had, that these reactions would not have taken me by surprise. They did. I realized how much of our reality and reactions are tied up in our personal histories.

The eastern German fall that year was glorious, a match for the beautiful Iowa fall of the year before. In many ways, our experience was just as strange and enlightening as their Iowa experience had been. I had spent plenty of time in Germany—both east and west—over the years but witnessing this new culture—east and west combined—emerge from its cocoon was astonishing. Unlike Berlin, this far eastern part of the country—spitting distance from Poland and the Czech Republic—had little exposure to western ways. Many people living there, even those critical of their government, believed in the system at its core. After all, they had all heard of the homeless problems in the US and other capitalist countries, a problem that didn't exist in East Germany.

Many East Germans were repelled by out-of-control capitalism and proud of their own frugality. All of Germany was ahead of the U.S. in recycling, but East Germany was way ahead.

I visited my cousin Benita. We shared a chocolate bar. When we finished, Benita looked at the foil wrapper and began to cry.

"What's wrong?" I asked.

"I used to be able to recycle foil, now I have to throw it away."

Most hoped that the newly reunited country would draw from both systems and combine their best elements. It didn't turn out that way. West Germany was, after all, the victor, and "to the victor go the spoils."

"The only thing left of our system is right turn on red," grumbled Olaf.

Reunification cost Olaf his job. The museum he directed was government-supported, and Olaf was a civil servant. As such, he was required to meet with the Stasi—the secret police—several times a year. He was expected to report any activities or speech critical of the government. These meetings—even though he never reported anyone— were enough to disqualify him from a job in the new government, and the Director job went to a westerner. Sonja's job, archivist in the rare books division of the Dresden Library, also went to a westerner.

Olaf became a full-time freelance puppeteer and Sonja worked as a freelance editor. Like all of their cohorts, they had to learn to function in a market economy, which Olaf did with relative success.

He was good at networking and had connections all over his region. He found us gigs at puppet theaters, museums, preschools, outdoor festivals, even a water mill.

The Zchoner Mühle (Mill) was a functioning watermill and a regional historical museum. It served as the home base for the Dombrovsky Marionettes, the last of the traditional traveling marionette troupes that had toured the countryside in caravans in the nineteenth and the first half of the twentieth centuries. The Dombrovsky family lived here in the winters in two caravans—one for the parents and one for the daughter and her young family. They had a table and chairs outdoors between their homes where they served us coffee and conversation. The talk centered around the usual—making a living as puppeteers in the market economy.

"How do you make a living? Does your government help?" they asked us.

We told them about our school residencies, our shows at festivals and libraries, the ways we kept our expenses low and patched together each month's income, and the ways we advertised and booked our shows.

"The state government helps with our school residencies", I said, "but who knows how long that will last. The others, well, if they want a show, they have to figure out how to pay for it. Every year we have to reevaluate.

"Isn't that stressful?"

Teri Jean nodded as I said,

"We're used to it."

"Our expenses are much higher than they used to be. So many things that were free or cheap under the old system are costly. Of course, we can get things we couldn't get before—this delicious coffee, for instance—but we have to have the money."

In the summers, the Dombrovskys traveled from town to town and set up in hotel courtyards where they hoped they would continue to cover their living expenses. In the winter, they were here, performing in a luxurious heated tent with a curtained stage and rows of chairs, dependent on ticket sales for their income. We performed in the morning, for a small but enthusiastic audience.

In the evening we returned to watch their adult show. The show was reminiscent of a nineteenth-century stage play—large-scale marionettes stiffly declaiming their lines in much the way their human counterparts had. The post-show, also traditional, featured a pair of variety marionettes playing the piano and dancing. It gave us insight into Olaf and Detlef's show. A variety show—like the one they had brought to Iowa—was really a collection of encore pieces from nineteenth-century plays.

I asked Olaf if they could get an ongoing gig at a museum.

"After all, they're living history!" I enthused.

"Oh! Don't say that in front of them! They hate that idea! They would never do that!"

"But why not?" I asked. "It seems natural!"

"They think their work is current and relevant. They wouldn't buy into the living history idea, even if it did increase their income."

Eight years later, during another eastern German tour, it appeared they had changed their minds. After we performed in the puppet theater museum in the spa town of Bad Liebenwerda, the director showed us their newly renovated exhibits. One room contained a beautifully painted proscenium marionette stage installed for the Dombrovsky Marionettes. I was happy to see evidence of a little more security for our friends.

Rolf Mäser, who had connected us with Olaf, invited us all for dinner one day. His garden, like so many German gardens, was a riot of fragrant and colorful flowers. Deep red roses, blue bachelor buttons, red and yellow gaillardia, feathery stalks of goldenrod, and pink and purple cosmos competed for space.

Frau Mäser, a typical old-school German "hausfrau" fed us solyanka, a deliciously sour Russian soup; boar roast—Herr Mäser was a hunter—sweet and sour red cabbage; potatoes; and dry white wine from Dresden. A typical meal for this part of the country, she topped it off with plum cake and apple cake. We thanked Herr Mäser for the many connections he had given us (and hoped fervently that he felt our shows had been worthy of his trust).

Several of our gigs were in "Kulturhäuser"—Culture Houses—another remnant of East German culture that has largely disappeared. Many towns had a Kulturhäus—a cozy meeting place with a bar in the back, chairs, and tables, and a stage in the front. Grandmas and Grandpas sipped beer and ate sausages in the back, while their grandkids sat in the front, watching Tortoise outsmart Anansi the Spider.

One Saturday we were scheduled as part of an afternoon of music and theater. Outside of the Kulturhaus, a large group of teens killed time till the late afternoon rock band arrived. With some trepidation, we talked them into coming inside for the puppet show. They turned out to be our best audience of all, hooting and hollering at Anansi the Spider's antics, and Leopard's frantic attempts to catch and eat the monkeys.

That evening our gig was in a restaurant performing hall, a common feature in that region. Elisabeth, a young puppeteer having career problems, attended the show and invited us to her studio to talk shop and dispense advice. Her studio was located in a half-ruined old castle surrounded by woods.

The night was dark—just a sliver of a moon peeking through the trees. We noticed a covered wagon parked in front of the broken-down castle wall. As we waited for Elisabeth to get her keys, we encountered a diminutive man, bearded, wearing a battered hat and a dark wool coat. He greeted us.

"Grüss Gott!"

The typical southern German greeting—loosely translated "God bless"—put me at ease.

"Don't be afraid. I live in this wagon."

I felt transported into a Grimm's fairy tale, talking to a gnome in the woods. He was one of the many displaced by reunification. With cynical good humor, he outlined his career path before and after. He hadn't always lived in a wagon; his post-unification income required downsizing.

The fairy tale image stayed with me as we wandered through the echoey halls of the castle until we saw a crack of light under a door and entered Elisabeth's cozy studio. She bemoaned her failure to find consistent artistic partners and good marionette string. Unable to help her with the former, we sent her good marionette string (black braided fishline) as soon as we returned home.

The air crackled with energy during this first eastern German tour. Despite the angst and uncertainty, joie de vivre and anticipation filled the atmosphere. No one knew exactly how things would turn out. Dreams could come true. New adventures were on the horizon. We performed at two outdoor festivals that were right out of 60's USA, with craft booths, impromptu performances, spur-of-the-moment parades, and the aroma of forbidden substances.

"This could never have happened before!" exclaimed Sonja.

We spent one of our last days wandering around the Old City of Dresden. I recognized the square where I had watched the miniature marionette show that so deeply influenced my artistic vision. Construction was in progress everywhere as crews rebuilt Gothic structures bombed out during World War Two. They had been left standing, skeletal buildings with stone in some places and "bones" of reinforcing rods in others. British and American firebombs had destroyed Dresden in February 1945, after the war had—for all practical purposes—been won. A photographic display of notes people had left in public places—in hopes their missing near and dear would see them—brought tears:

"Fritzi, if you see this, meet me at Gertrude's house. Our house is gone."

"Bärbel, I am alive and waiting for you at our bombed-out house."

Two years earlier, in 1992, I had visited Berlin for the baptism of my godchild Johanne, our family's first post-reunification baby. Her great-grandmother set the table for a typical get-together: filter coffee, cake featuring plums cut in half and laid out on a slightly sweet, yeasty crust; streusel cake with a crunchy brown sugar topping; and a large bowl of whipped cream. I sipped my rich, creamy coffee, and asked,

"How is reunification going for you?"

"I'm getting used to losing everything," she replied. "After World War One, our money was devalued, and we had to start over. After World War Two, we were the international pariah, our money was devalued, and the Russians took our country. And now, our money is devalued and we're the pariah again as the West Germans take our jobs."

I asked Johanne's grandfather, my cousin Peter, what he thought.

"I wouldn't go back," he said. I like being able to travel where I want. I like not having to worry about expressing my opinions in public. But I miss the simplicity and the slower pace."

It was the first of many performing trips to Germany and Austria, most organized by Olaf. It remains the most memorable. Witnessing the transition from East Bloc to West Bloc and the impact it had on my relatives and my professional peers was a once-in-a-lifetime privilege.

Just so you know: the only reason I'm not weighing in here is that I didn't

get to go along! Someone had to stay home and take care of things here, and besides, the airlines had gotten a lot stingier about how much luggage you could take. Can you imagine? I was considered luggage!

11. Owl Glass Puppetry Center

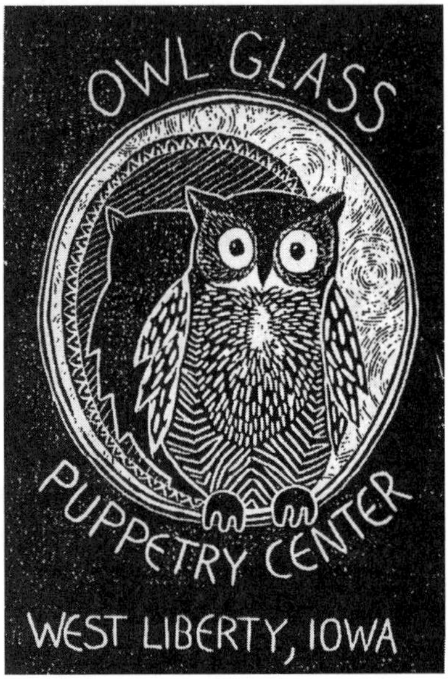

"The building next to Dos Amigos is for sale. I think you should look at it. It might be a good place for the puppets."

Dos Amigos in West Liberty was John's favorite small-town bar. He stopped there frequently to have a beer and work on his Spanish. John loved Mexico and traveled there frequently, sometimes with me and often alone or with a friend. He was the only Anglo who regularly frequented Dos Amigos, and the owners had taken him under their wings and taught him Spanish.

"Mi taverna es mi escuela!" John declared as he made sure to learn a few new words or phrases with each beer.

We had been wishing for a permanent space. A church in Iowa City let us rehearse in their basement, but we had to pack up after each session. Sometimes we set up in our house, but the space was small, and the puppet stage got in the way of daily living.

Our forays into so many small towns with active volunteer networks had whetted our appetite for community outreach and participation. We thought with a permanent space and a presence in the community we might be able to spend more time at home. We looked around Iowa City and immediately dropped the idea when it became clear that we could never afford it.

"How about one of the small towns around Iowa City?" I asked. "John found a place in West Liberty."

"I don't know," said Teri Jean. "Do you think people would come?"

"Look," I replied. "Worst case scenario no one comes. We still have a great place to rehearse, store our stuff, and run our business. And…I've heard granters take you more seriously if you have a permanent address that isn't your home. Let's go have a look."

"I'm warning you; the place doesn't look like much," said John as he unlocked the door to the modest storefront building with a brick facade and two large display windows, one cracked.

"Doesn't smell like much, either." The musty stench of a deserted building crept into my nose.

"Yikes!" said Teri Jean. "A puppeteer's nightmare," as she gestured to the walls. "No hands!"

During the building's most recent life as a Latino community center, someone had painted murals of Mexican dancers on the walls. The artist lacked the skill to paint hands, so all of the arms ended at the wrists.

The building was divided into two spaces, a large front area that had been a store in earlier days, and a smaller back room that had most likely served as a storage area. The back corner of the main area was sectioned off to hold a sketchy bathroom and a furnace. I opened the door to the smaller back room and almost plunged into the abyss.

"What's this?" I asked as I looked into the back room, a full foot lower than the front room. "There's nothing back here but the back door!"

I walked carefully across the rotting floor in the dark cubicle behind the main area and opened the door to the outside. I almost took another plunge two feet down into the alley.

"Is there a basement?" I asked. John opened a trap door on the floor of the main room.

"Careful! I don't want to scrape you off the floor!" I backed gingerly down the shaky steps.

"Wow! Nice basement! Look at those trees they used for supports! You can still see the branches. When was this built, anyway?"

"1886. One of the oldest buildings in town. Good foundation. No sign of rodents. Or water damage."

"What do you think, John?"

"Well, it needs work, but nothing I can't do with a little help from my pals. And what else are we going to find for $17,000?"

We took a deep breath, cleaned out our savings account, and bought the building in March 1995. I called Mutti with the news.

"Kind—Child—, you're a capitalist! You own two properties!"

"I know. I wish I could tell Vati. I have roots!"

John got to work, evenings and weekends. He headed up the street to City Hall.

"We bought the El Centro Unido building. It needs a lot of work. I'll need a building permit."

"A building permit! If that's what you want, we can issue one."

The next evening the locals started checking in: "We heard you applied for a building permit. you should'na done that! Now they're gonna want us all to get permits!"

John tore out and replaced the rotting floor in the backroom, built a staircase to the basement, and sealed off the trapdoor, but not before I had thoughtlessly walked into it and landed on my butt on the edge of one of the shaky steps. To this day, I have a dent in my fanny to prove it. He built two beautiful bathrooms and installed a three-part sink—a classic bar sink he had salvaged—into our new kitchen area. He ripped out the sketchy bathroom and furnace and put a new furnace into the now-accessible basement.

Teri Jean and I painted over the handless dancers in a bright yellow, and her stepson and one of my nieces painted the floor red. When John finished dry-walling the back room, he sent me to Fred's, our local feed store and everything vendor.

"Go get me a nice Mexican color for the back room." I came back with a glowing green. Now it was time to give the building a name. Should we call it Eulenspiegel, like the puppet troupe?

"How about something different? After all, we're going to do more than just our shows. We're going to have guest puppeteers and who knows what all else."

"Here's an idea: how about a name anyone can spell and pronounce?" joked Teri Jean.

My sister weighed in: "Why not call it Owl Glass? After all, that's the direct translation of Eulenspiegel and besides, there's a British folk hero called Owl Glass who's a lot like Eulenspiegel."

We painted Owl Glass Puppetry Center into the window. Our friend Deanne—who'd founded the troupe together with me—started painting a mural echoing the brick building front and incorporating some of our favorite puppet characters. It would be mounted on the top half of the building when it was completed to Deanne's satisfaction. We waited to see what would happen next. Walking down the streets, I could almost hear the gossip.

Schulz here! I did hear the gossip! In the coffee shop! These old farts were talking about YOU! "What are those gals doing in that building, anyway?" one of them asked. "I heard they're from Iowa City," piped up the other one. "That figures. Bunch of hippies. Puppets! You've gotta be kidding. That won't last!" added the first.

We had to do something to make a splash. We'd heard about the annual fair parade, one of the biggest local events. Even though West Liberty wasn't the county seat, it was the site of the annual county fair. The Sunday before the fair opened, West Liberty had a big parade followed by a community-wide party in the city park. We heard that everyone in town watched the parade. This was our golden opportunity.

I knew the middle school Talented-and-Gifted teacher.

"Jackie, can you think of any kids who would like to come over and help us build giant puppets for the fair parade?"

She sent us a crew of four, and we got busy. As the building hummed with activity and puppet heads migrated to the sidewalk to dry in the sun, other kids peeked in to see what was happening and stayed to help. Soon carelessly flung bicycles joined the puppet heads on the sidewalk to block the way and signal the buzzing hive inside. A young policeman walked in:

"Ma'am, there's been a complaint about the bicycles on the sidewalk." Kids leaped up, scrambled outside, and moved their bikes around the corner to the bike rack. Cousin Marie, visiting from Hamburg, had a thing or two to say:

"Oh, to live in a place so peaceful that the police have nothing better to worry about than mis-parked bicycles!

We made an "Owl Glass Puppetry Center" banner and built four giant puppets, one for us and one for each of the main ethnic groups living in West Liberty: an owl for Owl Glass; a sun to represent the Mexicans; a dragon for the Southeast Asians; and a European fairy tale witch to represent the Germans and Norwegians.

On parade day friends—old and new—of all ages showed up to help us walk the puppets in the parade. The puppets processed in time to the high school marching band, following the tractors and preceding the Shriners showing off on their tiny cycles. Everyone in town sat on curbs or on front lawns watching and cheering. Now everyone knew what we were doing and most wished us well.

The Monday after the parade a beloved retired art teacher walked in the door.

"When I saw the puppets in the parade, I knew my people had moved into town! What can I do to help?"

Soon she was helping Deanne finish the mural. Next, she was painting sets, helping make posters, and just hanging out.

But most people still thought of us as hobbying housewives until the school buses started rolling into town, bringing kids from all over the area for field trips.

Schulz here: you can say that again! I get around, you know! And I just happened to be at the coffee shop one day when the same two old farts were having coffee and gossiping about YOU—again! "Did you see the school buses?" asked one. "They came all the way from Tipton!" answered the other. "Those gals are rockstars!" We were in like Flynn!

Our storefront with the matching mural didn't last for long. A few years later a rogue SUV drove into the front of the building, shattering the facade and scattering bricks all over the sidewalk. All of the local kids seemed to know who'd done it, but no one wanted to say. I'm guessing it was someone's uncle. Maybe he'd spent a little too much time next door in Dos Amigos!

Since we had free labor in John, we used the insurance money to buy new windows and hire a friend to help. The new facade was wood—after all, John and his friend were carpenters—painted a beautiful Mexican blue. Our friend Peggy Fitzgerald—and a total of seventeen local volunteers—painted a new mural to match the new blue exterior. Our art teacher friend—grown old and beginning to show signs of Alzheimer's disease—painted a beautiful tree into the middle of the mural. It adorns our building and hangs as a memorial to its creator, the last painting she made before her descent into dementia and her death.

One of our very first public events came in the spring of 1996. We'd participated in the downtown holiday open house and had a couple of local school classes come for field trips, but we hadn't started doing regular public shows in our new space.

Then came the Russians! An East Coast puppeteer/presenter was bringing in a troupe from Russia—a couple whose work we deeply admired—and asked if we wanted in on the tour. The presenter claimed to have numerous opportunities for them, all around the country, and we agreed to present them and tour them around Iowa, an abbreviated weeklong version of the tour we had arranged for Olaf and Detlef. I figured out how much we could charge for their shows, subtracted the travel and housing expenses, and told the presenter how much money we could pay. I was delighted when he agreed!

We scheduled them to do an evening show for the public in our new center. We promoted the show heavily in the neighboring town of Muscatine, which had a sizable Russian immigrant community. When we opened the doors that evening, people of all ages flooded in, bought tickets and posters, and even made donations, until there was standing room only. They weren't the Muscatine Russians we expected; they were local residents curious to see "what those gals are up to!"

Even though no one could understand a word—expecting a Russian audience, we had given the translator they brought the evening off—the show was enchanting! Whether or not you could understand exactly what was happening to the main characters, a bear and a little girl, the puppets were so lifelike and the visuals so sweet that the audience was swept away into a magical fairyland. Our friend Mallory came with her four-year-old son. On the walk home, Tony recapped the whole story for her as if he had understood every word. That evening lives like a jewel in my memory.

The next day we left on our tour. There were five of us in my school bus-yellow Suburban: Vladimir and Irina, the puppeteer couple; their translator; me; and—oddly enough—their presenter, who had decided to come along on their travels. We traveled 300 miles to northwest Iowa where they performed at an art center and an elementary school; on to Mason City for a day at the MacNider Art Museum; and finally, a show in Cedar Falls, where a teacher who had attended one of our workshops brought her 10-year old daughter. That daughter, Liz Schachterle, was deeply inspired and has since become a highly regarded professional puppeteer!

We returned home, and I got ready to drive the whole crew to St. Louis, where I had arranged for them to perform next. I stopped at the bank and picked up the cash I had promised them through their presenter. I felt wonderful because we had taken in enough money at our public show that I could give them $400.00 more than I had agreed to.

I handed the money to Vladimir. He counted it. His face fell. He looked confused and panicked and spoke to the translator.

"He asks where the rest of the money is," she said.

"The rest of the money? That's $400.00 more than we promised."

"The presenter told them their shows were worth a lot more than this. They should be getting at least twice as much."

I glared at the presenter, the presenter whose motel and meal expenses I had been paying. "What did you tell them?"

"I told them what I thought their shows were worth. I didn't tell them they would be getting that much."

"How many other shows did you line up for them?" I asked.

"Well, I tried, but I could only arrange for two," he replied.

"Two?" I exploded! "And how much did those two pay?"

"Well, I could only get $100.00 each."

"So…you're telling me that the $2400.00 I just handed them is almost all they will be making?"

"I'm afraid so. I did my best."

"Your best! They're counting on this! They have a child at home! What were you thinking?"

"Well, they bought a bunch of sound equipment. They shouldn't have been spending money they hadn't gotten yet."

"But you promised them the money!"

"No, I didn't! I just told them what I thought they should be getting. We didn't have a contract."

"Don't you realize that East Bloc people are like children when it comes to understanding the market economy?" I shouted. "Your word was like a contract in their minds! What is wrong with you?"

I realized any more conversation was wasted time and breath, and we left for St. Louis with nothing resolved. I stopped at a gas station and got $200.00 in cash from the ATM. I gave it to Vladimir, explaining that we had made some extra money selling T-shirts and posters.

"I think this is a gift from you and not from sales." said the translator. I held my peace. My mind churned all the way to St. Louis and back.

Vladimir and Irina had been staying with a Russian/German couple I knew. I called them up for insight.

"They took out a loan to come. From a loan shark. At ridiculous interest. Computed and collected every MONTH! They were promised enough money to pay off the loan as soon as they got home."

"Do you know the total?" I asked. I found out that they would be $900.00 short.

When John came home, I threw myself into his arms and poured my heart out.

"I've always been afraid someday something would go wrong with bringing in puppeteers we've never met or seen, but I thought it would be a lousy show; I didn't think it would be this! I can't stop thinking about that loan shark!"

"Do we have more than $900.00 in our savings account?" asked John.

"Oh, yeah. There's at least a thou or more in there."

"Get out $900.00."

"Really?"

"We don't have a loan shark after us. But if I ever get hold of that @#$%^&*! so-called presenter…"

"You're right."

"Do you know anyone you can trust to get it to them?"

I called a puppeteer I knew in the same region as the presenter and told her what had happened.

"Not again!" she said. "Our puppetry guild has bailed out other groups he brought in."

She said they had an event planned to honor Vladimir and Irina; if I wired her the money, she would get it into their hands.

I heaved a sigh of relief and—once again—emptied our savings account.

Two days later we received an unsolicited donation from a friend and supporter. No one but Teri Jean, John, and I knew what had transpired.

The donation was a check for exactly $900.00!

12. The Nose

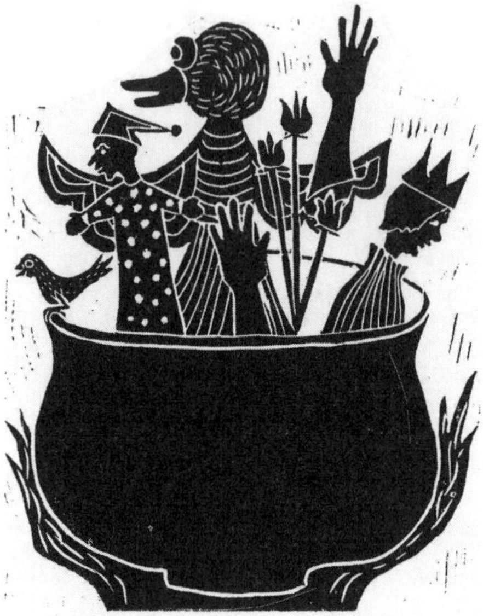

That was Teri Jean's jokey nickname for me after she quit her three to four-pack-a-day smoking habit. We were doing a residency at an elementary school in Dubuque, and TJ had gone to her grandma's house after school.

"That's it!" she said as she threw an almost full pack in the trash. "I'm making my grandma sick."

Grandma had emphysema. Listening to her cough with each puff was the last straw. Teri Jean knew smoking was bad for her. She'd tried to quit, but it took her grandma's discomfort to give her the willpower.

It was not easy. Not for Teri Jean and not for me. Withdrawal from cigarettes caused mood swings that she kept under control around strangers and people who had hired us. I was close—and safe.

"Mon, this place is a dump! We need to find a different motel!"

Twice during the same week. If the town had had four motels, we would have moved three times.

The mood swings ended after a few weeks, but they were replaced with a severe allergic reaction to cigarette smoke, causing migraine headaches, fits of anger, and—worse yet—loss of her voice. Smoking was still allowed everywhere, in restaurants, teachers' lounges, motels, and airplanes. It was my job to enter each space first and sniff for smoke; to tell sponsors we needed to stay in a smoke-free home or motel; to make sure no one could smoke in our performance venues.

Before too long she began reacting to perfume—and scented cleaning supplies, laundry detergent, deodorant, you name it. Her reactions once again included mood swings. I could tell when she'd been exposed by her sudden uncontrolled rage. I realized that almost everything was scented. And now I had more things to sniff out and more restrictions to insist on.

One week we stayed with a generous woman who did our laundry while we were in school. The next morning, as we arrived in the classroom, Teri Jean had one of her anger episodes. By that time I knew what caused her irritability, and I surreptitiously sniffed my way around the room, trying to find the source. I walked past Teri Jean. Oh no! The aroma came from her! It was our host's fabric softener.

Most people were kind and understanding, but I will never forget a scene with a school principal.

"Mr. Adams, Teri Jean is severely allergic to perfume and other scents. Can you please ask the teachers we're working with to wear unscented products this week?"

"What! I've never heard of anything like that! Is she doing that to get attention?"

"Mr. Adams, she does puppet shows. She doesn't need to get attention by faking an allergy."

"Well, this is ridiculous! I can't ask my staff for anything that extreme!" His voice rose. "I never heard of anything this crazy! Has she lost her grip?"

A wave of Old Spice wafted from him as he stepped closer and wagged his finger in my face. Teri Jean heard the exchange and burst into the office.

"How dare you yell at my partner like that!" she screamed as she stomped out.

I followed. Lo and behold, several teachers were listening at the door.

"That's telling him!" said one of them. They surrounded us and told us how satisfying it had been to listen to us confronting their abusive principal. Before we knew it, the story was all over school, and all of the teachers left their scented products at home. Mr. Adams did not relinquish his Old Spice, but luckily, he stayed in his office.

Teri Jean's chemical sensitivity lasted for at least half a dozen years, at its worst during the years she "lived" in Northampton. After she separated from Charlie and her stress level ramped down, her health improved, and gradually the chemical sensitivity—along with the migraines, irrational anger, and voice loss—went away.

In April 1986 we did a residency in a small school in rural Northeast Iowa. We stayed with a couple who lived in an earth shelter house built close to the bank of the Turkey River. It was a lovely house with an indoor swimming pool.

What did The Nose detect when walking in? Mold, of course, with all of that moisture. No big deal; neither of us had a mold allergy…yet.

Every day that week on the way to school, Morning Edition on Iowa Public Radio—the station permanently set in my Suburban's radio—told us about the nuclear disaster in Chernobyl.

Every evening we came home to the mold house. Teri Jean slept in a room that faced front and had a big window she opened every night. I slept in a back room—no windows. The dehumidifier in my room filled up so fast that I was afraid it would overflow if I left it on overnight. Every morning Teri Jean had to shake me awake.

"Monica, wake up! What's wrong with you?"

"I don't know. I had the strangest dreams. I always wake up by myself. But…thanks for waking me."

Saturday morning—home again—I woke up with a splitting headache.

When I tried to get out of bed, I could only stumble to the bathroom and throw up. Again and again. And the headache just got worse. We were supposed to drive to Laramie, Wyoming the next day for a week-long residency. The easternmost city in Wyoming, we could get there in one day.

"If I can just get out of bed and not throw up long enough to pack my clothes, you could drive, Teri Jean, and I'm sure I'll feel better by the time we get there."

"I'm calling our contact person."

"I rescheduled the residency for next week," she said after talking to our hosting teacher.

It was a good thing; it took most of the week for me to feel better. I realized I was having classic migraine headaches. I remembered my mother having them and I'd seen Teri Jean suffer, but I'd never had one myself. Before too long I realized it all had to do with the mold I'd inhaled every night for a week. For the next ten years, I got migraine headaches every time I was exposed to mold. Eventually, my immune system recovered, and the migraines ended.

So now there was one more thing to sniff out. As Teri Jean's chemical sensitivity improved, she became The Nose and scouted for mold. That was quite a trick in the humid Iowa summers. In Touring Arts Team towns, we frequently performed and taught workshops in church basements which almost always had hints of mildew. I loved the Touring Arts Team and was not about to let an occasional migraine stop me!

"Uh oh, Monica. I don't think we should be doing our workshop in the church basement. Let me see if I can trade for one of the upstairs classrooms."

And so, Teri Jean took care of me, just as I had taken care of her, the essence of partnership.

Schulz here: it was scary to see you so flaked out, melting into the couch and only getting up to puke! I know you; you've kind of buried that mem-

ory, but I haven't forgotten! It happened oftener than you would like to admit! Teri Jean would come over, bring you a movie to watch, and make you some chicken soup—she was a much better nursemaid than John was! I was so relieved when you finally stopped having those headaches.

13. Building Community Through Festivals

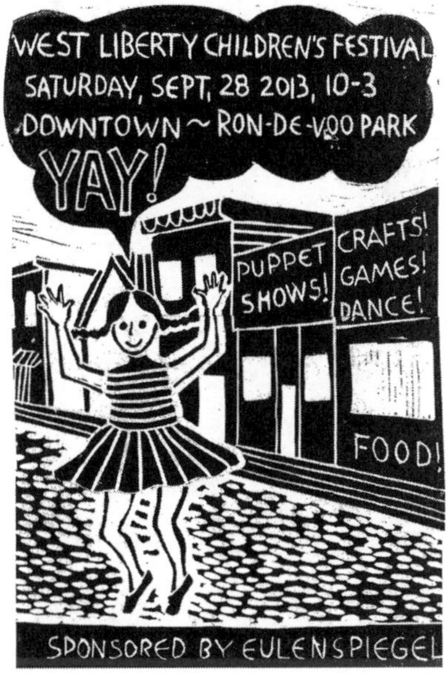

"I guess we'd better do this for our future," I said with a sigh.

It was 1989, and we had made a habit of applying for grants under the umbrella of our local arts council. Our contact person at the Iowa Arts Council had been urging (nagging) us to get our non-profit, tax-exempt status.

"Granting organizations will take you more seriously if you have your own tax-exempt status. It will open lots of doors for you."

That was the carrot. The stick was the unspoken threat that we would no longer get the Iowa Arts Council grants that we had come to depend on. We filled out the paperwork as best we could, not realizing this was a job for a lawyer. We heard nothing. I called the IRS, and we were assigned a contact person who treated our application dismissively.

Admittedly, I pestered her until she lost patience and hung up on me.

We waited. And waited. And waited.

"Teri Jean, you're going to have to call her this time. I've obviously pissed her off. She won't talk to me."

"OK." She made the call and reported back: "Guess what! We're in! Your contact was out on maternity leave. Her sub looked at our application. She couldn't see any reason to deny us, so she okayed it just like that!"

After celebrating with a glass of wine, we chose among our friends and supporters and assembled a Board of Directors. We wrote a mission statement:

Eulenspiegel Puppet Theatre is a non-profit, tax-exempt puppet company organized to promote the art of puppetry by producing and presenting high-quality performances and workshops. The company is committed to educating the public about the art of puppetry and enhancing the quality of community life.

The IRS designation changed us and our puppet company in ways I never imagined. We began to feel responsible for contributing to the common good. We'd been producing performances and workshops and educating for years. Now it was time to start "enhancing the quality of community life." At the suggestion of an art teacher on our Board, we decided to start by creating a "Young Puppeteers Festival," open to anyone in third grade and above—including adults—who was young to the art of puppetry.

We contacted teachers and scout leaders and sent news releases inviting the general public to create 15-minute—or shorter—puppet shows. We offered a free consultation on writing, puppet building, or performance to any person or group who signed up. We asked a magician friend to act as MC and do magic tricks between acts. We asked friends in theater to form a critique panel. Our Board members helped us assemble mini conference packets for each participant. The

Iowa City library agreed to let us convert their largest meeting room into a theater.

Ten groups signed up. Teri Jean and I took turns doing consultations—starting groups on the puppet-making process; introducing them to different styles of puppets; helping them understand how writing for puppets is different from writing for people; even attending and critiquing their rehearsals.

Saturday, May 2, 1992 was the big day! Our Board gathered and helped us set up lights, sound equipment, and a portable backdrop. We picked up donated cups, napkins, snacks, and drinks and set up tables and chairs. We commandeered a smaller meeting room for the critique panel. Our magician, Lee Iben, greeted the large audience, and the first Young Puppeteers Festival began!

Anticipation filled the air! Most groups had brought their own staging, designed to accommodate the show and style of puppet they'd created; a few used our generic hand and shadow puppet stages. The first two groups had their stages set up in the makeshift wings; each succeeding group quietly set up as the group before them performed. Props and staging were moved on and off as Lee entertained the audience with linking rings, disappearing quarters, and multi-colored scarves that came out of nowhere. After each group finished, they moved to another room to meet with the critique panel. Critiques were succinct and encouraging, completed during set-ups and strikes.

Each young puppeteer received a mini-conference packet with a program, coupons for local shops and restaurants, and the makings of a simple paper puppet. Mid-afternoon we took a break so everyone could assemble and show off their puppets.

The show I remember best from that first year was a shadow puppet show created by a group of 4th through 8th graders from Willowwind, a small alternative school in Iowa City. They told the story of Rosa Parks, showing a bus full of people.

Rosa Parks was a solid black silhouette while the white passengers had faces cut out to create a black outline with a white center.

The festival lasted ten years. Willowwind was an annual star. An area librarian and her young son, Amy and Jeff White, performed every year. Jeff is grown up now and working as a successful actor on the West Coast. I like to think his accolades at the Young Puppeteers Festival prepared him for later acting success!

Another perennial favorite—starting in 1996 when she first prepared a show—was Liz Schachterle, the girl who was so inspired by Vladimir and Irina. *Bear's Dream,* the Russian show, had featured a three-level stage: a top level for rod puppets, a middle level for hand puppets, and a bottom level for marionettes. Teri Jean and I watched Liz and her friend in delighted amazement.

"Look at that, Monica! They made that stage out of a refrigerator box!"

"And it has a stage opening at the top and one at the bottom! Where do you suppose they got that idea?" I replied.

"Shhh! They're starting!" Hissed Teri Jean.

Two hand puppets, a girl and a boy, appeared in the top stage opening—decorated to look like an American yard—carrying shovels. They began digging.

"What did you say we're doing?" asked the boy.

"I heard if we dig deep enough, we can get to China!"

"China?"

"Yep! It's on the other side of the world."

The two puppets dug furiously. Imaginary dirt flew everywhere. We could almost hear the shovels clanking. Soon the bottom opened up to look like an upside-down Chinese village. The boy and girl appeared in this bottom stage opening, upside down.

"Here we are!"

"I told you so!"

Wild applause from the audience.

"I sure wish Vladimir and Irina could see this!" I said.

Liz performed at every succeeding festival, each year outdoing the show she'd done the year before. After her second year, she turned to her father as a partner, and finally, in her junior high school year, she performed a polished, professional solo show.

If our festival did nothing else, it had a part in launching Liz Schachterle, who now performs nationally as *Liz Howls.* Every time I see one of her thoroughly original, whimsical shows, I feel like a proud mama.

We ran the festival on a shoestring. Local businesses donated money and useful items—snacks and drinks, fun things to put in the packets, cups, and napkins. We raised enough money to pay Lee and buy any supplies we needed, but Teri Jean and I worked free. We didn't mind doing free consultations—it was fun to see what the kids were working on—but the administrative duties became crushingly heavy.

The first problem was getting the word out. Publicity had never been our strong suit, and informing people felt like rowing upstream. Getting them to commit and stay committed proved even harder. We had a few strong core participants we could count on—Williowwind, Liz, an area librarian who created shows with her young son, and Buffy Quintero, the daughter of the teacher who suggested the idea in the first place. Others would be reliable and enthusiastic for a few years and then move on.

There was one teacher who finally pushed me too far. She was a highly regarded Talented and Gifted teacher in two local schools. Every year she signed both of her schools up. Her kids were great and had wonderful ideas. We always ended up giving them at least two consultations each, and the first few years we didn't mind. They worked hard and the results were good. We did get a little tired of being asked for more consultations than we offered, but we shrugged it off. Then the cancellations started. In our eighth year, the teacher called us mere weeks before the festival and pulled one of her groups out. She didn't think they would be ready. The next year she pulled both groups out. I was seething inside when she did it again in year ten, days before the festival. I hung up the phone and exploded.

"That's it! I'm not doing this anymore! This is the last year for this festival!" Teri Jean agreed. I think she'd been waiting for this.

I still pine for the Young Puppeteers Festival. When we recently interviewed for a new Outreach Director, I advocated for hiring Chris Eck because of the enthusiasm he showed for managing a revived Young Puppeteers Festival. I can hardly wait for May 2023, when the festival comes back!

By the time we ended the Young Puppeteers Festival, we had already launched another festival, the West Liberty Children's Festival, which still takes place every September. Mallory Smith was on our Board in 1997 when one of the members suggested a fall festival. Mulling over themes, Mallory pointed out that we had something that few small towns have: a large population of children, mostly thanks to our immigrant population. I told Mallory if she would help me organize and manage a festival, I would write a grant to pay for it. A few months later, I got her on the phone.

"Hey, Mallory, I got the grant!"

"What grant?"

"You remember! The one for a children's festival!"

"Oh…that. I'd forgotten. Well, we'd better get to work."

We had $1600.00 to spend. We spent some on publicity, programs, and T-shirts. I made a linoleum block printed poster—like the ones I made for our shows—and the image, a little girl with pigtails doing a cartwheel, appeared on the T-shirts and all of the publicity materials.

The rest of the money went to small honoraria for performers and a fee to Lee Iben, our magician friend, for MCing the day. I called in favors from musician and storyteller friends who agreed to perform for much less than they were worth. Mallory worked on the local clubs and businesses, getting as many as she could to put up activity booths. The Rotary

Club sold hot dogs, brats, and turkey tenderloin sandwiches. The street featured painting stations with easels, a fishpond, a duck pond activity, and a giant sandbox. Enough people showed up and enjoyed themselves to warrant a repeat the following year.

"You know you're going to have to put that pigtail girl on all of the posters from now on," Mallory said.

"Really?"

"Yes! She'll become the image people associate with the festival."

I've taken this seriously, and every year I wrack my brains to incorporate our girl in a new way.

After the first festival in 1998, it took a few years before the town got seriously involved. Every year it felt like pulling teeth to get people to participate. Like our experience with the Young Puppeteers Festival, we had a few consistent allies: a local women's club, the Rotary club, and our Board, but it seemed stalled; it wasn't getting any larger.

When we were preparing for year seven, I said to Teri Jean," If the town doesn't get more engaged this year, I'm quitting. We've done all we can!"

Just then Jenean, a retired school librarian, walked into the puppetry center.

"I have some ideas for the Children's Festival," she said, handing me a list as long as my arm.

I looked at the list and replied: "I'm guessing that means you'll be on the committee and help make these things happen."

"Ah! I knew you'd say that!"

Jenean was extremely competent and born to rule! To the distress of some of the other committee members, she took over. Along with a friend who was equally well-known in the community, she lassoed locals, helped them figure out what to do, and even prepared their supplies for them. All they had to do was show up for the day.

"She shouldn't be doing everything for people," one of my committee members wailed.

“Let’s just see what happens,” I said. “She’s a lot more connected in this community than the rest of us. Let’s see what she can do.”

Sure enough, that year the festival doubled in activities, booths, and attendees. Jenean had succeeded. She had gotten the town involved! It was beginning to become a town festival, not just ours. The following year, in 2004, she repeated what she’d done. Then, a few days after the festival, she resigned.

“It’s too much work,” she said. I’m not doing this again.”

“What now?” said one of the committee.

“I don’t think we should do what Jenean did. I think we should make people do their own work, but we can offer support and ideas. We can even provide some of the materials.”

The next year, all of the people Jenean had solicited returned. Now that they knew what to do, they were ready to do it on their own. It had truly become a town festival!

We still didn’t have much money—we raised a little from local businesses—but we still had to beg our friends to perform for little money. Then, at the end of an especially well-attended festival, one the local movers and shakers got my attention.

“Monica, why don’t you let us do your fundraising for you? We can suck a lot more money out of these people than you can.”

“Twist my arm!” I shouted ecstatically. The next year, our budget tripled, and we were able to pay our performers, even bring in guest puppeteers from other states! We added musicians and a juggler to the street. We had face painters and a balloon-twisting clown. Bit by bit, year by year, the West Liberty Children’s Festival also became a mini puppetry festival. In addition to thousands of local and area residents, it began to attract puppeteers who came to see their peers perform. We added a Friday night puppet slam for adults and asked our guest puppeteers to bring content. Eventually, we even added a few Friday workshops, open to local residents and visiting puppeteers. It had become a town festival and a puppetry festival!

In 2012, Our Great Plains Region of Puppeteers of America needed a host and location for the regional puppetry festival that was supposed to occur every other year. Our region hadn't had a festival since 2002. Shelly, my puppeteer friend from St. Louis, spoke up.

"Why don't you guys host it? You already do the Children's Festival. It's a mini puppet festival. You could build it around that.

We decided to give it a try. We scheduled it for a Thursday afternoon through Sunday morning, with the Children's Festival as the Saturday centerpiece. We put together a budget, decided on a registration fee that would allow the festival to break even with 50 participants, and put out our publicity, soliciting performance and workshop proposals.

One day I received a call from an East Coast agent working for the US State Department. Secretary of State Hillary Clinton's office was looking for performance opportunities for an Indonesian puppet troupe, Papermoon Puppet Theatre, who would be here on a cultural exchange called Center Stage.

"We're looking for an iconic American experience for our Indonesian guests," she said.

"You can't get much more iconic than a small town in Iowa with a large immigrant population!" I replied.

We needed to raise $2000.00 as our share of the expenses. We had to arrange housing and meals for nine people. Cara, our Outreach Director piped up.

"The local arts council voted last night to donate $2000.00 to the festival. Why don't we use that?"

I discovered that the guests included several vegetarians and one vegan. That was still a difficult concept for meat-eating Iowans. I talked to our local caterer who told me he made a mean veggie lasagna.

"How about a vegan meal?" I asked. He blanched.

"What's that?!"

"Don't worry. We'll get rice and beans from one of the Mexican restaurants."

Papermoon Puppet Theatre performed their evocative *Mwathirika* to a full house of puppeteers and West Liberty adults. The show was non-verbal but highly emotional and understandable. It told the story of the 1965 genocide in Indonesia, using full-body puppets manipulated by puppeteers sitting behind each puppet on a low platform with wheels. This placed the puppets' feet on the floor. They had distinctly expressive faces, making it easy for the audience to connect emotionally. As the show ended, the audience gravitated towards the stage, standing four deep for a closer look at the puppets and a chance to congratulate the puppeteers.

For the Indonesians, the high point of the weekend was the barn dance we held in an empty barn, part of an outdoor heritage display. We hired a bluegrass band. One of the attending puppeteers acted as caller, and all of the puppeteers, American and Indonesian, danced their hearts out.

After the festival ended, we received a thank you letter on State Department stationery with Hillary Clinton's signature! We hosted the regional festival again in 2018 and are preparing to host it in 2022.

Hey, Monica, don't forget about the festival that started it all, that funky little festival you used to do at Oak Grove Park. I think you called it the Eulenspiegel Fall Festival. Remember? It was in that little park between your house and Teri Jean's. It had that tiny little building in the middle that the city let you use. You called it the puppet house, but it was way too little to do us much good. But once a year, you opened it up, set us all up inside, and baked zillions of cookies. Let's face it, you're a sucker for festivals!

Schulz is right; I do love festivals! We started that fall festival in 1975, less than a year after our very first show. We asked friends to perform, and we did three shows ourselves. And Schulz is right; we did bake zillions of cookies—1000 to be exact—which we put on platters in the "puppet house". The delectable aroma outlasted the cookies, which disappeared post haste, many handfuls into the pockets of a couple of elderly ladies living alone in the neighborhood.

Our most faithful annual performer was Dave Morice, who mesmerized the kids as "Dr. Alphabet", wearing a top hat decorated with letters and doing a silly language-related show. We hadn't yet learned to control our audiences, and the kids crawled all over our props and staging. We had to shoo them away during the shows to make room for the puppets. One year Duffy DeFrance, the Muscatine children's librarian, did a belly dance. Other years she told stories that were just as wild as her dances.

After the festival, we hosted a big potluck at our house, just down the street from the park. We figured it was the least we could do to reward the friends who had performed free all day. 1982 was the last year for that festival. We had started it because we thought it would give us publicity and recognition. Then the realization hit us: the people who came thought we were hobbying housewives who played with puppets once a year. To top it all off, our after-party had gotten a reputation:

"Hey! I hear there's free food and beer at John and Monica's house. Let's go!"

It was time to pull the plug. That festival had been so much fun. It felt like the remains of the 1960s and 70s free-wheeling, pot-smoking, hippy culture, but maybe it was time to grow up, even if we did make our living playing with dolls!

14. Unlikely Meeting

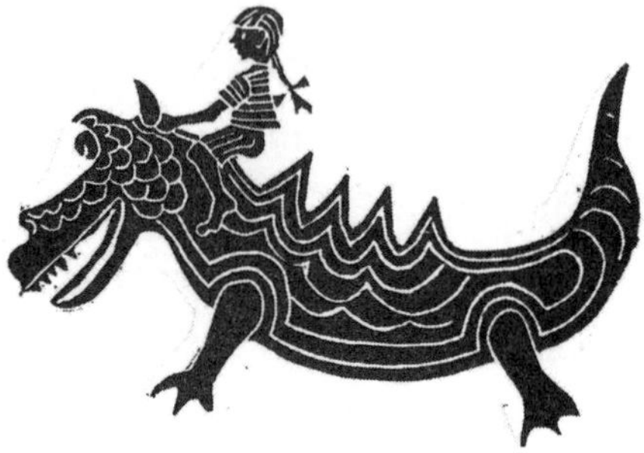

"Japan?"

"Yes," said the Board President of UNIMA-USA. "They always ask an American to lead the workshops; we have a reputation for being good at creativity education. But only one of you can go. You and Teri Jean will have to sort it out."

I knew right away it would be me. Although she was a good sport about all of our gallivanting, Teri Jean wasn't nearly as fond of traveling as I was. When I gave her the news, she didn't hesitate.

"You go! Send me some kitschy postcards…if they have kitsch!"

The *I Love You Puppetry Festival* was named after the American Sign Language sign for "I love you", which looks like a puppet skeleton—the hand formation used to work a traditional hand puppet. It took place every summer for three or four weeks, all over Japan. Four international puppet troupes were invited to perform; one American puppeteer led workshops for children and adults. Everyone traveled together from one city to another. Each town hosted its own celebration featuring the guest puppet shows and workshops as well as their local puppeteers. Each event lasted about three days, a sort of Japanese touring arts team.

I had to figure out what to do in my workshop. My first thought was my go-to shadow puppet workshop, but they had done shadow puppets the year before, in 1993. I had to use materials easily accessible in large quantities in Japan—I was told 100 or more people might attend a workshop. It had to be a project that could be completed in an hour or two, which knocked out hand puppets. I was advised to bring patterns since the Japanese were not accustomed to having to design things on the fly. They preferred to copy the teacher in order to learn the process. Creativity came later.

Inspired by Olaf and Detlef's trick marionettes, I finally decided on a poster board circus. I created jugglers, weightlifters, unicycle riding bears, acrobats, tightrope walkers, and more, using individual pieces put together with brass paper brads to create different types of movements. My bear had four parts: the head and body of a bear in profile; the thigh; the lower leg and foot; and the unicycle wheel. After putting the pieces together with paper brads, I attached "rods" made of barbeque skewers sticking straight out from the body and the wheel. Holding the rods at the ends, I could make the bear peddle furiously. The strong man worked similarly with barbells that went up and down; the tightrope walker had hip and knee joints. Designing them was an interesting challenge and decorating the white poster board pieces with markers was fun. John helped me create an environment for them out of tinker toys, with ramps, steps, and a tightrope. I played a recording of circus music as I demonstrated all of the characters at the beginning of each workshop. I made multiple patterns for each character and invited attendees to use the patterns or create their own designs. After the puppets were done, they could try them out on my tinker-toy jungle gym.

I packed all of my patterns and demonstration pieces into a small suitcase which I took as my carry-on, while I checked the suitcase with my clothes. I was supposed to fly on United Airlines from Cedar Rapids. Departure was delayed—and delayed again—and again. Finally, they told us the pilot had left the cockpit window open the night before.

It had rained on the instruments, and nothing was working. Passengers to Tokyo were sent to Chicago on a different flight and re-routed onto Japan Airlines.

Never before or since have I had such a luxurious flight! Large, comfortable seats, delicious seafood, little unexpected amenities like fuzzy slippers, and heated damp washcloths! I arrived in Tokyo rested and well-fed, but without my suitcase! It had gotten lost in the shuffle of substituted flights. Who knew when it would reappear? I was grateful I'd kept my workshop materials with me—much more important than a change of clothes!

After a day in Tokyo, the tour took off. My companions were puppet troupes from Bulgaria, Poland, and Mexico. With my love of Eastern Europe, I expected to connect with the Bulgarians and Poles. Instead, I felt an immediate kinship with Eli (pronounced Ellie), Camilo, and Tania from Mexico City. They did many of the same kinds of outreach and teaching we did and treated me as an equal, while it was clear from their behavior that the Eastern Europeans, as performers, felt superior to me, a mere teacher.

The opposite was true of the Japanese. After each workshop, I found myself surrounded by grateful adults thanking me and telling me how they expected to use what they learned. Two women followed me from workshop to workshop, building their skills. When we left their town, they came to see us off and presented me with a gift of markers I had admired.

The organizers had not exaggerated the size of the workshops. Most were groups of 60-80, but one day I had 120 participants. They could barely tear themselves away, and they stayed 30 minutes late, making ever more characters and performing little scenes. Luckily, they were conscientious about clean-up, and I never had to pick up after anyone! Most of my students copied my work, but every now and then, much to my delight, someone would design something completely new.

At first the slower pace made me uncomfortable. Most days I had only one workshop, much less work than I was accustomed to, but eventually, I got used to the rhythm and learned to enjoy my free time. I had an interpreter, Ike (pronounced Ee-kay), as my constant companion. She had been a puppeteer before becoming a full-time interpreter, and she was married to a puppet builder. She and her colleague Tamaki, whose show I had seen at a festival in San Francisco, worked for the Foundation Modern Puppet Center—the organizers—and shepherded us from place to place.

One day early in the tour, we went to Nishinomiya City, the birthplace of Japanese puppetry. We attended a ceremony at a Shinto shrine to Ebisu, the god of fortune, revered by puppeteers. The shrine was stunning, with a typical Japanese curved pitched roof. It was dark red, with gold embellishments and four pillars. A podium stood in front.

"Monica," said Ike. "They want you to say a few words on behalf of the puppeteers."

"Me? Why me?"

"You're the teacher, the only one."

I spoke a few sentences, complimenting the beauty of the shrine and the country and addressing the international importance of the Japanese puppetry tradition. Ike translated, and they presented me with a gigantic bouquet. Being singled out like that—although it was flattering—made me feel uncomfortably like a fraud. I passed out parts of my bouquet to all of the other puppeteers. That made me feel better—and still left me with a large bouquet of my own! I learned that the Japanese have great respect for people who make the financial sacrifice of working as professional puppeteers.

The Japanese summer was so hot and humid it made our Iowa summers seem temperate. It was a cicada summer—the air was filled with the humming of thousands of locusts from dawn to dark. The aroma of incense was everywhere, from insect-repelling coils as well as Buddhist shrines. Buildings were air-conditioned, but moderately—no more than a few degrees cooler than the outside air, making it easy to acclimatize to the heat. People were low-key and polite, much like Midwesterners. Most people could speak some English, but they were reluctant, fearful, I suppose, of doing a less than perfect job.

The hotel rooms were marvels of efficiency, tiny but equipped with everything you could possibly need, from freshly laundered robes to toiletries. All of the controls for the room—light switches, air-conditioning, TV, and radio—were located in the headboard of the bed. The tiny bathroom had a long faucet that swung around from the sink to fill the tub—small, but deep for soaking. In the morning, you could choose an American breakfast or a Japanese breakfast. I always chose the Japanese: miso soup, rice, fish, various pickled vegetables and fruits, and seaweed. When I remember that summer, miso is the overarching taste—it seemed to dominate every meal.

On many evenings I went with Tamaki, Ike, or other staff members to nearby restaurants for dinner. The evening meals were not that different from the breakfasts, many small dishes were passed around. They almost always included rice, miso soup, and pickles. The presentation was supreme: everything was artistically arranged.

A couple I met took me out for soup one evening. The soup was served with chopsticks! I looked at my hosts in confusion.

"How do I eat this?" I asked.

"Rest the ends of the chopsticks in the bottom of the bowl, twirl the noodles on them, and enjoy! Pull out the pieces of meat and vegetables with the sticks. When only broth is left, you pick up the bowl and slurp it directly from the vessel.

When my suitcase still hadn't arrived after a week and a half, I decided I'd better find some clothes to buy with the 10,000 yen ($100) the airline had given me. Luckily, I'd worn my favorite lightweight pants and top on the plane. The outfit was easy to wash and dried quickly without wrinkles. I wouldn't have cared if it hadn't been for the remarks every morning at breakfast:

"I see your suitcase hasn't arrived yet!"

"Aren't you tired of wearing the same clothes?"

"You poor thing! I hope your suitcase arrives soon!"

Enough with the misplaced pity! After our workshop that day, Ike took me to a large department store where I found exactly one dress and one pair of pants and top long enough for my 5'10" body! The dress, intended to be ankle length, hit me just below the knees. When my suitcase arrived the next day, I was glad I had decided against the $16.00 underpants.

We traveled from town to town in a large touring bus. The Japanese countryside rolled out in front of us, mountains always in sight. Light-colored low-slung buildings with curved rooflines echoed the flight of cranes, the quintessential Japanese bird. The bus stopped, and all of the Japanese staff lined up at an ice cream stand, or so I thought. I got in line and selected what looked like a chocolate chip ice cream bar. Mouth watering, I took a bite. YIKES! It was an adzuki bean bar. Instead of the sweet taste of ice cream and chocolate chips, I got a mouthful of beans!

As the days passed, I spent more and more time with the Mexican puppeteers. They realized that I was the only solo puppeteer on the tour, and they responded by including me in all of their outings. One day I went along to their performing site and watched their show. *The Moon and the Dragon* was an ethereal story of an old puppeteer who falls in love with the moon. After scenes from his life—including two short shows within the show—he dies, and the moon releases his spirit into a dragon. The show included lots of sound effects using an eclectic variety of instruments. The instruments were stationed on a table, stage left. Eli and Tanya took turns zipping to the table and adding sound effects, a technique I borrowed the following year when TJ and I created our T*ails From Africa*.

Camilo and Tania were excellent performers, but Eli's magnetism lit up the stage. We started talking about bringing them to Iowa for a tour. They told me about a Mexican folklore show they had that would be perfect for our emerging Latino population all over Iowa. Camilo was sure he could get grant support for a tour, and I was sure I could book enough shows.

Our last city was Iida, which billed itself as a "city of puppetry." It held an annual festival in August, bringing in puppeteers from all over the world and showcasing their local puppeteers, professional and amateur. Our group was part of that festival. The whole city was full of puppets, with window displays in all of the stores, free shows in the parks, and indoor performing venues for audiences of all ages. The festival started with an opening ceremony featuring welcome speeches by the mayor and other city dignitaries. The main square was embedded with tiles from each year's festival. 1994 was the 16th annual Iida Puppetry Carnival. In the square was a tent with ongoing puppet shows and puppet-making activities. Giant puppets wandered the streets. 279 puppet troupes, amateur and professional, performed; 2000 people attended.

A highlight of the weekend was a parade featuring all 279 puppet troupes! I had been asked to bring a puppet along for the parade. Of course, I didn't have room to carry a large parade puppet, so I packed Tinkle, a clown built on a slinky with a long body that could stretch and collapse. Tinkle greeted the crowds with a sign reading "Eulenspiegel Puppets, Iowa, USA". Now and then someone would shout:" Hello, Iowa!" Tinkle was awarded 3000 yen to spend at a local business. He took Ike and me out to lunch on his winnings.

What! You took Tinkle but you didn't take me? I could have been in that parade! I would have made you look terrific! Well, I guess Tinkle was less "luggage" than I would have been. Anyway, someone had to stay here and help Teri Jean. While you were out lollygagging around Japan, we were working at a Girl Scout camp in Northwest Iowa. Not as glamorous as going to Japan, but it paid the bills!

After the parade, we went to a performance by the Deaf Puppet Theater. *The Monkey King* drew on Japanese mythology to create a gorgeous, movement-oriented show. Two narrators, a giant bird, and a large cobra told the story, one by speaking and one by signing. Most of the puppeteers were hearing impaired or deaf.

I had put off shopping for presents to take home. Iida, with its compact business area, was a good place for this errand. I knew Teri Jean's three stepsons loved comics and I had seen many in shop windows, so I found a comic store and went in to browse. Good thing I looked before I bought! Most of them were pornographic! Who knew! I managed to find three innocuous ones for the three boys.

Next to find tchotchkes small enough to fit into my suitcase. Teri Jean had jokingly asked for kitschy postcards, assuming that everything in Japan would be refined. Not so! All through the trip, I was amused and amazed by the dichotomy of taste: small, carefully groomed dooryards with bonsai trees and artistically placed stones; classic, simple lines in furniture and accessories combined with the cutesiest of kitschy figurines. The only hard part was deciding if Teri Jean would prefer the kitsch or the beauty! I compromised by getting her examples of both: a cutesy ceramic cat and some beautiful, intricate paper cuts

I finished my shopping, packed, and attended a farewell party. Hordes of people descended on tables of food, beer, and saki. We could barely move, so we escaped to the outdoors. There I was shocked when I saw people setting off fireworks in the parking lot. Now I understood something I had marveled at. Every convenience store carried fireworks—shelved next to the bottled drinks and bagged snacks. There were no limits on their use. Anyone could light up the sky, and this evening, many did, another mind-blowing aspect of Japanese culture.

We spent one more night in Tokyo, the last night in a nifty, efficient Japanese hotel room. We spent the evening—all of us together—wandering around the neon-lit streets. Gigantic buildings lined the avenues. Noisy clubs packed with customers proliferated. Vehicles screeched around corners, honking their horns. The city made New York seem downright small-town!

The next morning it was time to board United Airlines—no water-logged control panels this time—for San Francisco, traveling together with my new friends, Eli, Camilo, and Tania.

We spent the trip hatching plans for the future. We knew we would see each other again in Iowa. I'd found the perfect offering for our new Latino residents in, of all places, Japan!

15. Goodfolk Puppets

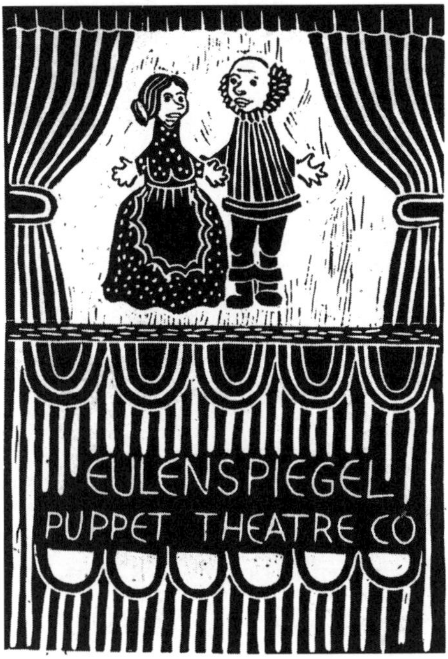

Twenty-four years in, in 1998, Teri Jean decided it was time to address her fear of running a business. She had always shied away from the business decisions, leaving them—and the dispersal of money—in my hands.

"Teri Jean, you've got to start paying attention. It would be so easy to cheat you."

"You're right, Mon. I've decided to sign up for a fast-track class for people who are running a small business. It's through the U, and the teacher seems pretty down to earth—and she has a Ph.D. in economics."

"Wow," I said. "You're moving past the money charm!"

A few years earlier, Teri Jean had consulted a book of spells and made me a money charm to pin over my desk. It was a piece of green fabric—to symbolize greenbacks—fashioned into a small bag. Inside were a coin, some herbs, a small crystal, and a picture of a puppet. It seemed to work. Our bookings increased, but—beyond the money charm—Teri Jean's involvement in the business was minimal. This would be a change!

As part of the course, the instructor offered to visit each of her students and consult on ways to build and stabilize their income. So one day the teacher—we'll call her Betty—arrived at Owl Glass. I told her about my history of making and selling puppets—something I had little time for these days.

"How about this: we create a cottage industry, hire stay-at-home moms to make the puppets, and we sell them."

"Selling them is the hardest part!" I objected.

I had discovered how difficult it is to compete with companies whose toys are made in third-world countries. But after all, Betty was an expert. What did I know?

"Why don't I come and work part-time for the business and get it established?" she said. "I've wanted to do something like this forever, and this is the perfect time. With the new Welfare-to-Work program the Clinton Administration just passed, we could hire someone and get half of her pay from the government for the first year. With any luck, we'd be profitable by then. The women making the puppets would work at home and meet together once a week for finishing, socializing, and coffee."

Mutti had recently died and left us a little money. I decided to donate $6,000.00 to the cause for Betty's pay. We rented a space in Mallory's building, and John installed workbenches and a bathroom with a shower. There was an extra room that we fitted out as a bedroom so we could also use the space as housing for guest puppeteers. We called the enterprise Goodfolk Puppets for the connection to folktales.

We decided to start with one hiree, and we found the perfect person. Brenda was a low-income mom with school-age children and sterling artistic skills. She loved making the puppets and made them at least as well as I did. I made the originals, created molds for the heads, and made patterns for the bodies. I taught Brenda how to pour liquid neoprene into the molds, empty them four hours later after a shell had hardened, take them out of the molds the next day, and sand them to perfection. She poured her heart and all of her talents into the process.

Betty had assured us that she had done detailed research and determined that the wholesale price we needed to charge to meet expenses—and pay Brenda a decent wage—was well within the range of prices charged by comparable companies. We marketed the puppets individually and in sets of six including such characters as kings, jesters, and wizards. We made them in all ethnicities, with faces sculpted to reflect different bone structures. Each kit included a sample script and instructions on manipulating the puppets to make them come to life.

One day Brenda called me into her workspace. There were two long tables set up in an L shape. The sewing machine sat on one, along with piles of fabric, scissors, pins, needles, thread, and yarn. The other held the molds, a gallon of liquid neoprene, sandpaper, modeling paste, paints, brushes, and empty jars that served as water containers. A coffeepot sat on the counter, the aroma emanating into the room.

Brenda was a slight, graceful young woman with olive skin, wavy black hair, and a ready smile. Her usually melancholy brown eyes twinkled with pleasure when she showed off her work.

"What do you think of these? I really wanted to make some animals, but we don't have any animal head molds."

She had used the head molds, painted them like children—with a few whimsical whiskers added—and given them animal bodies.

"They're adorable, Brenda! Good idea! They look like kids dressed in their animal jammies or Hallowe'en costumes! Let's call 'em Critter Kids!"

I stayed for a while and watched Brenda paint. With a steady hand, a sure eye, and a tiny watercolor brush, she enhanced the sculptural character of the different faces with fine, sensitive lines–whiskers, eyeliner, lip definition, wrinkles–and perfectly blended blush. She added sparkle to the eyes with clear nail polish. The expressive faces sprang to life.

We gave Brenda the option of working at home and checking in once or twice a week–Betty's plan for a business we hoped would employ several puppet makers–but she loved her workspace and showed up every single day.

Everyone who saw the puppets loved them but didn't necessarily buy them. Betty was discovering how hard it is to compete with companies—like Folkmanis, with their delightful plush animal puppets—whose products are made in China.

Still, ours were traditional human hand puppets. That type of puppet was almost always imported from Germany or the Czech Republic, not manufactured in the U.S. And Betty had researched meticulously, or so she said.

Schulz here: don't pretend you weren't worried about selling the puppets, Monica! You know darned well that you knew more about selling puppets than Miss-PhD-in-Economics did! Remember when you asked her about her research and it turned out she had done her fact-finding on EBAY?! All she did was find out how much people were charging for puppets, not whether they sold. SHEESH! No wonder this was turning into a pile of you-know-what!

After the $6,000 I donated was gone, Betty stayed on for another six months for almost no pay. She dearly wanted this experiment to succeed. I finally realized that organizing a female-centered cooperative workshop was a long-held dream of Betty's, and we were the vehicle she had been looking for. Our goal of having a sustainable regional puppetry center was irrelevant to Betty as long as her vision moved forward. I liked her idea—in theory—but it wasn't our main goal, and it didn't add to our income. Quite the contrary. I felt taken advantage of, but I had come to love Brenda, and I didn't want to pull the rug out from under her.

When Teri Jean and I went out of town for two weeks, I asked Betty to take our brochure to the printer, so we could mail them when we got home. I thought that was the least she could do after saddling us with extra work and expenses to fulfill her dream. She neglected it.

That finally put me over the top, and my face broke out in a bright red swollen rash. We had a few school visits scheduled.

"Uh oh, Teri Jean, how can I go to school looking like this?" I moaned.

"Don't worry. Wormwood and I've got you covered!"

Enter Wormwood, the bright red German hand puppet devil Teri Jean loved working in our demonstrations. He took one look at me, jumped backwards, and fell into a deep faint. I nudged him awake,

"What's wrong, Wormwood?"

"Monica, what happened to you?"

"What do you mean, what happened to me?"

"Your face. It's blinding me! It looks like a traffic light!"

"It's just a rash, Wormwood."

"A rash? Is it catching?" Wormwood backed up cautiously.

"I don't think you can catch anything from me that will make you redder than you already are, Wormwood!"

"Oh. Maybe I don't have to worry."

I had to worry, though. I knew it was time to pull the plug. I had come to realize that the efforts and money we were investing in Goodfolk Puppets were endangering Owl Glass Puppetry center.

I told Betty we would fill whatever orders we had and shut our enterprise down. We would try to recoup some money by gradually selling the remaining stock. As of January 1, 2000, Goodfolk Puppets would be gone.

I'll never know whether it was an intentional thumb in my eye, or whether Betty acted without thinking. Before the end of the year, she signed contracts to obligate us to Brenda's employment and all of our utilities for another six months. We couldn't face disappointing Brenda, so I didn't try to negate that contract.

I spent weeks contacting all of our other creditors and explaining our position. I felt like every day was spent furiously running from the puppetry center, through the alley, to the workshop, and back, dealing with a million things that had to be done in each space. I learned to work on the PC at Goodfolk, so different from the Macs I was used to. Every day was frantic.

When I had time to reflect, I beat myself up:

"Why don't you ever listen to your gut? You knew—from experience, for pity's sake—how hard it is to try and compete with companies whose products are made in third world countries! Why do you always assume other people know more than you do? Have you no consideration for John? Think of the work and money he invested in renovating the space and installing the bathroom, all for naught! What is wrong with you?

Luckily, I managed to get us out of the contracts Betty had signed. But what about Brenda? She loved this job! I talked through the problem with Teri Jean, and we decided to eke out a workspace for Brenda in the puppetry center. The basement already had a workbench and shelves. We installed Brenda there and gave her six months' notice. She kept making puppets and hoping we'd figure out better ways to sell them. After six months, we said a tearful goodbye.

Gradually, we sold all of the stock. Twenty-two years later, Brenda still stops in now and then to see if we might ever revive Goodfolk Puppets.

Recently, when Brenda popped in the door, she showed me some of her paintings. No surprise to me, they were skillfully done.

"Brenda, did you know the local arts council opened a gallery? You should join. You'd have opportunities to display and sell your work!"

Brenda joined, and her paintings hang in the gallery. She's still working at an unsatisfying job, but she has an outlet for her artistry, a door opened by Goodfolk Puppets.

As for the puppets, I kept the molds and still make a few each year, but we've given up having an American company making European-style puppets.

16. Evangelism

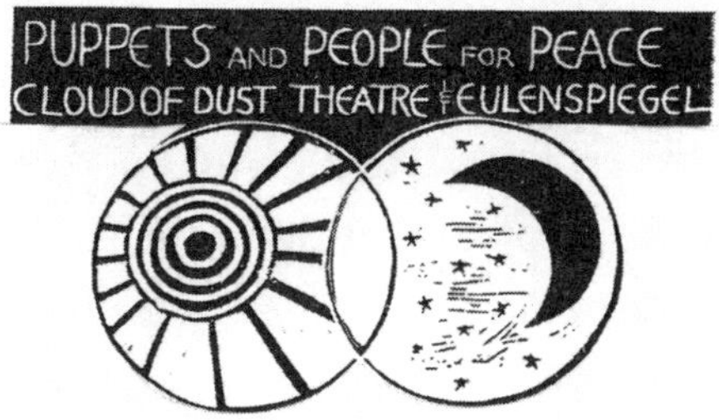

"Oh, darn it all!" sighed Mutti from her bedroom.

It was the spring of 1998, and Mutti, age 96, had received a diagnosis of stage 4 terminal lung cancer. She'd never smoked more than an occasional mosquito-repelling cigarette, so she assumed it was the result of years of inhaling sulfuric acid fumes in her metal work. At least that's what she chose to believe. It made her feel better about her impending demise to think that it was directly related to her beloved art.

The shortness of breath was so bad that she was confined to her bed with an oxygen tank. A rotating cast of children and grandchildren took care of her, along with daily visits from hospice nurses. An endless stream of visitors, mostly thirty or forty years younger, poured in and out of the door. They weren't charity visits to an old lady; they were her friends, wanting to talk to her while they could.

"Did you think you were going to live forever?" I asked.

"I just wanted to see the rest of the century!"

"You have seen most of it, 1901-1998! That's pretty good!"

I spent my days in the room opposite her bedroom, making mock-ups for the pop-up book stage I was planning to use in a small production of *Little Red Riding Hood.* Every time I finished a page, I took it to her bedside and showed it to her. Her delight and amazement were all of the encouragement I needed to start afresh on the next page.

Mutti was our biggest fan. She sat in the front row of the audience—on the floor with the little kids—and talked back to the puppets. She loved going to out-of-town shows with us and insisted on helping with all of the schlepping.

"Mutti!" exclaimed Teri Jean. "You have to put that trunk down! What are people going to think of us, letting Monica's tiny little 85-year-old mother carry our stuff!"

"If they don't like it, they can lump it!" American slang was especially juicy in her German accent.

When I awoke on April 10, Good Friday, I had the feeling it would be Mutti's last day. She spent most of Thursday sleeping. At 3:00PM I felt a subtle change in the atmosphere of her room. Then the phone rang. It was her devout Catholic neighbor.

"Can I come over and see your mom?"

"Sure. Come on over, but it might be too late."

Moments later he walked in the door. By that time, I knew she was gone.

"I'm sorry. I'm afraid she just died." He looked at his watch and gasped.

"It's 3:00 o'clock. And it's Good Friday! The same time Jesus died!"

"A sense of drama to the end," I replied.

Deborah, my niece, lit every candle in the house—hundreds, it seemed—and we spent the evening telling Mutti stories.

My siblings and I stayed to clean out her house, put it on the market, and help plan her memorial service. The house looked tidy, but it was full of buried treasure. I spotted Christopher, my brother, carrying a stack of magazines out for recycling.

"Stop! You can't just get rid of those magazines!"

Why not?" he asked.

"I'll show you," I said, handing half the stack to Anne.

We held the magazines upside down and shook them, one by one. Drawings, watercolors, and scissor cuts fluttered out.

"These magazines were her portfolio!"

We finished with the house the day before the memorial service. We donated most of her sketches to the Wartburg Seminary archives, the Lutheran seminary where Vati had taught and where she had been the unofficial artist-in-residence for the last twenty-five years. The service was held at the seminary, The president spoke alongside the Abbot of the nearby monastery. A five-piece jazz band composed of Wartburg students accompanied her second-youngest granddaughter carrying the finely crafted box John had made for her ashes. We buried her on my father's grave, under the copper relief she made for him. We found a rough chunk of limestone and took it to a monument maker for the inscription we wanted: "Eva Dittrich Leo, 1901-1998. Born in Germany, emigrated in 1939. Creator of Paul Leo's grave marker". We figured 1939 would tell future generations why she left Germany and the rest would give her age and occupation.

As I left Dubuque with Mutti's little orange kitty riding shotgun, I thought," There goes my last connection to the Lutheran Church."

I decided to stop at the puppetry center on my way home. I walked in the door to a ringing phone. It was Mallory, calling from her gift shop, which served as an unofficial community meeting place.

"Can you come over here? The new Lutheran pastor wants to meet you."

That was the beginning of a long friendship—sometimes partnership—with Pastor Terry Mahnke. He'd come into the ministry in middle age, studying theology in St. Paul. There he'd attended an Easter Vigil service with puppets by *In the Heart of the Beast Puppet and Mask Theater.*

"I always scorned puppets before. I saw such trivial stuff passed off as religious puppetry. But the power of that Easter Vigil service made a big impression. I'd love to do something like that here. What do you think?"

“Well,” I said, “I think it’s a great idea, if you don’t expect me to attend your church. My dad was a Lutheran minister. I’m still on comp time.”

He laughed. That was all the answer I needed. This might be fun.

As it turned out, the Easter Vigil was not to be. Pastor Terry couldn’t get his congregation and the other pastors in the Ministerial Association on board. But that didn’t stop us from lots of other collaborations.

Puppet Bible School replaced the traditional Vacation Bible School. Terry picked a story and we figured out how to translate the story to a puppet pageant. The kids made puppets and scenery. One of us—usually Peggy or Buffy, who both led our after-school puppet club at various times—worked hands-on with the kids, and the week culminated in a public pageant-style performance.

My favorite year was the year they did the story of David and Goliath. Terry built Goliath out of plastic bags stuffed with more plastic bags. He was gigantic—about nine feet tall—but lightweight. Terry suspended him on a line between two poles in the church yard. Under Peggy’s direction, the kids made flat cardboard cutouts of David, a flock of sheep, and a slingshot, and painted them with vibrant tempera paints.

The day of the pageant arrived. Nine-foot-tall Goliath made threatening noises and shook his fist. David arrived followed by his flock of sheep. He stopped short, heard Goliath’s threats, and bent his arm with the slingshot attached. The kid with the stone placed it adjacent to the slingshot and ran towards Goliath. Crack! At the sound of a slapstick worked by another kid, the cardboard stone pierced Goliath in the heart! Terry released the line and Goliath crumpled to the ground, accompanied by more noisemakers. Roars of applause from parents and neighbors!

On September 11, 2001, another Goliath crumpled to the ground as planes hit the twin towers of the World Trade Center. Everywhere we looked in West Liberty people sobbed and talked in hushed tones. Teri Jean crossed the street from the liquor store with a bottle of wine in her hand.

"The owner of the store was sitting in front of the tube, tears rolling down his cheeks!" she reported.

"Americans have short attention spans," I said. "This will be forgotten in no time." I couldn't have been more wrong. Twenty-some years later, 9/11 still lingers daily in our consciousness and politics.

Pastor Terry stopped over soon after, and he and Teri Jean got into one of their deep philosophical discussions. They both had the same speaking style, starting in the middle of a thought and moving to both ends simultaneously. They could always understand each other, even when no one else could follow them. The topic of the day was how a community should respond to the events of 9/11. They agreed that working on a creative community project would be a positive step, and Terry immediately proposed a community puppet show. Much to my amazement, Teri Jean, who was usually leery of loosely controlled projects, agreed. As one who loves unpredictable collaborations, I jumped right on board.

The Iowa Arts Council offered a grant for projects addressing the tragedy of 9/11.

Our project was chosen for funding. It was full speed ahead.

Puppets and People For Peace began to shape up. We looked for stories that featured people working together and discovered a Native American tale, *Pushing Up the Sky.* It was a creation myth, telling how earth and sky became separate. It featured an entire village working together to push up the sky. We envisioned it as a shadow puppet show and asked John to make us a large round shadow screen. With the help of our community, especially Cara McFerren, who had majored in art and relished an opportunity to create, we crafted stark images with colored accents, showing animals, humans, and constellations.

We asked our friend Bob Aiken, a former Iowa puppeteer who'd moved to Colorado, to come for a week and bring *The Circle of Creation*, a show that fit our theme, that he and his wife performed together. She couldn't come along, but Bob offered to reorganize the show, split up her part into sections, and teach it to West Liberty residents.

Bob hauled his ten-foot diameter frame into the puppetry center and set it up in the middle of the floor. A cast of local residents and friends of the puppets arrived to rehearse.

"All right, everyone, we'll start by helping this spider weave these strips across the circle to form a spider web. Al, you take this end; Lou, you take this one. Now cross in the middle."

After the spider web took shape, it was time for the group to move in tandem, draping fabrics across the web to create a landscape of rolling hills. The landscape filled out, and animal puppets came to life. The puppeteers took turns stepping in front to recite passages from Native American writings alternating with verses from the book of Genesis. Everything dealt with circles and cycles.

"It's more of an animated theater piece than strictly a puppet show," Bob mused.

We decided to start and end with a parade of giant puppets into and out of the theater. We made a sun and a moon, each about ten feet tall, and lined their fabric bodies with battery-operated twinkle lights. We made a twelve-foot Mother Earth character. Her cloth body was composed of a patchwork of every kind of ethnic fabric we could find. At Teri Jean's suggestion, her face became a collage of many faces of all different skin colors. Our elementary art teacher worked with her second graders to create the faces in the collage. Each child chose a piece of paper closest to their skin color and made a self-portrait. We cut them out and glued them onto the puppet's head.

The three giant puppets marched into the theater to music, an impromptu jam session by musician friends who'd agreed to add their talents to our extravaganza. The puppets perched in stands flanking the puppet stages, our large circular shadow stage, and Bob's larger frame stage. With our cast of ten, who had spent a week's evenings rehearsing with us, we performed *The Circle of Creation* followed by *Pushing Up the Sky*. We ended by marching the sun, moon, and Mother Earth back out of the theater.

The audience was large and enthusiastic. It wasn't an Easter Vigil, but it bestowed a similar spiritual experience and the same community cooperation.

A few years later, Terry and his family moved to a different parish in a new town. A few years after that, cancer took him, just as it has taken so many of the people I've cared about and worked with. Their voices, including Terry's, resonate in my brain as I imagine their part in every new project.

After that first year, community shows became an almost annual event. Participants included people from all walks of life—a school superintendent, the chief of police, a Spanish exchange teacher, a plumber and his young son, a phys ed teacher, a lawyer, and children and adults of all ages.

Eventually, we started designing the shows we liked the best for touring. We took (and still take) our favorites—*Portraits of the Prairie, Immigrant Stew at the Chat 'n' Chew, John Brown's Journey, Five Suns of the Aztecs, The Flea,* and *Don Quixote*—to other towns in the framework of three-day residencies. Local sponsors organize a cast and crew, and we sail in, set up the stage and puppets, and rehearse with them just as Bob rehearsed with our locals. Our collaborating musician comes in on day three for a dress rehearsal and performance. This is still one of my favorite parts of my job. I bask in the energy generated as people discover the power of puppetry for the first time.

One community show residency that stands out was in Adel, Iowa, where we rehearsed a classroom of second graders—our youngest group ever—into *Portraits of the Prairie.* The stage is a three-level landscape of rolling hills. It resembles a Grant Wood painting and was designed and painted by Peggy Fitzgerald, the sometime Eulenspiegel staff member/friend who'd also done the *David and Goliath* pageant with Pastor Terry.

Seven or eight kids lined up behind each of the three panels. Each child had a stack of flat puppets at their feet. Dressed in a painter's smock and mask and wielding an oversized brush, I played the part of a painter painting a portrait of the prairie. My co-puppeteer stayed backstage with the kids, managing them but also working a sassy squirrel who talked back to the painter.

In the first scene, native prairie, the front row had coneflowers that grew up and waved back and forth in the wind. The second and third rows had butterflies, birds, and prairie mammals. The whole scene was a gently moving landscape led and punctuated with live classical guitar. It was followed by a series of other scenes documenting the history of our land. The second last scene featured vast fields of corn, a hog confinement, and cornstalks marching back and forth as we all sang a chorus of a rousing song written by our collaborating musician, Ron Hillis.

"Can't get away from corn, can't get away from corn.

Everywhere, sure as you're born, can't get away from corn!"

The show ended with a reconstructed prairie, a replay of the first scene. At the end, the kids filed out, row by row, faced the audience and bowed.

After rehearsing for two days in their school gym, our second graders were scheduled to perform as part of the Adel Book Festival. Adel was a typical midwestern small town, the Main Street lined with a hardware store, flower shop, bakery, quilt shop, and antique store.

We set up the prairie scene in the empty firehouse on Main Street and held our dress rehearsal early Saturday morning. As we rehearsed, people began to filter in to watch. By the time the rehearsal was over, the firehouse was full to overflowing. I motioned the front row to file out and line up. The first child stepped out, looked, gasped, and lurched backward. This repeated with each succeeding child! They had no idea they had attracted an audience.

As long as Pastor Terry stayed in West Liberty, we continued to hatch projects together. He told us about the tiny, elderly parishioner who looked up at him, shook her finger in his face, and admonished,

"Do you want to be known as the puppet pastor?"

Of course, that became his nickname! One day it dawned on me:

"Terry, I know why we get along so well. We're both evangelists. You evangelize for Jesus and I evangelize for puppets!"

17. Collaboration

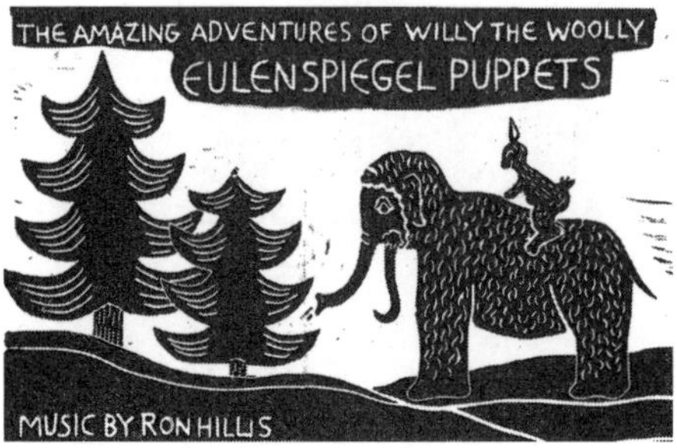

It was 1996. We were home for a while, using the time to build our sesquicentennial show, *Sal Fink, the Mississippi Screamer.* Guy Drollinger had agreed to add live music to the show, and he wanted to involve another musician, his friend Ron Hillis. Teri Jean ran into him in our favorite coffee shop.

"Say, Ron," said Teri Jean, "how would you like to work with Guy Drollinger, Monica, and me on a show?"

"A puppet show? Are you serious?"

"Dead serious! Guy says your music is just what we need, and that you two like playing together. Talk to him about it."

Guy was right; Ron's music was perfect. Sal Fink turned out to be the beginning of a twenty-five-year, on-and-off, partnership that resulted in ten shows elevated by Ron's evocative music.

Ron has a special talent for writing topical songs and the musical knowledge to write in different styles and key signatures. Once we had a script, we simply told Ron where we thought a song would work. He read the script, figured out the topic for a song and decided whether it should be a waltz, a tango, in a minor key, whatever. *Storm on the Water* from Gertie's Journey is a tango; *Johnny's Song* in *Appleseed!* is a waltz. He wrote a Spiritual for *John Brown's Journey.*

The biggest lesson we learned working with Ron was how to fill time with movement and illustration. Ron liked writing lyrics—multiple verses—and there's nothing interesting in watching a puppet bobbing around pretending to sing. So—we had to come up with creative ways to engage the audience visually during the songs.

First challenge: three verses of *The Iowa Catfish Song.* At the direction of Michael Sokoloff ("Work that fabric, Girl!") we spent that song dancing fabrics in shades of blue into an arrangement that resembled a river. In *Freedom Star: Gertie's Journey on the Underground Railroad* we illustrated the songs with shadow puppets, and that became our go-to in other shows as well. Our shadow screens were integrated into the scenery, peeking through the forest in *Freedom Star,* through a window in *Don Quixote* and *John Brown's Journey*, through a wintry sky in *The Amazing Adventures of Willy the Woolly.* An overhead projector perches backstage to provide a light source and magnify the puppets.

When The Des Moines Symphony asked us to do a performance with them, they told us we could choose the show. Since Michael had helped us with several projects not of his choosing, we decided to let him pick the symphony piece. Did he choose *Peter and the Wolf* or *Carnival of the Animals*? Of course not! Michael wanted to do serious, cutting-edge theater, so he chose Stravinsky's *L'Histoire de Soldat* (*A Soldier's Tale*). It was challenging artistically—the concept, the puppet building, the performing—but it turned out to be even more challenging to book. The music was difficult and used only eleven instruments. Most small-town symphonies found it too challenging. Even if they could master the music, most wanted pieces that used the whole orchestra. We performed it only eight or ten times.

I didn't begrudge the time and effort because I've rarely learned or stretched so much. We'd never played with sizes to the extent we did in this show. All of the main characters—the soldier, the princess, and the devil—existed in two sizes. Rod marionettes of all three characters were two and a half feet tall. The soldier also appeared as a four-foot tabletop rod puppet while the princess was a human-size stuffed doll. Michael directed and played the part of the narrator. He'd been a dancer in his youth, and he relished the opportunity to dance with the princess! Teri Jean donned a flowing velvet gown, wore a mask, and played the devil.

The devil had to blow up at the end. How to do that? We'd built him on an inflated balloon which we planned to poke with a pin at the perfect moment. We needed a visual effect to punctuate the moment. Teri Jean and I went to our favorite toy and magic store to consult with the owner, Mark, who always kept us in mind and let us know when he acquired a gadget he thought we could use.

"Mark, what do you think? Could we use flash paper for a nice flame while the balloon deflates?"

"What are you wearing? A flowing velvet robe?" Mark shook his head. "It's not a matter of whether you'll catch on fire. It's a matter of when!"

Instead, we filled the balloon with mylar glitter. When it burst, it released the glitter into the air, a larger effect than a small flame would have been. And Teri Jean didn't burn up.

Michael influenced our work forever. He only directed a few shows—it became apparent that his heart was in adult theater—but his voice rings in my ears with each new show. "Work that fabric, Girl" syncs perfectly with my love of beautiful fabrics and different ways of using them in puppets and scenery. Left to my own devices, I would not have thought of highlighting their movement as I position the fabric into its place in the scene. Before Michael's mantra—"more glitter!"—I thought glitter was gauche, not realizing how it made the scenery glisten, the magic and other-worldliness it created. I only use glitter glue or glittery fabrics since I've learned how damaging loose glitter is to the environment.

In 1997 we spent the better part of a month with late renowned puppet guru, George Latshaw. We got a grant from the Iowa Arts Council to pay him to come to West Liberty and direct a show, *Till Eulenspiegel Tales*. He built on Michael's fabric use by teaching me to make puppet costumes and hairdos with internal movement—capes weighted with beads that made them sway, feather boa hair that picked up the slightest breeze, stocking caps with weighted ends that made them flop.

We asked George to suggest a style of puppet for the show:

"Write down everything the puppet needs to do, and it will become apparent." he said.

"Hmm. The innkeeper needs to stir the stew and catch a rat. Till needs to carry a dead wolf. The boy needs to place a dunce cap on the university rector's head. Hand puppets. They're the only kind that can actually pick things up, the only kind of puppet with muscles."

Every day I brought the puppets I was creating to rehearsal and showed them to George.

"Isn't that marvelous?" He enthused. I waited for the other shoe to drop.

"What would happen if…" and George gave me suggestions for improvement, my assignment for the coming evening.

George was determined to break Teri Jean's worst habit, stopping for a do-over every time she made a less-than-perfect movement.

"Keep going!"

"But…"

"Keep going!"

"But I want…"

"Keep going!"

After George left, Teri Jean had me take a photo to send him: her, backstage, with a gag around her mouth and two puppets on her overhead hands.

We bought a special comfy chair for George to sit in as he directed us.

It still sits in the puppetry center. Every time one of us needs inspiration, she sits in the chair to absorb "George vibes."

I love collaborations! I love that the final product is different from anything any one of us would—or could—have done alone. I thrive on the uncertainty and the shifting balance of power. I love not being in sole charge.

It all started with Teri Jean. The shows we created were a complete blend of our differing personalities, interests, upbringings, and life experiences. I was raised on *Grimm's Fairy Tales* and Hans Christian Andersen. I have a larger collection of folktale books than any library I've ever been in. Teri Jean was raised on Looney Tunes and *The Three Stooges*. She loved Monty Python and gave me my love of slapstick. We both loved puns and turns of phrase. Our shows—mostly—were adaptations of my favorite folk and fairy tales since I knew and loved so many. We adapted the stories to puppets and modern audiences, but we made every effort to preserve the heart, the true meaning of the story. Our rabbit tales—*The Adventures of Great Rabbit*, *The Lion in the Well*, and others—drew inspiration from the antics of Bugs Bunny, who was their true descendant.

We brainstormed the scripts together. I kept my eye on the big picture—where the story was going—while Teri Jean fleshed out the delightful details. I made the puppets. Teri Jean mocked up staging and scenes using cardboard boxes and anything she could find. She used puppets from other shows—and my sock monkey, Terence Eugene—as understudies while she figured out the scenes. When I finished a puppet, I turned it over to her ruthless scrutiny.

"This puppet needs to go back to the shop. I want more arm movement." Or…

"I want puppets that move themselves."

Our rehearsals were fraught with anxiety. Teri Jean, a perfectionist, wanted to stop and burnish details. I wanted to go all the way through to understand the flow of the story. Sometimes we reached a stalemate, and frustration stopped the process. Eventually—once we'd gone all the way through a few times— it was fun. We had to remind ourselves this would happen.

We were rank amateurs when we started, flinging puppets around carelessly, looking at the audience instead of watching what we were doing, but together we grew into professionals with carefully crafted shows. In spite of disagreements and difficulties, we never stopped having fun.

Alfred Schulz here: Hey, wait a minute! Don't trash our early work. We had a ball acting out scenes from our private lives—remember? Remember when my body got so worn out that you had to give me a "soul transplant" into a new body? You couldn't bear to throw the old one out, so suddenly there were two Schulzes. The other one decided to be my good-for-nothing twin brother, Albert, and, whoa, did that cause problems! He was so obnoxious—pinching Moms in the fanny, saying rude things—and everyone thought it was me! Ha ha; that was fun! We couldn't do that once you guys got so..."professional!"

Eli was the next puppeteer I collaborated with. We started our work together over email, a brand-new experience for both of us. Eli knew from the beginning which story she wanted to develop. The story of *The Rabbit in the Moon* was embedded deep in Mexican folklore and in Eli's soul. It tells the story of Rabbit's battle of wits with Coyote. When Coyote finally appears to win, the moon comes down out of the sky and rescues the rabbit, Juan Conejo, and takes him with her into the sky. That's why Mexican children when they look at the moon, see a rabbit whereas our children see the man-in-the-moon. I realized how this story personifies the Mexican attitude towards death, accepting the transition to the other side and seeing it as beautiful.

I had to find a Mexican folktale that spoke to me. I combed my collection of folklore books and found a little-known tale, *The Musical Ant*. An ant finds a flute, learns how to play it, and makes music instead of working. The queen evicts him. He finds another colony and is evicted again. As he starts to leave, he sees an invading army. He plays dance music, and the army dances instead of invading. I loved the story! I added a scene or two and a few more characters. I traded the flute for a piano since a hand puppet can actually play a toy piano. I asked Ron to write me a couple of tunes that could be played on a toy piano.

When Eli arrived in late July 2007, we both had scripts and music. We had each built a couple of puppets or props. We discovered that we worked together in harmony with little or no stress. When I realized that Eli could play piano, we set up a keyboard and the pressure was off. Hormiguita could play a few tunes on his piano, but most of the music came from Eli's keyboard. We called the pair of tales *Stories and Cuentos*.

Every show and workshop we developed over the next twelve years was pure pleasure.

In 2015, we decided to create a bilingual community show. Once again it was up to me, as the folktale aficionado, to find the right story. I was struck by a series of Aztec creation myths that Eli knew but hadn't considered.

The stories, *Five Suns of the Aztecs*, tell about the creation of the world and the battle between the gods Quetzalcoatl and Tezcatlipoca. After earth-shaking battles, things go smoothly when they finally decide to work together. The scenes were dramatic, and the message was compelling. There were enough parts to keep a large group of community puppeteers busy.

I applied for a grant which enabled me to pay community artists to help create the show, making colorful birds and fish, a glittering sun, and a hand-dyed silk ocean.

Eli created a musical score, using indigenous melodies and percussion instruments. She trained an ensemble of rag-tag, multi-age musicians to work with her as she sang her Spanish narration. I narrated in English.

We presented the show in West Liberty and took it to seven other communities, where we rehearsed and performed it with groups of all ages, six years old through adult. Maybe someday we'll be lucky enough to meet another Latina to learn Eli's part so the show can live on.

Even though I've been called a political junkie, I never wanted to write didactic shows. Somehow or other, many of them end up revealing my left-wing peacenik leanings. Juan Conejo, the star of *The Rabbit in the Moon*, has to leave his home in a little village to find a job elsewhere. He crosses a wall and a desert to look for work. John made us a wall—out of corrugated metal—that looks suspiciously like the border wall. Eli spray-painted "No Pass" onto the wall in black. Juan Conejo has to figure out how to get across.

The Musical Ant features an army of ants dressed in camouflage. When Hormiguita plays the piano, they forget about attacking and dance with abandon. "Make art, not war."

A year or two after we created the show, we performed it on the little stage in our tree-shaded downtown pocket park located next to the movie theatre in West Liberty. Families gathered to watch, sitting on the bleachers, the benches, or the latticework chairs and tables. The aroma of popcorn wafted out of the New Strand door, attracting people who returned with bags full of the salty, buttery snack. Our fellow lefty friend Rod arrived with a pal and his family, who came to every show. As the puppets took their bows, his friend whispered,

"I wish they'd do political theater."

"What do you think this was?" Rod countered.

Community shows have been some of the most interesting, unpredictable collaborations. Take a topic or story, add an eclectic group of people with widely varying talents, and mix in specific requirements—enough parts for a large cast, flexible narration that can remind everyone what comes next, and a sequential story that allows people to appear one by one, not bunched together. Make sure that the topic or story is one of general interest. Take a deep breath and relax. Expect a fine product but be supportive and not overly critical. Everything works best when people enjoy the process!

My overall favorite community show is *Immigrant Stew at the Chat 'n' Chew,* another show with a shrouded political message. We created it in 2006, at the end of Teri Jean's tenure in the troupe. We asked our friend, author Mary Swander, to help us write it. We wanted a light-hearted history of immigration into the Midwest, especially in view of all of the little Iowa towns besieged or blessed—depending on your point of view—with Latino immigrants.

"Let's just get together at my house and hammer this out," suggested Mary.

We lounged around Mary's home in the country, early spring fields and vast midwestern skies visible through the large windows. Mary typed furiously on her laptop as Teri Jean and I volleyed suggestions.

"OK. Let's not lose track of the story!" that was me, in my usual role.

"Wait, wait! Let's give her a good midwestern, multi-cultural name: how about Cathy Schmidt-McGillicutty!"

"OK, but is Cathy Irish with a 'C' or German with a 'K'?"

"The café. What should we call the café?"

"Chat 'n' Chew, of course. Every little town has a Chat 'n' Chew!"

"How about Immigrant Stew at the Chat 'n' Chew? The stew can be the leitmotiv that carries the story."

"Great idea! Each ethnicity can be represented by an ingredient! Corn for the Native Americans…"

"Cabbage and potatoes—Irish *and* German!"

"We've got to have jalapeños, of course!"

We ended up with a common tale: Cathy, the mother, is upset when her daughter wants to marry the son of Mexican immigrants. By the end of the story—when she's examined her own family history through a series of flashbacks—she transforms and welcomes Juan into the family.

We asked Bob Aiken, who had worked with us on our first community show, to come help with this one as well. He built a gigantic papier mâché stew pot and huge papier mâché and fabric vegetables. He directed the show. I played Cathy; Lauren played Jesse, her daughter; Teri Jean ran lights and sound; community members played out a series of flashbacks about Cathy's family. Ron wrote the Immigrant Stew Polka and directed a crew of kids with sound-effect instruments. We all sang while Bob danced with a life-size puppet.

In the years since, Pam and I have taken this show to over twenty communities for three-day residencies. We rehearse every morning for three hours; then do puppet-making workshops in the afternoon. On the third day we perform for the public. It's always fun! Bonus: it delivers a timely and important message.

Mary Swander had been part of our close circle long before *Immigrant Stew*. We'd horsed around together, creating silly entertainments, like the massage "demonstration" that Mary did on Teri Jean as I provided the sound effects: ratchets, boneshakers, clackers, anything dangerous sounding we could find in our noisemaker stash. When we decided we'd each do a solo show, I created *Little Red Riding Hood*. Teri Jean decided to bring to life three of the quirky characters in Mary's *Driving the Body Back*, a collection of narrative poems telling the deathbed stories of her eccentric relatives while painting literary portraits of their rural Iowa lives. TJ's eclectic show—using objects, shadows, and Mary's words—was deeply moving. A geode became George's throbbing eye; an apron lifted to reveal a life-size puppet of a Native American chief; a headscarf moved from her head to her hand and transformed into Mary's grandmother. When Mary published another book-length narrative poem, *Girls on the Roof*—about a mother and daughter trapped on the roof of their catfish house as the 1993 flood raged around them—we had more traditional puppet fun. Our intern Lauren, a wildly talented visual artist in addition to all of her other talents, painted a backdrop that doubled as a shadow screen. The story played out with rod puppets of the two women over the top of the backdrop, shadow puppets behind the screen, and a hand puppet of Crazy Eddy, a skeleton washed out of his grave by the flood.

One of Teri Jean's and my many school residencies in the 1980s was in Cumberland, a tiny town—population 100—in western Iowa. We stayed with the retired high school drama teacher, a vibrant, active, opinionated lady.

"You girls have to meet Floyd. I'm inviting him for dinner!"

Floyd Pearce ran a small press, the Pterodactyl Press, which specialized in books by Iowa poets that he printed by hand on his antique letterpress. He had grown up in nearby Lewis and moved to San Francisco as a young adult, at a time when being gay was anathema in small-town Iowa. He had a successful career as a dancer and bought a house. When he aged out of dancing, he apprenticed himself to a printer and learned the art. When he reached retirement age, he realized his San Francisco property had vastly increased in value. He sold it and used the money to buy a building in Cumberland, pay his living expenses, and launch his press. We became fast friends!

Floyd had always wanted to publish a children's book. I had always wanted to illustrate one. Anne, my sister, was a writer who had published two children's books with major publishers. Her favorite manuscript, *Marcel and the Dirtball* had been rejected again and again. Based on a true story that played out in her New York City apartment, it featured a senior cat unhappy with the stray kitten interloper brought in off the street by his boy. A common story told in spare poetic prose.

Floyd loved the manuscript. I told him he could only have it if he let me illustrate it. We decided I would make woodcuts which he would print on his letterpress directly from the block. He said he needed absolutely level (within a milligram) blocks. I bought rosewood—the wood least likely to warp—and John asked a machinist friend to machine the blocks to the right height for the press (type high). Meanwhile, he edited Anne's manuscript, making it even stronger. He edited my sketches as well, giving me a lesson in the importance of negative space, a lesson I carry into every aspect of my work, including performances. The blank areas—in visual and performing arts—strengthen and emphasize the whole.

Floyd designed the book with input from Anne and me. He chose a lovely, flecked mustard yellow paper. It looked—maybe it was—handcrafted, but it was a tricky color when it came to choosing colors for the prints. We all contributed ideas, but the final decision was up to Floyd as the book designer. He picked a palette I love but never would have chosen. That is the essence of collaboration.

A serendipitous collaboration occurred in the late summer of 1999. Teri Jean and I were good friends with Bonnie and Andrew Periale, puppeteers from New Hampshire. We met and connected at puppetry festivals, and Teri Jean nurtured the friendship during the years she lived in Massachusetts. After we opened the puppetry center in West Liberty, we presented their shows several times over a few years. We often talked about attending an intensive puppet workshop that took place at the O'Neill Theater Center in Connecticut every June.

"I wish we could go to the O'Neill," I said, "but June is the worst. We do so many library and festival shows in June."

"Well," said Bonnie, "let's do our own O'Neill."

She got to work. She invited two other puppeteers, Caleb Fullam and Lynnie Raybuck, and two Canadian musicians, Daisy DeBolt and Tiina Kiik. Daisy was about to release a powerful new album, *Just Mountain Songs*. She agreed to let longtime fans Andrew and Bonnie use the songs as the subject of a puppet collaboration. She even agreed to participate and to include her accordionist friend Tiina.

Caleb, Lynnie, Daisy, Tiina, Teri Jean, and I invaded Bonnie and Andrew's rural New Hampshire paradise for a week in late August. Teri

Jean and I pitched a tent, inflated blow-up mattresses, and camped in the pine woods. The others camped out all over Bonnie and Andrew's house. Each of us puppeteers—except Bonnie, who acted as a doula and helped us all—chose a song to illustrate and dramatize. We all took the lead in our chosen song but enlisted help from the others.

Andrew set the parameters: we were limited to a few materials: corrugated cardboard, paper, masking tape, and wire. It would be a shadow puppet show on a large screen, using a pair of overhead projectors to create overlapping images. By the end of the week, we had to be ready to perform. We were scheduled for a local show in Strafford and one in Boston for their puppetry guild. Daisy and Tiina supplied live music.

I chose a song and froze. I was used to adapting folk tales; I'd never done anything so abstract. And…I had to accomplish this in a week and in front of all of these people I admired. I didn't know where to begin.

"Tap into your emotions," said Teri Jean. "What have you experienced that calls to mind the harsh beauty of that song?"

The album captured the merciless realities of rural life in the mountains. The song I'd chosen, icily beautiful, was a wintry scene of wolves stalking and killing sheep. I dug deep and remembered my grief when our darling goats—the same ones who had amused our German partner puppeteers by eating their luggage tags—had been chased down and killed by wandering, marauding dogs. I created a shadow scene with falling snow, blood, and two tiny goat carcasses. It was a good thing I didn't have to speak—I couldn't perform it without weeping.

That week was pivotal in my continuing artistic development. It blew the cobwebs out of my brain. I glimpsed so many new, non-linear storytelling ideas. A few years later, I created *Finding Home*, a trilogy about my parents' immigration experiences, using candlelight, shadows, objects, paper puppets, and scenes made with my mother's watercolors. I don't think I could have done it without that week in New Hampshire.

One last collaboration, not artistic but definitely creative—and a huge learning experience—was with Mallory, whom we met when she hosted our Mexican puppeteers for a month. She became our Board president, later on, our booking agent, and always our friend. She and I were both committed to community outreach. We started the Children's Festival together. She clued me into the many ways of getting involved in a small town. Every now and then she'd appear in the door to proclaim, not suggest:

"Come on, it's soup lunch day at the Methodist Church. Let's go have lunch!"

"Outside, all of you! It's Veteran's Day. They'll be appearing in front of the American Legion with the flag in a few minutes at 11:00 AM."

She opened my eyes to smart, inventive business practices, too. When the Iowa Arts Council introduced a mini-grant that topped out at $1500.00 and required matching funds, she lost no time.

"We need some good, versatile programs and residencies priced at $3,000.00."

And, of course, when they introduced one for $500.00, super easy to apply for, we offered programs for $1000.00. Why hadn't I thought of that?

So many things I've learned from the people that have appeared in my life. I've been lucky in love, friendship and work. What else is there?

18. Gone, But Not Forgotten

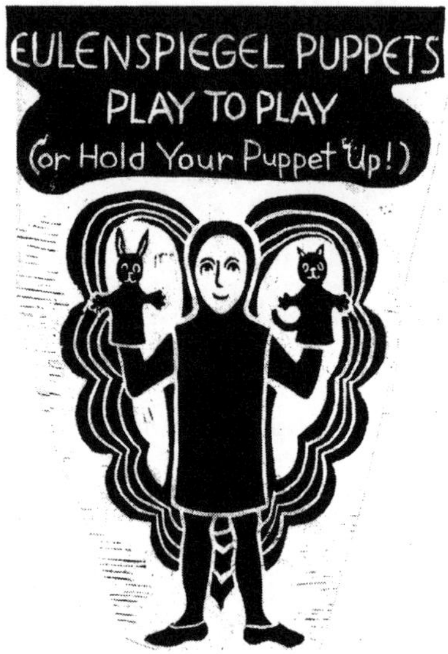

It was January 2006. The Christmas tree was still up, candles burned down. The puppets were still on their holiday break. Teri Jean walked in the front door, headed for the stove, and poured herself a cup of coffee. She sat down at the round table.

"Monica," she said. "We have to talk."

"Oh?" I poured a cup and sat down with her.

"I don't know how to tell you this, but I have to quit the puppet troupe."

"You WHAT?!"

"I need better health insurance. Mickey's operation cost us $30,000.00. Who knows if his back will hold up. You know back surgery doesn't have a great prognosis. We can't afford for that to happen again."

"Isn't there another way?" I asked.

"Mickey likes working for himself. He says he won't work for anyone else, especially not a corporation. That means I have to get a job with health insurance. And I suppose that means I better go back to school and finish my degree."

I met Teri Jean just after she dropped out of college. She'd been in a pre-med program and had gotten a job in the hospital. Working there had convinced her she didn't want to be a doctor.

"I love the puppet troupe," she said, "and I want to keep being involved in some way. But if you don't want to do this alone, I understand. I don't expect you to keep it going for me."

"I don't know what else I'd do, Teri Jean. Or—more to the point—what else I want to do. I'll just have to figure this out."

After Teri Jean left, I found John in his workshop and broke down in sobs.

"Why can't that deadbeat get a job?" he fumed.

"It's not up to us, John. It's Teri Jean's decision."

John was not mollified.

"Look, John. Teri Jean feels bad enough. Making her feel worse is not going to help."

Teri Jean had thought about moving on before. Every few years she'd worry about money and stress about the fact that she hadn't finished her BA. If the puppet troupe failed, I could get a teaching job; if work slowed down, I could substitute teach. She worried about having no concrete options. In the past I'd been able to calm her fears by getting on the phone, lining up some more jobs, and increasing our income.

This was different. I could tell that no amount of cold calling, lining up residencies, or making puppets to sell, would calm her fears. We spent the rest of the semester—we still had bookings and residencies to complete—speculating about different paths she could take to reach her goal of a well-paid job with—yes!—health insurance!

Teri Jean was gifted in languages. She could learn and pronounce new tongues with remarkable ease. She thought she'd study Spanish. Surely with all of the new immigrants from Latin America, she'd find a good job.

One evening, as we spread out on our separate beds in a small mom-and-pop motel googling local restaurants on my laptop—I was looking for a good fresh salad bar as usual—an email came in from our musician friend, Ron. He knew about TJ's plans.

"Tell Teri Jean that the profession with the most job openings, now and projected, is nursing," I read aloud.

"Well, God knows it would be familiar," she said. Her late mother had been a nurse. Her sister was a nurse. Her brother was a paramedic.

"It's kind of the family profession, I guess. Mom was disappointed when I dropped out of pre-med," she remembered.

She decided to forego the BA and get a nursing degree instead. She would start her studies in the summer and finish three years later. We hadn't booked anything much past June and she figured she could do a show now and then. She got a job working overnight weekend shifts in the hospital to provide the health insurance she needed.

I have always been a one-foot-in-front-of-the-other-keep-going person, but this knocked me in the gut! What now? I had workshops I could do and a nice solo show—the *Little Red Riding Hood* I'd worked on while Mutti was in hospice care—but there was a basement full of two-person shows that had suddenly become obsolete. I taught one of them—a fun demonstration show we called *Puppet Potpourri*—to our intern, Lauren Haldeman, hoping to keep touring commitments and nurture a young puppeteer, but before long she discovered she hated being on the road. Besides, she was a talented poet and needed to pursue that path.

Every day when I walked into the puppetry center, I felt like I was entering a black hole that sucked me in. There was so much to do, so much to consider. The bills—the phone calls—the emails—the events—

the workshops—the guest puppeteers—the messy basement—just kept piling up!

We'd scheduled a residency—doing *Immigrant Stew at the Chat 'n' Chew* with a group—for July, and Teri Jean had thought she could get away for three days. In late June she called.

"Monica, I'm sorry, but if I cut class for three days, I'll be way too far behind. This class is hard, and I'm rusty!"

I called Peggy. She was busy. I called Lauren. Ditto. I didn't think I could do it alone. Despair was setting in.

You were in a tizzy, Monica! I was worried sick about you, and I wasn't the only one! You weren't doing anything fun. You weren't even playing with me! You walked in the door with blinders on and went straight to your desk. Then you'd sit there with your head in your hands. I kept trying to get your attention. You did perk up a little after you talked to Pam.

Schulz is right! I remembered Pam Corcoran and Puppetfest Midwest, a weeklong workshop-intensive festival in Missouri. Pam was a puppeteer who taught there every summer. Puppetfest Midwest was the week before the Des Moines residency. My home in Iowa was halfway between Pam's Wisconsin home and Puppetfest Midwest. I called Pam and explained about the residency, about our community show concept, about *Immigrant Stew,* and about the timing. I asked if she'd like to come to Iowa after the festival and help me with the Des Moines residency.

Much to my relief, she agreed, and that was the beginning of a partnership that continues to this day. Pam and I have done countless community show residencies together. I do the narration; she's the "Queen of the Backstage," super-organized but adept at the forbearance it takes to let kids remember their own parts and only help when absolutely necessary. She works peripheral characters like the sassy squirrel.

In the fall, things began to feel a little more normal. I taught Lauren Teri Jean's part in *The Dragon's Three Golden Hairs.* Sound familiar? It was our reworking of our favorite, *The Devil's Three Golden Hairs*. After the late 1980s Satanist scares—totally fabricated but pervasive—it became impossible to book a show with a devil character. We put it away for ten years. Then I came upon a Russian tale, similar except with a dragon, and we got it back out and made a spectacular dragon body puppet (non-puppeteers might call it a costume and mask).

Lauren toured it with me for a few months. She did a great job, but it was clear she didn't like traveling. Then we got a request to bring the show to Birmingham, Alabama for a week. Lauren chewed her knuckles every time I mentioned Birmingham. I had to show mercy:

"Lauren, you don't have to do this," I said.

"Are you sure? "She heaved a sigh of relief.

Once again, I found myself calling Pam.

"Pam, would you be interested in learning a show and taking it to Birmingham, Alabama for a week?"

"Yes! That sounds like an adventure!"

"Do you mind leaving a day or two early and going to my niece Deborah's wedding in Tennessee? She's marrying into an Old Order Mennonite community."

It was an adventure! We arrived at Deborah's home in time for dinner the evening before the wedding. Deborah, the same niece who had clued us into what the girls in the youth shelter thought of *The Fisherman and His Wife*, the girl who helped at Mutti's deathbed, was marrying Abram, a member of an established Old Order family—no electricity, cars, telephone, computer, even radio. We sat on her porch after dinner, Deborah in her long skirt, apron, and head covering. Was this the same girl who had hitch-hiked around the country in her extra-short cutoffs and tank top? The girl who had talked me into getting my first email account? I wondered how much her intended knew about her past life.

The wedding involved a half-day church service followed by a delicious lunch of chicken salad—made for the crowd by the bride, who had also raised, butchered, plucked, and cleaned the chickens! Deborah always had been a practical girl who was ready for anything!

It boggled my mind to see "our girl"—John, Teri Jean, and I had always considered her one of us—in her long skirts, deferring to her husband-to-be. The can-do part of her new life fit right into my idea of her, but dressing modestly and especially deferring to men, was completely out of character. Her husband, who had been raised Old Order and had only finished fourth grade, seemed so naive compared to her. Could this go well?

Now—15 years later—Deborah is still married with four children. It's going well, I guess, but it's still a mystery to me.

After the wedding, we continued to Birmingham. We performed in two schools a day and were struck—horrified—by the discrepancies between the schools in the wealthy neighborhoods and the ones in the poor neighborhoods. The wealthy schools had everything you might want; the poor ones had clocks that didn't work, bare wires hanging from electrical outlets, no toilet paper. I asked one of the principals how this could be, and she told me the schools were financed not by state taxes, but by property taxes in their neighborhoods. All the way home we kept saying,

"Thank goodness for state funding for schools in the Upper Midwest!" Of course, there were discrepancies in our schools, too, but nothing like this.

Grateful for Pam, I was also grateful that Teri Jean remained engaged. In what little spare time she had, she helped me plan the future.

"Monica, why don't you reorganize some of our shows so you can do all of the puppets? You could ask Ron to add music, and that would make for a bigger show and better transitions."

We already knew that Ron was a gifted songwriter and instrumentalist. We already knew he could perform with puppets. He had been part of *Sal Fink, The Mississippi Screamer* a few years earlier. He wrote and performed evocative music for *Freedom Star: Gertie's Journey on the Underground Railroad,* which he, Teri Jean, and I had been performing for several years.

It was easy to reorganize *The Adventures of Great Rabbit,* a Native American tale we did as a shadow puppet show. It involved moving faster and placing puppets carefully on two small tables, so I could work one while picking the next one up.

Sal Fink—tall tales about the legendary daughter of the keelboat man, Mike Fink —presented more of a challenge. I decided to rewrite the script, remove a part I'd never liked, and add a tall tale or two. In the original version, Sal battled a bear and vanquished him by turning him inside out. It was a neat visual trick, but I felt sorry for the bear. Instead, I had her fight the bear, then tame him, teach him to dance, and take him home to do the housework. I found the precedent in stories about Sally Ann Thunder Ann Crocket, Davy's legendary wife. To distinguish it from the original, I renamed it *Sal Fink, Catfish Wrangler,* since Sal navigates the rivers riding on a giant catfish.

Teri Jean finished her studies in 2009 and got a job at University Hospital. We still talked almost every day.

"Hey, Monica, guess what! Today one of my patients asked where she knew me from. She recognized my voice from a puppet show."

That happened frequently and pleased her immensely. Her first year on the job she suggested I do a small production of *The Snow Queen*. We'd done that show years earlier but had never been satisfied with the script, especially the ending.

"I think you should try rewriting it. You're the one who loved that story!"

"Hmm. That's an idea."

"I think you should do it the way you do Little Red, with a pop-up book stage and little marionettes. People love Little Red! And I'll direct!"

As I rehearsed, Teri Jean watched from the audience view and told the puppets where and how to move, just as a director of human theater does.

I followed her advice—and her direction—and I've been doing that show ever since.

It was January 2011, five years after she decided to quit puppets and barely over a year since she got her nursing job. Her health insurance had kicked in with full coverage.

The phone rang at the puppetry center. A trembling voice answered my greeting.

"Monica, I have cancer. Stage three ovarian cancer. That's why I've been having those back aches."

She thought her back aches had been the result of helping lift a three-hundred-pound patient and that her abdominal pain was from something she'd eaten.

Shortly after, Teri Jean had surgery and started chemo. She was too sick to go back to work, but at least she had health insurance. Every day on the way home I stopped at her house. Every day I was on the road I called her. On days she felt well enough, she often came to the puppetry center to hang out and help. One day one of our recurring contact people called.

"Are you ever going to bring Gertie back? It's such a good show, and I'd love to present it here again."

I explained that *Freedom Star: Gertie's Journey on the Underground Railroad* used Teri Jean in addition to Ron and me, and that she had quit the puppet troupe. When I got off the phone, she had an idea.

"Listen, Monica, I bet we can reorganize that show so you and Ron can do it without me. I'll help you figure it out, and I'll direct the new version."

We hauled Gertie and the other puppets, sets, and props out of the basement and set everything up.

"Let's see," said Teri Jean. We can keep the script, music, and scenes, but we have to reorganize them so you can do them without me. Ideas?"

"I could build new puppets to replace the hand-and-rod puppets. If I make tabletop rod puppets, with only a rod out of the back of the head and no arm rods, I can work two at the same time. That way we can keep the scene with Gertie and Samuel, when he tells her the way through the woods and they sing *Freedom Shoes.* I sure hate to sacrifice the harmony singing you and I used to do."

"Ron's just going to have to step up and sing! I'll tell him that."

"I guess we can also keep the scene in Springdale with Gertie and Mrs. Haverkorn. But how can I put Gertie's new shoes and cape on and work Mrs. Haverkorn and Gertie at the same time? Hmm."

"That just might have to happen offstage. Gertie can come back on with her new things," said Teri Jean.

"Naa, there's gotta be a way for the audience to see her getting her shoes and cape… Wait! Remember that show we saw where the puppeteer held a puppet between her teeth? I could hold Mrs. Haverkorn's head rod in my teeth and have both hands free for the cape. And…if I weight Gertie's butt, she can sit by herself. And we could use the tree stump instead of a table for her to sit on! After all, the scene is in the woods."

It's beginning to come into focus," said Teri Jean. "I think we can do this!"

She was right. With Teri Jean's input and directing, the new version was as satisfying as the old. We still perform it today. Every time I work Gertie, I feel like I'm channeling Teri Jean, who performed that character with such empathy.

As we began to face a future without her, we talked about a puppet show inspired by our work together, and I wrote *Play to Play (Or Hold Your Puppet Up!)* It was fun to relive our old adventures together as I decided what to put in the show. Teri Jean remembered things I'd forgotten and vice versa.

We decided the stage should be a pop-up book and all of the characters should be paper puppets.

Wait a minute! There's one 3D puppet in that show—ME! I've even got my own director's chair!

Schulz is right. The play is written as a dialogue between him and me, with comments directed at Teri Jean. Schulz sits on the tabletop stage, next to the pop-up book, in his director's chair. I asked Michael, who had directed so many shows, for suggestions. He looked at the script and solved my main problem, how to integrate the comments to Teri Jean.

"Place an imaginary Teri Jean in the back of the audience, greet her early on, and talk to her throughout." he suggested. It works brilliantly. We rehearsed in my workshop. TJ—already weak—reclined in my soft chair, one that folds down into a bed. I talked to a real Teri Jean and an imaginary one simultaneously, both of us aware that the real one would soon be gone.

She directed all but the last scene. By that time, she was already under hospice care and too sick to participate. She asked our friend Susie Gilbert to finish the job, and she asked me to make a puppet of her as an angel. I agreed. It was painful but immensely touching, for me and the audience.

It was clear to all of us that the end was drawing near. Teri Jean's 58th birthday, July 7, 2012, was days away. I was due in Tennessee to teach at a weeklong workshop at the Tennessee Arts Academy. I stopped at Teri Jean's house before leaving.

"I can cancel," I said. "I can find someone to take my place. Do you want me to stay here?"

"No," she said. "This is my puppet troupe, too. Go to Tennessee and make us look good."

Halfway through the week in Tennessee, I got the message: Teri Jean had passed to the other side. Present or not, she will always be part of Eulenspiegel. On our website, in the "About Us" section, she's listed as our Guardian Angel. Our artistic visions were so intertwined that I don't know what mine would have been without her. Every time we work on a new show, I still hear her voice:

"Remember! A surprise in every scene!"

19. Mexico in Iowa

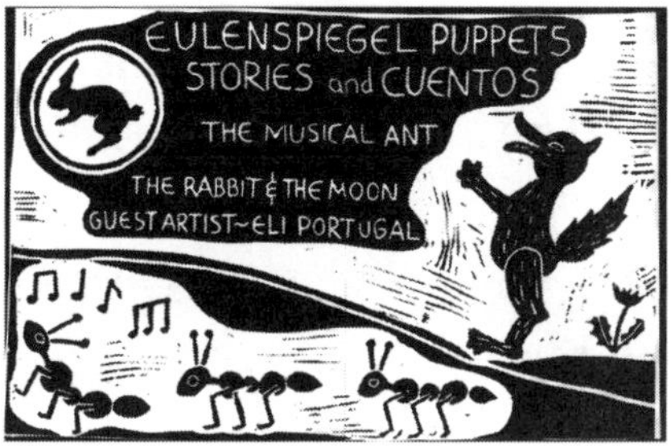

August 1994. I could hardly wait to get home from Japan and tell Teri Jean and John about my big surprise, my new friends from Mexico! John had a long-standing love affair with Mexico. Teri Jean would be excited about my plan to bring Eli and Camilo to Iowa. Scores of Mexicans and Central Americans were resettling in the state, and little towns—rife with residents of German, Scandinavian, and Irish heritage—grappled for the first time with the reality of diversity. Eli and Camilo, with their gorgeous, evocative shows reflecting Mexican culture and their warm personalities, were the perfect ambassadors. We decided to tour them around Iowa in October of 1995.

Camilo assured me that he could get grants to cover their travel from Mexico and their performing fees. That meant I only had to raise enough money to take care of their US travel and lodging. Easy-peasy! I called some schools and libraries in targeted towns and lined up enough shows to cover expenses.

RRRRRR. Fax rolled out of the machine on my desk in late July 1995: "Monica, I am afraid the grants have fallen through. Camilo."

Now what? Not only was I looking forward to their visit, I had promised their show to a dozen communities all over the state. I made a block-printed poster and produced a brochure. Their show, *Big Ol' Wagon (El Carreton)* was scheduled to open our performing season. I was not ready to give up. It was time to make more phone calls.

You were nailed to that desk and glued to that phone! You barely moved for the whole month of August. John and Teri Jean and I had to fend for ourselves! Now and then I'd hear a curse—or a cheer—and I'd know something was happening. Finally! "Schulz, I've booked 31 shows for them! That should do it!" you announced. Whew! We could get back to normal.

Camilo sent me a list of sound equipment they needed and measurements of their puppet cases. It was more equipment than we owned and more cases than we could fit into our Suburban. Our friend Jean stepped up and offered us the use of her pick-up truck—with a topper—and her services as a driver for the month. We checked into equipment rental prices and discovered we could save money by buying the equipment. The anticipated fees from the 31 shows I had booked made all of the numbers add up.

The only thing left was housing. Without the expected grants, we couldn't afford motels for the days we were within commuting distance from home. We needed to find a Spanish-speaking home to welcome them; struggling with language in their time off seemed too cumbersome. One morning in September, Teri Jean was shopping at The World Marketplace in Iowa City, one of our favorite places to look for third-world rhythm instruments. The phone rang and was answered by the manager, a young woman with light brown hair, blue eyes, and an open face. After an initial exchange, she gave a lengthy answer in fluent Spanish before hanging up.

"Excuse me," said Teri Jean. "I don't usually eavesdrop on other people's phone calls, but I couldn't help hearing you speak Spanish." She went on to explain our situation.

"I live in West Liberty. We have lots of Spanish-speaking families. I'm sure I can find a place. By the way, my name's Mallory Smith. My husband's name is José. He's Mexican."

"Really! We just bought a building in West Liberty. We're going to open a Puppetry Center!"

Mallory called back a few days later and invited Eli, Camilo, and their young co-puppeteer, Marcos to stay with them for the month. We were ready!

Mojiganga Arté Escenico—their troupe—arrived in Minneapolis on October 3 and performed *Big Ol' Wagon* at *In The Heart of the Beast Puppet and Mask Theater* before we drove up in both vehicles to pick them up.

For the next month, we operated like a well-oiled machine. Four of us—Teri Jean, Jean, our intern Macy, and I—took turns: two drivers/roadies for each job. The other two stayed home and took care of business. Halfway through the month, my niece Anna arrived from Berlin to study music at the University of Iowa. She bonded with Marcos and took her turn helping.

Camilo was tall with an aquiline nose, light skin, and high cheekbones. He'd lived in Mexico for decades, but he'd been born and raised in Brazil. He showed his Portuguese roots in his features and body type. Eli's short, curvy body, round face, caramel-colored skin, and fleshy nose pointed to indigenous heritage. Marcos was young—almost puppyish—and textbook Mexican in his appearance, a perfect blend of Spanish height and indigenous features. Camilo was clearly in charge and not entirely happy when he realized that all of his roadies were female.

"Marcos! Don't let Monica carry that speaker; you take it," he yelled the first time he spotted me lifting the sound equipment

Eventually, he realized that our tight schedule necessitated everyone pitching in, and he made peace with women carrying the heavy sound equipment.

The show was vibrant, colorful, active, and fun! It resonated Mexican culture and folk art. At one point in the show, Camilo liked to invite some audience members to join the troupe onstage and dance.

In West Liberty, we took the show to the Middle School, with 300-plus 6th through 8th graders in the school gym. Camilo—overcome with enthusiasm—invited the entire audience onstage to dance. Teri Jean rushed to clutch one of the speaker stands and Macy wrapped her body around the other one. The rafters rang! The floor shook! The speakers shivered precariously. Teri Jean and Macy held on as best they could, but storm clouds gathered on TJ's face as she glared at Camilo. After the show she confronted him.

"Don't you ever do that to me again!" she roared.

Camilo wasn't sure what he'd done to upset her. For him, it had all been good fun. I began to understand the sources of friction between restrained Euro-Americans and happy-go-lucky Mexican Americans.

Another source of potential friction revolved around time. Camilo had a hard time understanding why things had to happen on such a tight schedule. Quite a few of our days had us in one school in the morning and a different school in the afternoon. With set-up and strike in both locations, it made for a short lunch break. Our Mexican friends loved restaurants with salad bars and buffets, but there was never quite enough time to sample the creamy cole slaw, jello and pasta salads, pickled herring, pea salad with chunks of Velveeta cheese, and savory deviled eggs.

"Time to get going," I said, consulting my watch.

"Already?" complained Camilo.

"Yes. The next show starts at 2:00, and we still have to set up."

"Does it have to start at 2:00? All I want is a little cup of coffee and a little piece of cake," he moaned.

"We'll get one after school."

Camilo held up his left arm and looked at his wrist. "I will remember you like this, Monica."

On the whole, Camilo was happy with the tour I'd scheduled. He had no idea how tedious my August had been and how liberally I had complained to John and Teri Jean!

"Monica, would you like to be our agent in the United States?" he asked me one day.

"NO!!"

Camilo was taken aback by my vehemence.

It was another beautiful fall. Our Mexican friends reveled in the panorama of autumn leaves and their crunch as we walked through the playgrounds. At the end of October, we had our first transient snowfall. Marcos skipped down the street and whooped. He opened his mouth and caught snowflakes on his tongue. He had never seen snow.

After thirty days and thirty-one shows, it was time to say goodbye. We were sad to see them leave, but we knew we would see them again.

And we did, five years later when they came back with the show I'd seen them do in Japan, *The Moon and the Dragon*. This time they brought their teenage daughter, Maira, to be the third puppeteer. Maira had her father's nose and cheekbones and her mother's skin color, humor, and sweet disposition. This show was smaller, so we only needed one vehicle.

Something else had changed. Eli was beginning to feel her power. She didn't always defer to Camilo as she had in the past. She watched me perform my solo show, *Little Red Riding Hood*, and she was entranced.

"I would like to do a little solo show like that!" she enthused.

"You could never do that, Eli," said Camilo, dismissively.

Teri Jean and I exchanged glances. This did not bode well! Camilo's attitude towards us had changed, too. Pleasing us was no longer one of his priorities. He thought nothing of canceling a show because he was coming down with a cold. A show that 200 local school kids in our school's brand-new dual language program planned to attend. As the visit progressed, we felt closer and closer to Eli and Maira as we distanced from Camilo.

It was no surprise, a few years later, to learn that they had divorced, and Eli had moved from Mexico City back to her hometown of Xalapa, Veracruz, taking Maira with her. She was pursuing a degree in music and psychology and learning about flower essence therapy, an alternative way of harmonizing the imbalances between mind, body, and spirit, and achieving mental health. Camilo had gotten custody of the puppets and the shows, but Eli had Maira and her independence.

One day in early 2007, when I was beginning to get used to performing without Teri Jean, she stopped over and settled down at the round table.

"Monica, I have an idea."

"Oh?"

"Why don't you get in touch with Eli and see if she wants to do a bilingual show with you?"

"That's an interesting idea," I responded.

"Maybe you could work on two shows, a solo show for each of you, and do them together. Then Eli could take her show home and you could keep yours."

I liked the idea and contacted Eli immediately. It came at the perfect time for her. She had finished her studies and was practicing as a therapist, but she missed puppetry. Since she was in practice for herself, she could determine her own schedule.

We began to plan. We each chose a Mexican folktale, wrote a script, each in our own language, and thought about ways the show could be staged. We made sketches which we scanned and emailed to each other. We thought about ways we could combine our staging ideas and use the same staging for both shows.

In late July 2007, Eli traveled to Iowa. We knew we had one month to create our combined show, which we called *Stories and Cuentos* (Stories and Stories). We figured out how to perform them together for the time being and separately in the future. Mallory, who had hosted Eli and her troupe for a month in 1995, had become our "booking angel," arranging all of our touring shows. She was straightforward and no-nonsense, with a good head for business. She was a creative thinker who made unexpected connections, bringing us work we never would have found on our own.

She arranged for us to premiere the show at the Tumbleweed Festival in Garden City, Kansas, the last weekend in August, then on to Salina, Kansas for shows in six schools.

Eli once again stayed with Mallory and José. I picked her up every morning, and we spent the day in my workshop tucked into the woods, windows on all four sides looking out into a leafy paradise. We created puppets, props, and scenery, each of us doing the things she did best. I sculpted the heads and made patterns for the stuffed fabric bodies while Eli painted faces and props. After everything was built, we moved to the puppetry center and spent the remaining days rehearsing.

We set up two simple backdrops that doubled as puppet stages, with a playboard topping each at a little less than six feet, tall enough to hide us when we stood behind but short enough that Eli—much shorter than me—could easily reach it. In front, we put a four-foot table. Some parts of both stories played out on the table; the rest over the top of the playboard. On one side we put a stand holding the keyboard Eli played in *The Musical Ant.* A soft-sculpted tree stump covering an upside-down bucket completed the scene. I sat on the stump and played percussion instruments as Eli played the jarana—an indigenous stringed instrument about the size of a ukulele—during *The Rabbit and the Moon.*

Rehearsing with Eli was an undiluted pleasure. She stayed calm and cheerful even as we fought our way through the early stages. When we finally worked our way through without having to stop, we traded high-fives.

"Good work, comadre! We're a team!" she enthused.

By August 25, we were ready to go. Juan Conejo, the rabbit hero of Eli's story, and Hormiguita, the ant hero of my story, eagerly awaited the first performance. We set up on the grass in front of the elevated children's stage so kids could sit close. Hormiguita made his entrance, schlepping the piano he found home to his queen. Irate, she kicked him out.

"We can't eat that!" she screeched.

"Hmmm. What's it good for if you can't eat it?" he mused.

He played around with it till he figured out how to play melodies, and the story took off. The kids hung on every word and melody.

When Hormiguita finished, Eli strolled onto stage in a long hand-woven skirt and ruffled white blouse, playing the jarana. She sang the introduction to the next story, *The Rabbit in the Moon.* Kids watched expectantly as Rabbit and Coyote engaged in a battle of wits. At the end, the moon, singing a hauntingly beautiful song, cradled Rabbit and carried him into the sky with her.

The show was a triumph! Best of all, when we performed in the Salina schools, we reached Latino kids who needed validation. One of the Salina teachers sent us a note:

"The show was great! Thanks so much for giving the kids a chance to see it. Our Hispanic kids really got a kick out of it. We have one little boy that started the year speaking no English. He had a big smile on his face the whole time."

This was exactly what we had hoped. Any thought of dividing our shows flew out of the window, and instead, we talked to Mallory about booking our joint appearances only in the spring or fall so we had plenty of work in a specified time. We developed a winning strategy that worked for audiences and made sense to us. My puppets spoke English and Eli's spoke Spanish. Everyone understood the stories.

Our models were shows I had seen by Magical Moonshine Theater, Michael and Valerie Nelson. I met them when Michael and I were on the Board of UNIMA-USA together, and I loved their shows when I saw them at festivals. When our West Liberty schools added a dual language program, we started inviting them to bring their bilingual shows to our town. I admired the way they included both languages without becoming hopelessly redundant. Eli and I could do that, too!

Eli began coming to Iowa twice a year—May/June and September/October. We developed bilingual workshops and a bilingual community show, *Five Suns of the Aztecs.* Children all over Iowa and Kansas learned and performed the Aztec creation myths featuring the battles between the gods Quetzalcoatl and Tezcatlipoca. They whipped silk fires around and covered the puppet stage with silk floods. They donned cardboard giants and stomped around, shaking the imaginary earth. Latino kids connected with their heritage and Anglo kids learned to appreciate their darker-skinned peers in new ways
.

In 2017 we decided we needed another show. We created *Uncle Rabbit's Adventures (Las Aventuras de Tio Conejo)*, a story about a rabbit and his greedy landlord, a goat. We combined two stories in creating our script. *The Goat in the Garden* is a Puerto Rican tale and *Tops and Bottoms* is a world tale—one that can be found in many different countries and cultures. We gave ourselves a challenge: use every cute little prop that we had collected over the years. We used the watering can, the tiny clothespins, the picket fence, and even the Barbie grill, but there was still a little mailbox.

"That mailbox is so cute. Can't we use it? We could put it in front of Tio Conejo's house." urged Eli.

"Only if Tio Conejo gets a letter. Props aren't just for show. They have to be used." I insisted.

Then it dawned on us! Tio Conejo could get a "cease and desist" letter from the lawyer—abogado—of his landlord, Señor Cabra (Mr. Goat). That turned out to be the favorite scene for any adult in our audience!

Eli and I both loved traveling, especially finding oddities in unexpected places. I knew she would love Lucas, Kansas, with the Garden of Eden that had astonished Teri Jean and me a dozen years earlier. It was located sixty miles from Salina.

"Eli, if we hurry, we can get to Lucas before the museum closes. You have to see this place!" I said one day after shows in two Salina schools.

"Let's go, comadre!" Eli was always ready to go!

On the way to Lucas, we drove past several farms with large sculptures made of discarded farm implement parts.

"Look at that, comadre!" Eli shouted.

"Get ready for more!"

We got to the Grassroots Art Museum just before it closed, and after our tour, the director steered us to the new public toilet downtown.

"Thanks," I said." I don't have to go right now."

"Go anyway. We got a grant to build it. We needed a restroom for the tourists, and we discovered that you can't get money for restrooms but you can get grants for public art."

That sounded intriguing, so we walked down the street. We saw what looked like a giant concrete toilet paper roll unspooling to form a sidewalk. The restroom building was shaped like a toilet tank. In front was a gargantuan concrete toilet bowl full of porcelain water speckled with objects, the kinds of things that might get flushed: toy cars, dolls, bottles, goldfish, and more. The "bowl' was encircled by benches representing the toilet seat. The inside restroom walls were mosaics incorporating pop-culture symbols of each gender: Barbie dolls, lipsticks, doll furniture on the women's side; cap guns, and toy trucks on the men's side.

We toured the Garden of Eden and walked the streets, spotting curiosities in people's yards, before getting supper at the café.

"This place is lucas!" said Eli.

"That's right," I said. "Lucas, Kansas."

"No," said Eli. "In Mexico, we say 'lucas' for crazy. This place is lucas!"

In August 2018, Eli and I were scheduled to bring Uncle Rabbit to the

Tumbleweed Festival, where we had premiered our first show together. In early August, I got a video call on Facebook.

"Comadre, I can't come. I have cancer."

"What?! Oh, no!"

"I'm afraid so. I plan to beat this, but I have to stay here for the treatments."

I couldn't believe this was happening again! I tried to be optimistic, and I was, in our weekly video calls, but I kept having flashbacks to Teri Jean's final months. As time passed, I became more hopeful as her treatments began to bring results. Her doctor gave her a good prognosis, and I booked shows for May and June of 2020. And then, on January 13, 2020, I got a call from Maira.

"My Mami has died." I couldn't believe my ears. John had died the previous April, and now Eli was gone, too!

"But she was getting better," I cried!

"Monica, please. Mami told me she wants you to remember her with joy, not with sadness."

"I will always remember her with joy, Maira!"

I do remember her with joy, but also with sadness, when I think of all the stories we'll never tell, the trips we won't take, the lost exploits. Eli was my only friend and collaborator with a sense of adventure that matched mine.

I sometimes imagine John, Teri Jean, and Eli hanging out together on the other side. I try to honor Eli's wishes by remembering all of them with joy. I still feel their presences in the blue building in West Liberty that loomed so large in all of their lives.

20. John

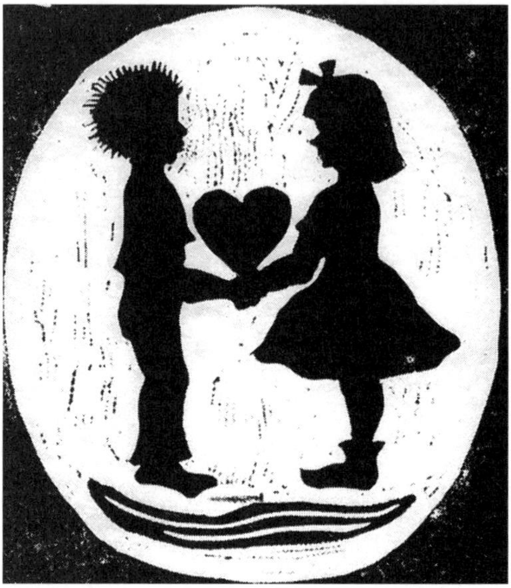

I met John in the summer of 1968. My childhood friend and roommate, Susan, and I had just graduated from college and had both decided to stay in Iowa City for the summer. I was taking a drawing class.

"Come on, Monica," said Susan, rattling her car keys. If you want to find this guy's house, let's get going!"

We drove north out of Iowa City towards North Liberty, passing through Iowa's summer quilt, alternating fields of corn, beans, alfalfa, and milo, dotted with free-range pigs. Monoculture and animal confinements were still in the future.

"This guy" was John. I had met him the day before when I stopped at my favorite watering hole for a Seven Up. He and a friend were in an adjoining booth, and I eavesdropped on their conversation which centered around the little boy he had custody of. That was unheard of in 1968, and I was intrigued. When they asked me to join them, I did, and spent the evening talking, riding around in his pick-up truck, and briefly stopping at his house, a one-room schoolhouse he had renovated. It had a large, high-ceilinged central room with stairs to a two-bedroom loft. Much to my liking, he had been generous with colors, no beiges or grays in sight.

When he dropped me off at home, I left my drawing portfolio behind the seat of his pick-up truck. I needed that portfolio for my drawing class, but I also kind of wanted to see the guy again. He'd been so quirky—full of puns and silly jokes and verbal gymnastics—not at all like the stuffed shirts I usually attracted and politely ignored. I hoped I'd recognize his house.

"Stop! That's it!"

I hopped out and knocked on the door. I didn't recognize the fellow who answered.

"Does John live here? My name's Monica, and I left something in his truck." He broke into a grin.

"Yep! And he's going through the phone book right now, looking for people named Monica. He's up to the 'c's.' You might say he'd like to see you again. JOHN! JOHN JENKS!"

That was the beginning. I got my portfolio back, and John and I started seeing each other. He was a carpenter and a dad with sole custody of his barely three year old son, Little John. His face was dominated by a sizable Roman nose and a bushy, reddish full beard. His smile was in his twinkly hazel eyes, not in his mouth. He had a broad, muscular back and shoulders and skinny bowed legs. In spite of a slight hitch in his walk, he was nimble as a mountain goat. He leaped around on roofs—scaring the living daylights out of me—when roofing was part of his job. He'd lost the middle finger of his right hand when he was still a teenager. A construction accident had caused an infection that ended up costing him the digit. He used it as a launching pad for jokes, telling kids a vicious mouse had bitten it off and giving adult friends "the finger" with his stump. He further delighted kids by offering to let them help themselves to the contents of his "booger jar," which he claimed to have in his workshop.

He'd had a pretty miserable home life as a child. His parents fought constantly. He was the oldest child, drawn into the middle and expected to choose sides. He felt responsible for conflicts out of his control. At age 16, he left home and moved in with a farm family as an after-school hired hand. On our first "date", we visited the farm and cleaned out the hog pen, shoveling piles of poop into the compost heap. He was never boring!

That first date set the tone for the next fifty years. We never felt obligated to do things the way other people did. We sang our own tunes, sometimes together and sometimes separately. I came from artists and intellectuals; he came from farmers and carpenters. We came together through non-conformity and whimsy.

I was immediately drawn not just to John but also to his darling little boy, Little John, who was just past his third birthday. Little John was drawn to me, too, which gave me a heavy sense of responsibility.

"I can't mess around," I said to Susan. "I can't take the chance of breaking this little boy's heart."

I decided to continue with a plan I'd made before I met John. I would move to Milwaukee, where a college friend lived with her family, get a job, save the money to start the toy-making business I had in mind, and think things over. I was hired as a girls' supervisor at the Milwaukee County Detention Home and found myself working with troubled teens, girls 11-15 who'd gotten into some kind of difficulty, including many who were "runaway and uncontrollable." I loved the job! I worked the 3:00 to 11:00 shift, so school was over for the day when I arrived. One of the other supervisors, a kind-hearted middle-aged woman, had taught the girls how to knit. They taught me. We knitted, played board games, went to the gym, and talked about our lives, theirs and mine.

One day, arriving at work after a two-day break, I read the logs from the previous two days—when my unit had been in the hands of a young colleague—and noticed we had a new girl who had been locked into her room since she arrived. I knocked on her door, unlocked it, and let myself in. A tall, skinny, African American girl—12 or 13 years old—huddled on her bed.

"Gwen, I'm Miss Leo, your supervisor. Can you tell me why you're in your room?"

"Miss, I didn't do what they say," she sobbed.

"Can you tell me what they said?"

"Oh, Miss, I didn't do nuthin' with no boys! I'm a good girl!"

"Is that what they said?" Her sobs grew louder.

"Miss, they said I had to take a test…down there," she said, pointing to her vagina.

I realized she was talking about the pap smear routinely administered to every girl on intake. No one had bothered to find out why she refused. I sat down on the bed with her and put my arm around her.

"Gwen, that doesn't mean they thought you're a bad girl. It's called a pap smear, and every girl has to have one when she comes in. Some girls have infections, and they have to find that out so they can give them medicine. I get one of those when I go to the doctor."

"You're not funnin' me, are you, Miss?"

"I'm telling you the truth, Gwen. Can I take you to the nurse's office to get a pap smear?" Her sobs calmed.

"OK, Miss."

After that, Gwen was my best pal, waiting for me every day.

I had been hired as a temporary civil servant. After eight months the other two young women who'd been hired along with me—one of them the woman who'd locked Gwen into her room— got their permanent status, and I didn't. I wasn't planning on staying much longer, so I didn't really care, but I was insulted all the same. I went to the boss's office.

"Why didn't I get my permanent status? Ms. Kennedy and Ms. Nelson did."

"Well, we don't think you're tough enough to lock a girl in her room against her will, and they are."

"Hmm. Can you check my records and tell me how often I've had to do that?"

He looked at my records. "Never. That's my point. Both of them have."

"Excuse me, Sir, but has it occurred to you that I'm able to manage them without using force, and that that's good?" He didn't agree.

That was all I needed. It was time to move back to Iowa City and commit to my Johns.

For a few years, we lived in an attic apartment in Iowa City with slanted ceilings over a large living/dining area—a tiny kitchen tucked into the corner. It had one bedroom and a huge closet. I painted jungle scenes on the walls and converted it to a bedroom for Little John. The living room walls alternated white and royal blue. Windows gave a view to all four sides of the house. I loved this place; it felt like me. We ate in the living room since the round table was always covered with puppet heads, fabric, paint, and a sewing machine—my workstation as I made puppets and dolls to sell. I sold at art fairs most weekends in November and December—and in the summer—and made puppets in between.

Mutti had come to visit for the weekend. She loved going to art fairs with me. We left the apartment with a floor knee-deep in fabric scraps. We gathered the finished puppets and took off to set up my display. That evening—our dinner plates balanced on our laps—Mutti looked at John.

"How can you stand this mess?"

"What mess?" asked normally tidy John.

"This mess!" She gestured to the table and scrap-covered floor.

"I don't see a mess. I see money." That sealed John into Mutti's heart forever.

His standard remark on weekends with lousy sales—even if we really needed the money: "Some people have no taste!"

We started selling puppets at the Chicago Renaissance Faire—King Richard's Faire—in 1972. It was brand new and such an adventure—for everyone, including the promoters. It was in session for six weekends, mid-June through late July. I made an eight-foot square mock medieval tent out of awning remnants. We dug a fire pit, added a cooking grate, and slept in the tent. We drove up every weekend and furiously made puppets the week between. During fair hours, we hammered sharpened dowel rods into the surrounding ground and used them as puppet stands.

Renaissance Faires cropped up all over the country as the last gasp of hippy culture. Craftspeople paid a rental fee for their booth space and attendees paid admission. Everyone—exhibitors and spectators—dressed in costume to add to the fantasy. Roving performers—jugglers, musicians, rat catchers, town criers—staged impromptu shows, and food booths sold goodies that were exotic for the era—falafel, roast turkey legs, mead. Most of the booths were built to resemble fairy tale images: Tudor style cottages, Hobbit huts, witches' shacks. Our tent fit right in. The fairs stimulated mainstream imaginations and soon they were swamped with admission-paying fantasy lovers.

By the third or fourth year, the promoters realized they had a cash cow. They decreed that everyone had to have a booth made out of wood or stone. With our foundations on their land, we would be dependent on them. We would have to give in to any demands they made to save our investments. A dilemma. I wanted to keep selling at the fair, but I didn't want to relinquish my power or build a structure on a piece of land 300 miles from home.

"John, can you think of any kind of building made of wood or stone that would be portable?"

Our friend Larry, who was staying with us between apartments, weighed in:

"How about a gypsy wagon?"

We all loved the idea and got to work. John found an old-fashioned farm wagon—wood with large metal-clad wheels—to serve as the base. The wooden spokes were covered with tar which had protected them from rot. Teri Jean and I scraped the tar off and painted the wheels and the wagon bed. John used his carpentry skills to make a round top, front, and back. I sewed a canvas cover. My friend Judy—who carpooled to the fair with us every weekend and specialized in fantasy art—painted a magnificent dragon on the back. John put a platform bed inside, where Teri Jean and I slept during the fair weekends. We set up the old tent, too, and turned it over to Little John and any friends he brought along.

The afternoon before opening day, John and Larry hauled the wagon to the fair on a trailer—following Teri Jean, Judy, assorted children, and me in our pick-up truck with the topper. I asked the promoter where our assigned spot was. He showed me to a corner about the size of a pocket handkerchief.

"We need a bigger space than this," I said.

"Where have you been? You should have been here building your booth. How much can you possibly build between now and tomorrow morning?" he replied angrily.

Just then John and Larry appeared in the old Ford truck pulling the trailer with the gypsy wagon. The promoter gasped.

"Wow! Who does that belong to?"

"Me!"

"Put it anywhere you want!"

For the next few years, John pulled the gypsy wagon 300 miles to the fair and—six weeks later—pulled it back. Little John changed his costume. Instead of dressing as a prince, he became a Romany boy in an embroidered velvet jacket. We still displayed the puppets on dowel rods, but the dolls got to sit on the steps of the gypsy wagon.

That's when you started making us big puppets! You needed extra large dowel rods for us! Of course, I was never for sale, but I remember you made Bartholomew to sell as a wizard. Someone almost bought him, too. It was someone you didn't like very well and you didn't want her to have

Bart. So…you gave him to Teri Jean. Pretty clever! You could honestly say he'd been spoken for. Good thing. Think of all the shows we wouldn't have had without Bart.

Our weekend routine began Friday evening. Just before 11:00PM, while we were finishing the last of the puppets, I looked at Teri Jean:

"Let's get over to the Dairy Queen before it closes!" We each gobbled the largest cone they sold and—sugared up—returned home to complete our work. With only five days between trips, we had to make use of every minute to rebuild our stock after our weekend sales.

At 3:00AM, we woke Little John and whatever friend was coming with us. They stumbled into the driveway, got into the back of the pick-up truck, stretched out on the mattress, and promptly went back to sleep. We filled the biggest travel cups we could find with coffee. We took off and drove fifty miles to Judy's house, where she joined us in the cab, and six-year-old David crept into the topper and fell asleep next to the other boys. At 6:00AM, we stopped at a café—always the same one—for breakfast. They had a source for tiny pullet eggs and gave you twice as many as you ordered. I felt so rich ordering two eggs, sunny side up, and getting a plate with four shiny yellow yolks staring up at me!

By 9:00AM, we reached the fair and busied ourselves setting up for the crowds who began arriving at 10:00. After the fair closed at 6:00PM, the real fun started. We built a fire, cooked dinner, sang songs, and wandered the grounds socializing with other exhibitors. We were young, and adrenaline carried us.

When I awoke the next morning, Little John sat by the fire he had started, toasting marshmallows for breakfast. I started the coffee percolator and—lured by the aroma—other exhibitors arrived, empty cups leading the way.

Sunday, as soon as the fair closed, we packed the pick-up truck and left for home. We always arrived at Spaghetti Basketti in Freeport, Illinois, just before they closed. I'm sure they dreaded our arrival. We got home in the wee hours, and spent Monday morning cleaning up. Then it was time to make puppets for the next weekend.

We moved out of our attic apartment into a house next door to John's Uncles, Dan and Paul. We added another Renaissance Faire to our summer schedule for a total of twelve weekends. I needed a better workspace than the round table.

Our house had an attached garage, used mostly for storage. We moved the tools into the basement and John insulated the walls, built rows of shelves and two workbenches. We bought a stove from Sears—brown and black enamel—that was designed to burn both wood and coal. We scoured the brushy hill behind our house—a hill that eventually became the site of a mini-mall—for dead wood to burn. Little John searched along the railroad track next door for chunks of coal that had dropped out of train cars, earning a few dollars for each box he filled.

I had my first warm, cozy workshop and we had a table for meals!

In the summer, we opened the garage door and welcomed the breeze. Of course, the flies felt welcome, too! Teri Jean, hands covered with sticky wood putty, eyed the flyswatter:

"The next time I take a break, three of you will die!" They weren't intimidated.

1978 was our last year. Little John—for the first time—had to be nagged to get into costume. We had shows and workshops that were ultimately more lucrative and just as much fun. It was time to switch gears and focus on shows and school residencies.

When John built our house in the country, workshops for each of us were part of the plan. He had found an old semi-trailer he could buy and turn into my space. He insulated it, put in lots of windows, counters, shelves, and a workbench, and installed a wood stove. He placed it steps from our front door and painted it bright red. It served me well for a dozen years before damp intruded and signs of mold appeared on the walls.

"I could tear the sheetrock out, clean everything, and put in new walls, or....we could use the money we inherited from Mutti to build you a new workshop. I think Mutti would like that."

"I think so, too," I said, remembering the wistful memories she had of the octagonal workshop she had left behind when she fled Germany.

John outdid himself. My workshop, 20' x 24', is lined with bright yellow metal cabinets he salvaged. We painted the walls yellow to match. Yellow seemed like an active color that would lift my spirits and encourage me to work. The trim, inside and out, is my favorite deep red. The building, nestled into the woods behind the house, sports gray siding. Windows on all four sides give a view of wildlife and trees. The roof hangs over the front to form a sort of porch, a place to gather my thoughts. Cast aluminum dragon lights shine into the woods. Every time I walk in the door, a feeling of calm energy engulfs me.

John's workshop was as individual to him as mine was to me. We had our love of color in common. The outside of his workshop stands as a reminder: color-blocked in yellow, red, blue, and green. The inside walls are still covered with Mexican religious art—and kitsch.

It all started in 1994 when we traveled to Mexico together for the first time. We drove through a tunnel, the only entrance to Real de Catórce, a small town John wanted to show me. We emerged from the tunnel to see a vendor by the road, selling statues of saints, religious candles, and lenticular prints—sometimes called flickers—that changed from The Last Supper to a portrait of Jesus when viewed from different angles. John was entranced and stuffed our van. Before we returned home, we'd added a hand carved and painted statue of Our Lady of Guadalupe and several ceramic saints.

Home again, John lined his workshop walls with glass-fronted display cases. He added to his collection every time he went to Mexico and—in between trips—with the help of Ebay. He drove to Missouri to pick up a Confessional he'd bought. He brought it home and installed his beer refrigerator in the Priest's seat.

"This is what happens to people who are raised without religion," I told him. It was hard to tell how much of his interest was genuine and how much was tongue-in-cheek, but his insistence on visiting the shrine to Our Lady of Guadalupe in Mexico City—a city he'd carefully avoided in the past—convinced me of his sincerity.

When he decided he'd had enough of building and renovating other people's houses and crawling around on roofs, his whimsy took over. He became a junker. Always interested in salvage, it became his full-time occupation. He collected discarded items, dismantled them, sold the metal for scrap, and kept oddments that he reassembled into funky outsider art: mobiles, wind chimes, birdhouses, even an angel that flew across his workshop on a pulley.

Our home is surrounded by birdhouses of all kinds, all repurposed and all occupied: a red teakettle, black and silver percolators, a few made out of multi-colored plexiglass. My favorite is one made out of a toilet plunger. John attached a motor that makes it go up and down—like a plumber's friend—when a switch is flipped. We've always been careful not to make it move in the summer, when it's occupied.

John almost never came to shows. It made him nervous to see me perform, just as it had always made me nervous to listen to Vati preach. I understood what was going on in his brain. What if people don't listen? What if kids start running around? What if some jerk says something mean? I'd have to knuckle them! John was protective—overly, sometimes—of the people he loved.

He may not have come to shows, but he made us anything we wanted. I learned not to tell him how I thought things should be made; he would think he had to follow my amateurish directions. Instead, I sketched my idea of the finished product, told him the size and how we planned to transport it. One time I did have a clever idea for a backdrop that was held up by the puppet trunks. John put it together for me:

"This works. I'm glad I thought of it!"

"You didn't think of it; I did!" I reminded him.

"Yeah, but it's the kind of thing I would have thought of, so it's the same thing as if I did," he said with a twinkle.

John's health began to fray in 2017, but I was not ready to see it. His taut, agile body had gradually changed. His back, shoulders, and arms were almost as strong as ever, but a broken foot, improperly set over twenty years before, came back to haunt him with a limp. His midsection had thickened, and his tripping walk had slowed to an amble.

A few times he briefly lost consciousness—twice while driving on mercifully deserted country roads—and was hospitalized. In absence of a coherent diagnosis, we blamed dehydration, and drinking more water did make a big difference—his balance improved, his hand tremor disappeared. His neurologist, stumped by not having a diagnosis, delayed his cataract surgery.

Then his foot began to hurt. It was winter and the skin on his heel was cracked, so we blamed our favorite villain:

"Winter wants to kill us!" John was fond of saying.

In December 2018 we decided to drive to Mexico and spend Christmas with Eli. She and John had hatched that plan in the spring, the last time she had been here. They were playing music together in his workshop—John on the accordion, Eli on the guitar—singing El Rey, his favorite macho-parody Mexican song. They were surrounded by John's obsession: his extensive collection of Mexican religious art. Eli looked at a Mexican Nativity and said,

"Why don't you and Monica come to Xalapa for Christmas?"

In the meantime, of course, Eli had had her cancer diagnosis, which made us even more anxious to go and give her our support.

We left on December 18. I got in the passenger seat.

"Why don't you drive?" said John. "I'm tired. And my vision isn't the greatest."

I ended up driving every mile—2000 each way. In the past, I had done much of the driving in the U.S. and John had taken over in Mexico. But this time John was simply too tired and too nervous about his eyesight.

As we drove, we reminisced about other trips, driving through villages we recognized and others that were new to us. We loved the same kinds of things: hamlets decorated with whitewashed rocks and tree trunks; roadside stands selling everything from honey to cords of garlic to stone sculptures; homes that doubled as restaurants, with tables in the living room and Mama stirring a pot of fragrant caldo de pollo—chicken stew—in the kitchen.

"The sunshine and warm weather will be good for you!" I was convinced his foot would improve in the summery weather.

We had a lovely time celebrating Christmas with Eli's family: her parents, siblings, and of course Maira, now a mother of two. We loved seeing the charming little home Eli had created for herself and Milo, her cat. She had bought a patch of land in a neighboring village and, with the help and labor of a local craftsman, constructed a bright, airy one-room house. Large windows and a balcony looked out on the wild surroundings. Scrambling down the hill behind the back door, Eli and I explored the lush vegetation—bushes, trees, blooming plants—that proliferated everywhere. John—not feeling well enough to join us—watched from above.

We wandered a Mexican market, John's favorite. We stayed in our favorite hotels on the way home and stopped to buy painted pottery, as we always did. But John's energy didn't improve. His foot hurt more, not less.

He saw a podiatrist who told him he had a clogged artery in his leg, preventing blood flow to his foot. After that it was all downhill. Botched artery clearing, insufficient follow-up from the doctor, premature discharge from the first hospital which led to six days in ICU in the second hospital, six additional days in the second hospital, then three weeks in rehab. By April 10, when he finally got home, he knew he was facing below-knee leg amputation. The long delay between the podiatrist's diagnosis and the clearing of the artery had killed his foot.

He loved being home. He putzed around in his workshop, sat in the sun, visited with friends. We didn't talk about the upcoming surgery. It was a given.

One day an old friend visited. They'd worked construction together for years. Both jokesters, they had developed an impromptu comedy routine that lifted the mood and lightened the hours at work.

"This coffee tastes like mud," he said as he entered John's workshop, coffee cup in hand.

"Of course. It was ground this morning!" John replied. "Ba-bum!"

They cycled through several more jokes and decided to go on a junk run. He couldn't have suggested anything that would have pleased John more. In his current condition, he was afraid to drive, and he missed his daily rounds, checking in on friends and collecting scrap. Who would have guessed that it would be his last adventure.

The next morning, April 17, 2019, he woke early coughing uncontrollably. I called 9-1-1, but by the time they arrived, John had left the planet. They said it was a heart attack. I can't help but think that maybe he picked his moment. He'd always been so active that the prospect of losing a leg may have seemed insurmountable. His doctor and I both suspected that a recommended colonoscopy would have revealed cancer, the Jenks family curse. Did he suspect that, too?

When we met—both in our twenties—John was convinced he wouldn't live past 30. Forty seven additional years—Seventy seven—was a triumph! We were part of the youth-worshipping, burn-out-like-a-flame, never-trust-anyone-over-thirty generation, but we stayed together for over fifty years and made it well into our seventies.

Now that he's gone, I sometimes reflect on what my life might have looked like without him. I'm fairly sure I would have been a puppet and doll-maker. I had made that decision by the time I met him. But a puppeteer? Deanne, the friend who helped me do my very first shows—and suggested the idea—was our neighbor when we lived in the house that belonged to John's uncles. Would I have started performing without her? She was the performer, not me. And Teri Jean: it was John who brought her into the fold and initiated our thirty-one-year partnership that influences my work to this day.

My beloved son? Would I have even had children? I certainly wouldn't be living in a log cabin in the woods, which has become a large part of my identity, connecting my old age with my childhood and the woods in our back yard. I wouldn't have bought a run-down building in West Liberty—not without a partner willing and able to renovate it—so Owl Glass Puppetry Center wouldn't exist. No West Liberty Children's Festival, no bilingual shows with Eli, no Stephanie living three blocks away. One step leads to another, winding through our lives. It's mind-boggling to try to walk the intertwining paths backwards, but one thing I know for sure: I miss John terribly, but his footprints are all over my life and my work.

21. Young Blood

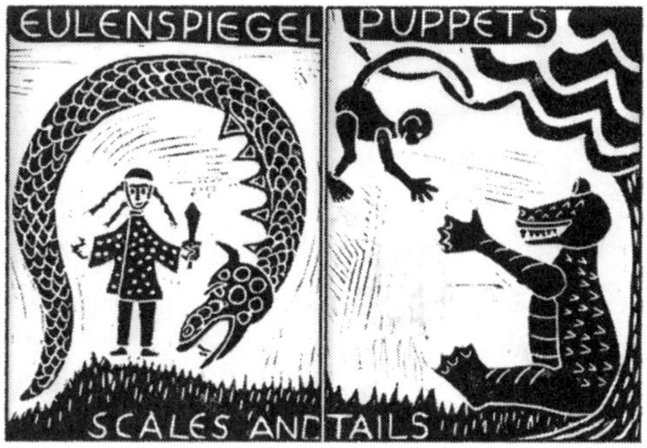

During the spring of 1998, my life and work meant taking care of Mutti and, after she died, working with my sister to go through her belongings and clean out her house.

"Anne, why don't we go to Germany together when this is all over?"

We left on our trip the following November. Our last stop was Hamburg, the home of several cousins. We drank strong coffee with evaporated milk and ate Streusel Kuchen—a buttery cake with a crumbly topping, not too sweet—tastes that always took me straight back to my Art Academy days.

"Isabel wants to study directing. She'd like to do a six-month internship with a theater company in the U.S. Would you happen to know of a company, Anne?" asked my cousin, guessing my New York City sister might have connections for her daughter.

"As a matter of fact, I do! It's a puppet theater company in Iowa, Eulenspiegel."

My cousins laughed sheepishly. Why hadn't this occurred to them? No matter. I was confident we could think of plenty of ways to keep Isabel busy. She arrived the following September.

Isabel was tall, brunette, and young. At 6'2", she made me look short. She had a quick smile, twinkling eyes, and a lively sense of humor. She was outgoing and immediately made friends with two West Liberty youth, a German exchange student and a young artist.

She arrived just in time to help with the West Liberty Children's Festival, the third one, and Puppets and Pastries Dessert Theatre for Adults, only the second one. It was still early days at Owl Glass Puppetry Center.

I was worried. Some of our fall work had fallen through, and I had no idea how we would keep this eager dynamo busy. She made a new portable shadow stage for us. She changed the window displays. It felt like busywork.

Then Old Creamery Theater called. They were a professional regional theater company located in the Amana Colonies, an hour from West Liberty.

"Teri Jean! Old Creamery wants us to do *A Christmas Carol* with them this year! They want the ghosts to be giant puppets, and they want us to work them for twenty-five shows!"

"That sounds exciting," said Teri Jean, "but we can't! We don't have a lot of gigs, but we have enough to interfere with that."

"There's gotta be a way! It would be so great for Isabel!"

"Wait!" said Teri Jean. "How about we build the puppets with Isabel's help and have her and Michael work them. He said he doesn't have much work. Jeez, he wouldn't be bothering with *puppet* shows if he had enough 'legitimate theater' gigs."

Michael was Michael Sokoloff, who had pulled our fat out of the fire with Sal Fink a couple of years earlier. He had directed another show or two since then and collaborated with us on Stravinsky's *Soldier's Tale* which we performed with the Des Moines Symphony that summer.

He loved the idea! He and Isabel connected immediately and developed a nice rapport on stage. They got along so well that he asked her to be his assistant director on an upcoming job for another theater.

The four of us visualized the puppets together. Isabel and I did most of the building, making frameworks out of wire and cardboard that we covered with layers of papier mâché, my preferred medium. Christmas past was an ethereal-looking figure with a flowing robe and a detached head that transformed from a face to a flame. Christmas present was ten to twelve feet tall, jovial looking. Buried in the folds of his robe were two small, desolate-looking figures, representing ignorance and want. The ghost of Christmas future was simply a large hand with a pointing index finger, gesturing toward the future and Scrooge's death unless he changed his ways. This project kept Isabel—and all of us—busy through December.

Then came the Global Volunteers! This organization sent volunteers all over the world to spend their vacations helping with local projects. At the suggestion of Iowa Governor Vilsack and his wife, Christie—who were members—they had chosen West Liberty as the low-income, diverse community for their "Millennial Project," to be completed during the last week of 1999.

West Liberty needed a volunteer project. We had plans with the young owner of the local movie theater, the New Strand. Built as an opera house in 1910, it became a movie theater in 1929 when a screen was installed. Wouldn't it be great to get a push-back screen so the stage could be cleared for puppet shows and the screen could be pulled forward for movies? Days before, the owner had told us about a portable screen he could buy for $4000.00. We agreed to kick in half if we could use the theater.

Mallory suggested a theater renovation as our volunteer project and offered to coordinate the volunteers. We were off! More work for Isabel. Tom and Christie Vilsack (they insisted they weren't Governor and Mrs. for the week!) drove over every day from their home in Mt. Pleasant, fifty miles south of us. Tom helped re-upholster seats while Christie scraped gum wads off the floor. We painted walls, cleaned, installed the screen, and repainted the decorative carvings around the proscenium arch. In January, we performed Stravinsky's *A Soldier's Tale*, the first live theater on that stage since 1929!

The day of the show was exciting! Local residents were thrilled to see a live show on the stage of their opera house. Students and professors in the music and drama departments at the University of Iowa decided it was "serious" enough to warrant their attendance. Best of all, an old woman who had—in years past—played piano for the silent movies there, attended with her son, the former janitor!

Isabel found lots of ways to keep busy. She kept our windows decorated with unemployed puppets from retired shows and kept the puppetry center tidy. With Teri Jean's teenage stepson, she painted the blemished wood floor barn red. She helped with our after-school Kids Club and served as our roadie whenever we took our shows on tour. She sharpened her directing skills by helping with our new show, *World Tales,* a collection of three stories—all existing in different versions in many cultures— from three distinct parts of the world.

The first one, *Tio Conejo (Uncle Rabbit) and the Hurricane,* came from Mexico. The second one: a new version of our much-loved *Fisherman and His Wife* from Germany. Lastly, *Li Chi Slays the Serpent* from China, one of the oldest recorded tales in the world and the first-ever with a female hero. I echoed folk art from the various countries in the puppet and set designs and made a fascinating observation. Folk art has similarities all over the world. Even the colors are similar with tonal differences. Mexican colors are bright and clear; central European tones are the same with a little subduing black mixed in. Chinese colors are bright and hot, almost neon.

When Isabel's six months were up, she took three glowing recommendations with her: from us, from Old Creamery, and from Michael. We missed our 6'2" "little girl", as Teri Jean loved calling her, looking up from her own 5'4" stature.

Ten years later it was time for another German intern. My Godchild Johanne from Berlin wanted to be an au pair and work on her English. I suggested she come to West Liberty, work on her Spanish and her English, and help with the puppet theater. One of our Board members stepped up. She could use help with her three young children, the oldest of whom was enrolled in the school's dual-language program, learning alternate days in English and Spanish. Her husband taught Spanish. They lived a few blocks from the puppetry center.

Johanne arrived. Average height with brown hair and a neat figure, her open face reflected those of her father and her aunts, the beloved cousin children I had delighted in visiting in East Berlin in my art academy days. Born in December 1990, she was our family's first "Reunification Baby."

By the time Johanne came in 2010, we were doing lots of community show residencies. Pam and I loved taking her along to help backstage or, in the case of a Mexican folktale, to be the second narrator, throwing in Spanish narration between my English.

Shortly before her time was up, I was invited to perform *Little Red Riding Hood* at a puppetry festival in Seattle. Why not drive cross country and give Johanne a tour of this vast landscape? To make it affordable and even more fun, I lined up shows at eleven libraries in Oregon for the week after the festival. Our friend Gretchen decided to come along for the ride and put herself in charge of food—mainly salads, my favorite—to eat in rest areas on the road.

We left at "early thirty" on Wednesday, July 28, with Little Red—all six inches of her—riding shotgun. Her pals were packed in their decorated suitcase, but Gretchen wanted to document our trip by photographing her at scenic places along the route and posting them on Facebook, still in its infancy. Spirits were high as we left West Liberty and headed north to Sioux Falls and west on Highway 92. When Little Red got hungry, we stopped at a rest area and made a huge salad with spring greens, cucumbers, peppers, tomatoes, and every other tasty morsel Gretchen had bought at our tiny farmers' market. We added a generous portion of blue cheese, a dollop of dressing, and feasted.

When we reached the badlands, Gretchen snapped Little Red gazing out over the scenic landscape. Of course, we had to stop at Wall Drug! This tourist trap was built in the 1930s and became famous—and wildly successful—by offering travelers a free glass of ice water. You can still get a glass of water, but you might be distracted by the wall-to-wall tchotchkes: mugs, shot glasses, t-shirts, perfume, homemade fudge, jackalope baseball caps! And speaking of jackalopes, there was a giant sculpture of one—a huge rabbit with antlers—in the courtyard. Johanne and Little Red had their picture taken riding on its back.

The next day we reached Montana and the headwaters of the Missouri River. Little Red dipped her toe in the water and smiled for the camera. We got to Seattle in time for the Friday night opening of the festival—held in a college—and headed for the dining hall, full of puppeteers, most of whom I knew.

"I always thought you were an anomaly," said Gretchen. "This place is full of people like you!"

On Monday morning, after the festival ended, we started down the Oregon coast, stopping at two libraries each day to perform for their Summer Reading Programs. We spent the evenings in a park next to our motel—a Motel Six in Albany, Oregon— relaxing and walking the park's trails.

On the last day, we had a tire blowout on the highway, a precursor of things to come. After changing to the spare, we went to a tire store and waited for our new tire. A grim-looking employee came out.

"Ma'am, I'm afraid your brakes are bad. We can replace them for you."

"No, thanks." I hadn't noticed any problem with the brakes.

We started home, and at the end of the second day, another tire looked bald. I pulled into a store, the same brand as the one that had replaced my blown-out tire. We found a nearby motel, checked in, and waited.

"Ma'am, I'm afraid your brakes are bad. We can replace them for you."

"No, thanks." This one wasn't taking no for an answer.

"Ma'am, these brakes won't last one hundred miles in these mountains! If you want to get home alive, you'd better have us replace them."

"I'll think about it and get back to you."

"I'm serious, Ma'am. I don't want to be responsible for your untimely death!"

I called my mechanic. He'd serviced the minivan—known as Vanna—before we left home.

"Mike," I said, "my tire blew, the second one. These mountains are really hard on them. Anyway, both shops have been telling me I need my brakes replaced. What do you think?"

A loud guffaw on the other end of the line. "They saw you coming, didn't they?"

"Really? That's why I'm calling."

"Your brakes are fine. That scam is as old as the hills."

We made it home without further incident. I dropped Gretchen and Johanne off, went home, gave John a hug, and got on the phone with the second shop.

"Hi. This is the person from Iowa whose tire you replaced. May I speak to the nice young man who waited on me and warned me about my brakes?"

"Sure! Gene, get on the phone!"

"Hello?"

"I drove another 1200 miles on those "bad" brakes, and they're still working just fine! Quit trying to take advantage of people, you scumbag! I slammed down the phone and grinned at John.

Early in 2012, I sat at my desk in the puppetry center updating finances when the door opened and a tall, thin young man walked in.

"Hi! Remember me? Justin? Justin Cornett?"

"Give me a hint!"

"I was working at Great Arizona Puppet Theater in 2004 when you and Teri Jean performed there. I'm moving to Iowa. I want to work for you!"

"Good luck," I said. "We can't afford to hire a puppeteer right now."

"Then I'll do what I did at Great Arizona! I'll hang around and volunteer. You'll figure out a way to hire me soon enough."

"Volunteers we can use! Welcome! As a matter of fact, we have a community show coming up. We're performing *Portraits of the Prairie* with local residents in a few weeks. We can definitely use you there!"

Justin was right. Before the year was half over our Outreach Director and I were figuring out ways to pay Justin for his work. He helped run our after-school puppet club. He did odd jobs around the center. I put him on the festival staff when we hosted the 2012 Great Plains Regional Puppetry Festival for Puppeteers of America. We dubbed the event The Great Plains Puppet Train with a nod to West Liberty's railroad history.

In the meantime, Angela Polowy had also started hanging around and helping out. We met her in 2010 when Pam Corcoran and a dancer friend brought their puppet/dance production, *The Pied Piper,* to present in West Liberty with our kids, adults, and dancers, our community show offering for the year.

The plan was hatched a year earlier. The dance studio up the street agreed that their teenage dancers would rehearse and perform while our after-school puppet group worked the puppets. We had a fourth-grade teacher on board; his class made masks and acted as the rats. I got a grant to pay for the residency.

Then, just two weeks before rehearsals were to start, all of the dancers pulled out. They had a conflict—a soccer game—the day of the show. We panicked! Beat by Youth Sports for the umpteenth time! It was the repetitive story of our work with kids—sports trumped everything.

There was no way to do the show without dancers. Our Outreach Director, Chris, had an idea. A second dance studio had recently opened across the street. The director specialized in young kids four to seven years old. We figured it was worth a try.

"What do you think?" Chris asked our neighboring dancer.

"I think it sounds like fun but, if the dances are choreographed for teenagers, my kids won't be able to do them."

"I'll tell you what. Why don't we put you two dancers in touch with each other and you can decide if it's feasible."

The visiting dancer found out what our local kids were capable of and re-choreographed the whole show. Whew!

We still needed a few adults—besides Johanne, who was eager to participate— to dance the parts of the mayor, his wife, a baker, a supplicant, and some townspeople. Chris's husband was the mayor of our town. It would be too perfect to have our mayor dance the part of the mayor of Hamelin! Only one problem: he had never danced. So, our dancer—seven months pregnant—taught him the dance and danced with him as the mayor's wife! We put out the call for other adults, and Gretchen agreed to be the baker.

"I'm bringing Angela along. She's new to town, but she's interested in puppets. She needs to get to know you," said Gretchen.

Angela did brilliantly in the part of the supplicant, throwing herself on the floor with outstretched hands in front of the mayor.

Soon she began coming over just to hang out. She talked about ideas and planned projects but seemed unable to go from A to B. I heard stories about her challenging childhood and her health problems and realized how lucky I was to have grown up healthy in a functional family. A year after The Pied Piper, Gretchen raised money to send her friend Angela to "puppet camp"—Puppetfest Midwest—with me in July of 2011.

Puppetfest Midwest was a weeklong, workshop-intensive puppetry festival in Missouri, created and sponsored by Peter and Debbie Allen of Parasol Puppets. Each attendee signed up for one workshop that met a total of twenty hours. I taught one of the workshops and Angela signed up for a different one. It was an eye-opening, life-changing event for her. She saw adults approaching puppetry as a serious art form and making a living at it. She realized I was part of a large community and not the oddity she had thought I was.

Over the next year, Angela worked hard to get her health in order. She still hung out with us and made friends with Justin.

"Monica, why don't you teach Angela and me one of the shows you and Teri Jean used to do?" asked Justin one day.

"Hmmm. That's an interesting idea! Which one, I wonder."

I realized I had a good recording of *Eulenspiegel's Circus*, the show we'd created with our intern Macy and later tweaked and reworked for two puppeteers, Teri Jean and me. It was imaginative and silly. I gave it to Justin and Angela to watch and designated Justin Head Puppeteer with instructions to work with Angela on puppet manipulation, his strong suit. I directed.

What fun to see different puppeteers bring new ideas and talents to the show that Teri Jean and I had so much fun with! I wished there were still programs like the Touring Arts Team and Iowa Arts Council-sponsored school residencies so Justin and Angela could be immersed the way we had been.

Well, there weren't, so maybe it was up to me to create one. In the summer of 2013, we organized our first Summer Neighborhood Tour. I raised money to cover over three-quarters of the cost, and we offered outdoor shows to neighborhood groups in low and middle-income neighborhoods for a tiny fee. The purpose—in addition to my goal of giving Justin and Angela numerous opportunities to perform *Eulenspiegel's Circus*—was to build community. The shows were snapped up by groups all over eastern Iowa. Some were official groups—neighborhood centers, lunch programs, and the like—and some were simply neighbors who got together to host an event.

After a couple of years, the City of Iowa City got on board and reserved a dozen of the available shows for their neighborhood parks. Volunteers in each neighborhood promoted and facilitated the events. It's a match made in heaven: the City gets popular events at a minimal cost and my booking chores are reduced to almost nothing!

The circus show, with Justin and Angela in tow, turned out to be a popular touring offering. They took it to the MacNider Museum in Mason City; to an international festival in Northwest Iowa; to the Smoky Hill River Festival and lots of other summer festivals. Justin built a solo show, *The Monkey and the Crocodile,* and Angela created a couple of short pieces for adults to perform at Puppet Slams.

It seemed as if I finally had a team!

Schulz here: Yep, you guys had a blast! It was fun watching you three work on Peter and the Wolf, playing with the puppets, dancing around to the music, and working in a scene with the frog, the rabbit, and the worm. You guys were barfing ideas! Oh, and the wolf you were working on; when you had it facing the door in your workshop! Haha! I watched you jump out of your pants every time you opened that door and saw it looking at you! What a hoot!

It didn't last, of course. Nothing does. In the spring of 2015, Justin moved to Texas. His ex-wife had moved there, and he wanted to be close to his son. He did his solo show at libraries all over the San Antonio area—as Eulenspiegel in Texas—and he still comes back to tour *Peter and the Wolf* and help with community shows. Still, the team was broken. Angela lasted two more years, but a large part of her mojo left with Justin.

She pulled up her socks and created a high-energy solo show, *Mother Goose's Neighborhood,* which she did for the 2016 Neighborhood Tour, but she didn't feel like touring anymore, so Eli learned her part in *Peter and the Wolf.* By the summer of 2017, she didn't feel like committing to the Neighborhood Tour.

I enlisted Buffy Quintero, who had grown up across the street from us and did her own puppet shows. She had a delightful show about Baba Yaga, the Russian witch, and she kept our Neighborhood Tour going that year and the following year, when she learned one of our shows, *The Lion in the Well.* I tried my best to hire her to replace Angela, but I couldn't lure her away from her first love, teaching art.

Just when I had about lost hope of ever finding a younger team, Stephanie walked in the door, but that's another chapter!

22. Stephanie Saves the Day

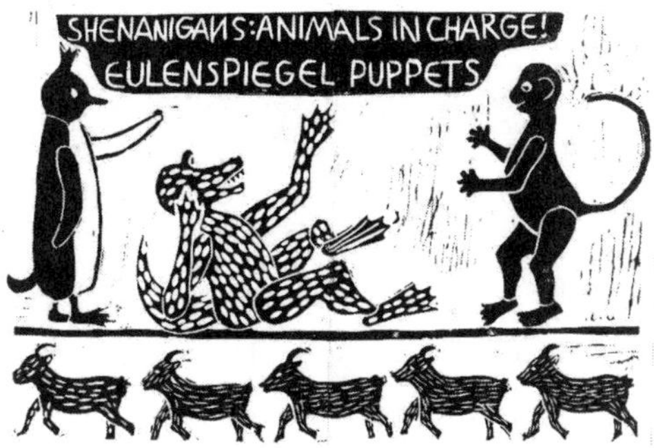

I've been lucky. The people I've worked with have all become good friends. One of these is Cara McFerren, who was our Outreach Director from 2011 to 2019.

It was November 2017, the day of West Liberty's annual downtown Holiday Stroll. All of the downtown businesses opened for the afternoon. A local grandfatherly sort played Santa Claus, carolers sang on the street corners, little girls in tutus entertained in the window of the dance studio, and smiling, red-cheeked loiterers consumed mountains of Christmas cookies and gallons of hot cider. Aromas of pine boughs and cinnamon filled the air. Everyone knew there would be a craft activity in the puppetry center, and families hurried in to make pop-up holiday cards.

A few days earlier, Cara had asked:

"Monica, how would you feel about my friend Stephanie selling some of her dolls and miniatures here during the open house?"

"Why not?" I said. 'Sounds like it would fit right in!"

I liked Stephanie Vallez immediately. She was tiny with long, blonde, curly hair. She'd acquired her Latino last name—and her young son—in a bygone marriage. She had a sharp wit tinged with sarcasm but leavened with cheerfulness. Her dolls and miniatures were clever—some a little dark—and irreverent. She wrote for the local paper and interviewed lots of our residents for the weekly rag. Even though she hadn't grown up in West Liberty, she had family history here and lived in the house her grandfather had left her.

Cara and her husband, Cliff, had opened a successful printing business a couple of years earlier, and Cara was busier and busier, working for the business, raising their son, and active on the City Council. It seemed natural to ask Stephanie to add a part-time job as Cara's assistant to her roster of part-time work.

As the months passed, Stephanie took over more and more of Cara's duties until, by the Children's Festival in September 2019, she had taken over, as Cara focused on her printing business. Stephanie was the perfect combination of relaxed and detail-oriented. She did all of the necessary contacting, volunteer coordination, and prep work so that she could relax and let the volunteers do their thing on the day of the festival. It was just as much work as ever, but Stephanie was able to do it without succumbing to undue stress.

Schulz here: She was cool as a cucumber. I couldn't believe it! I was expecting her to run around like a chicken with its head cut off, but she just strolled up and down the street, calmly answering questions and telling people to talk to the volunteer in charge. Wow!

When John and I decided to spend Christmas with Eli in Mexico, I realized I'd be gone for our annual winter break show.

"Shoot! I guess I'll have to cancel the winter break show. Too bad! It usually brings in a pretty good-sized audience."

"Don't you have a show you could teach me?" asked Stephanie.

"Hmm. I guess I could teach you *Puppet Potpourri*. It's fun. It's interactive. People love it. It wouldn't be too hard to learn."

Puppet Potpourri is a demonstration show that grew like a weed. It started informally, as Teri Jean demonstrated hand puppet movements and couldn't resist having her hand puppet do obnoxious things like farting, sneezing, volcanic snoring, and loud nose-blowing. Naturally, it was a hit. We added little guided vignettes that we did with volunteers from the audience. After Teri Jean quit, I crafted the demo and vignettes into an organized one-person show, adding shadow puppet and marionette segments as well as sound effect instruments worked by audience members. Stephanie learned it and performed it while I was in Mexico.

"Who's that new puppeteer you've got?" asked one of our long-time audience members when we met on the street.

"That's Stephanie, our Outreach Director."

"She's great. I hope you have her do some more shows. She had the audience eating out of her hand."

You'd think the penny would have dropped—I would have realized what I had— but I can be a little dense at times. I had already hired a young artist who was scheduled to move to West Liberty in January and learn puppetry. She was a talented visual artist with a delightful sense of whimsy and a love for kids. She was eager for the opportunity, and I thought she'd be a natural. In February, as we were getting ready for our annual *Puppets and Pastries: Dessert Theater for Adults,* I thought it would be fun to teach her a little vignette Teri Jean and I used to do with Schulz.

"I don't perform!" she said, so I did the vignette with Stephanie.

Boy, when I heard that, I knew we were in trouble! I kept trying to get your attention. I kept pointing at Stephanie and clearing my throat. You didn't hear me! How could you have not seen what was so clear to me!

Schulz is right; the penny still didn't drop. After all, my new hire had wanted to do this job badly enough to move from several states away. I got her started on the basics of developing a new show. Then John got sick. After going to one doctor's appointment after another, then spending every day in the hospital with him, I had little energy left for anything else. Who knows how things would have turned out if I had had the time and stamina I expected to have? But in the end, she moved on. It probably turned out just the way it was supposed to.

"I like to perform," said Stephanie.

"Oh. Of course. You and I can perform the election show." I replied.

I'm a member of our local LULAC (League of United Latin American Citizens) chapter. Since West Liberty has so many immigrant residents, voter registration is our biggest issue. One of the other members suggested a puppet show to teach kids the importance of voting.

"This is something I can wrap my brain around!" I said to Stephanie.

We began brainstorming ideas for a show. Worried about the 2020 election, we wanted kids to remind their parents to vote. I read every folktale I could find about how animals choose their leaders.

"We need two main issues, one for each side. Preferably things that aren't immediately identified with one party or the other," I said.

"Well, there's progress, development. That could go both ways," added Stephanie.

"If we do progress and development, we should counter it with environmentalism."

"But that's a Democratic issue!"

"It wasn't always. And it shouldn't be!" I insisted. "But which animals should we use? Wouldn't beaver be a good choice for development? He could build a huge beaver dam!"

"Turtles are one of the first creatures to suffer from polluted water."

"And I love turtles!"

"We need a reporter or a commentator." Stephanie looked around the center and fixed on one of our many owl images.

"Madame Owl! She could be a sort of Rachel Maddow. She could run her show from a treetop!"

We were off and running. We developed a story about an election for Leader of the Beasts and called it *The Big Election*. Benny Beaver wants to build the world's biggest beaver dam. Terry Turtle wants clean air, fresh water, and green growing trees. Madame Owl keeps abreast of what's going on and keeps us informed.

A colony of ants, a duck, a worm, and Mr. Bunny are peripheral characters, taking sides and moving the plot along.

After listening to campaign speeches and watching the antics of the various characters, the kids vote, marking actual ballots and donning "I voted" stickers. Mr. Bunny counts the votes. So far, Terry Turtle has won every election; it seems kids are environmentalists.

"We need a catchy song about voting," I said.

The next day I came into the puppetry center and checked the phone messages. I heard Stephanie's voice, singing a lively little tune:

Everyone gets a vote
Everyone gets a choice.
However big or small you are
You've got an equal voice.

Whether you're rich or poor
Everyone has a say
We decide our destiny together on election day.

The penny finally dropped! This woman, thirty-plus years younger than me, who just happened to live three blocks from the puppetry center, had every skill—and the desire—to be an excellent puppeteer.

She and I discovered that we have good chemistry onstage. We enjoy performing together and audiences seem to delight in watching. We added live clarinet—Stephanie's instrument—to *The Big Election* and took it all over Iowa, performing it for 4000 kids during the next nine months.

Working on this show kept me afloat after John died. Some people process grief by taking time to think and rest. I need productive activity. Instead of dwelling on the emptiness of my house, I spent my evenings in my workshop, building Benny Beaver, Terry Turtle, Duck, Worm, and a host of ants. My bonus daughter—a treasured neighbor who treats me like a beloved relative—stopped over regularly to check on me and admire Benny and Terry. Life began to seem normal again. And then…

Lockdown!

On March 13, 2020, we got the news. Due to the Covid 19 pandemic, schools would not reopen after the following week's spring break. The phone rang. The emails poured in. One cancellation after another. First March shows, then April and May, then summer, and before we knew it every live show for the rest of the year had been canceled. It was time to regroup.

"Well, Stephanie. We may as well work on new shows. With any luck, we'll be able to perform them sooner or later."

Stephanie dug into *Kate Shelley's Train Rescue*, a show she'd started about the legendary Iowa teenager who saved a train from plunging into Honey Creek in the 1880s. She decided to create a pop-up book stage and tell the whole story, beginning with Kate's parents' immigration from Ireland and the long journey across the ocean and overland to Boone County, Iowa.

I decided to work on a three-part show, *Magical Fish and Mermaids*. It was my third version of *The Fisherman and His Wife*, coupled with a Canadian folktale about a canning factory, a little girl who wants to be a mermaid, and a plethora of different kinds of fish. I joined the two stories with a cranky—a long illustrated scroll wound onto two spools and loaded into a box with a viewing window. I sing a folksong, *The Eddystone Light,* as I crank the scroll to show the illustrations.

I hadn't been home this much in decades. Between working on the show, I took long walks in the woods with Miss Kitty. Within less than a year, I had lost John, then Eli, then all of my work. I think I would have sunk into a deep depression without the artistic outlet of the show I built. I've learned—to keep my spirits up—that I need to work on something creative every single day.

When it became increasingly obvious that we were in for a long haul, we realized that we would need all the ingenuity we could muster to get through.

We bought a webcam and took turns making how-to videos for the kids we would have been working with in better times. We agreed we would only use materials they were likely to have at home and only show them things they could do without adult supervision. Stephanie started by showing them how to make their own anti-covid masks. I showed them how to make a shadow puppet stage out of a cardboard box and a piece of computer paper and puppets out of cereal boxes. Stephanie showed them how to make a cranky out of a cereal box and two pencils. I showed them how to put on a puppet show using kitchen utensils—corkscrews, whisks, egg slicers, and more—as characters.

"Grrr!" said the kitchen tong in the role of an alligator with a snapping jaw. The garlic press—acting as a drawbridge—came down on top of the alligator, stopping it in its tracks. The corkscrew rushed over, flapping its arms and yelling. The whisk fluttered by and told them to quiet down.

We loaded the videos onto YouTube and put the links on the school website.

We added links to videos of some of our favorite shows so the kids could watch them at home. We knew they were preferable live, but we were in "better than nothing" territory.

With summer approaching, we got a Zoom account and designed a three-part shadow puppet workshop which we presented through the local library and later through an area art museum. The first session was devoted to writing stories; the second to making a stage and puppets; and the third to performing for each other. I was gratified at how well it worked over Zoom: I could hold my example close to the camera to increase visibility and we could see clearly what the kids were doing. An unexpected bonus: we had participants from afar, including my great nephew in British Columbia, whom I met for the first time on the computer screen.

Buoyed by the summer workshops, I agreed to do zoom workshops for two West Coast puppetry guilds. The San Francisco Guild and the Puppetry Guild of Puget Sound wanted to learn my techniques for building pop-up book stages. The San Francisco folks decided they also needed to learn how to make the miniature rod marionettes I use in most of those shows. It was a treat to see so many faces I knew on the computer screen.

As luck would have it, two young men opened a video studio in West Liberty. They recorded and live-streamed shows for us so we could still provide programming to our audiences.

We missed performing live, so we decided to take a leaf out of the book of our colleagues at Great Arizona Puppets. They had been doing drive-in shows since lockdown.

"What a great idea!" said Stephanie. "Let's get to work! What's our story?"

The next morning, I was listening to public radio—as I always do—when I heard a report of an alligator seen cruising a deserted shopping mall in Myrtle Beach.

"That's it!" I exulted.

Stephanie and I researched other tales of animal activities during lockdown when humans had seemed to magically disappear. We read about city monkeys brawling with Temple monkeys over a yogurt cup; penguins touring an art museum; geese strolling down the Las Vegas strip. On top of that, all sorts of wild goats were stampeding city streets all over the world. We added a healthy dose of fantasy and a giant Mother Earth puppet, who entered, singing Stephanie's words:

I am land and sky and sea, the sun that shines, the storms that rage
You may call me Mother Earth, and I look real good for my age.
During the pandemic, humans stayed at home
With no one there to spook them, the animals started to roam.
Mountain lions sleep in my trees in downtown Denver.
In San Francisco, coyotes hope you'll stay inside forever.
There are gators in the shopping mall, goats graze in the park.
Penguins roam museums, raccoons don't wait till dark.
Geese enjoy the neon lights on the Las Vegas strip.
Monkeys bored without tourists decide to take a trip.
Wild boars stampede the streets in downtown Barcelona.
Fish swim in Venice canals all because of corona.
So while you're isolated my friends are roaming free.
When this ends take care of them, and please take care of me."

We asked our musician friend, Laura Kittrell, to write a melody for Mother Earth and add a musical score on the keyboard.

At the advice of our friends at Great Arizona, we made the puppets large—at least two feet tall—and made sure the playboard—the puppet floor—was six feet off the ground. The final scene was with shadow puppets. Cara came back into the fold to paint the shadow scenes, which we showed with an overhead projector. The show started at sundown when the sky was still light. Gradually the sky darkened, and when total blackness descended, we turned off the stage lights and turned on the overhead projector for the last scene. We called it *Shenanigans: Animals in Charge!*

We bought a transmitter—one of our techie friends taught us how to use it—so we could broadcast the show into the car radios of the three rows of cars with excellent visibility. Our friend Bonnie joined our team and took charge of parking and sound transmission. We got a grant to tour the show so we could offer it at a bargain price. In September and

October 2020, we performed it fifteen times all over eastern Iowa. That time glows in my memory as a magical interlude.

When winter set in, we needed something else to fuel our creativity. The Cedar Rapids Opera contacted us. They realized they couldn't send singers into the elementary schools for a show as they usually did. They asked us to create a puppet show using the soundtrack of their singers, and we built puppets, props, and scenery for *The Enchanted Forest.*

It was not an opera in the usual sense. It combined the music, especially the familiar arias, of several operas in a new story designed for children. I made hand puppets of two of the main characters and rod puppets of the others to accommodate for the height difference between Stephanie and me. I worked the hand puppets at a comfortable height. Stephanie—eight inches shorter—worked the rod puppets, holding them up to the height of my hand puppets. My experience working with Ron—the musician—and learning ways to fill long musical passages with interesting movement and visuals, came in handy as we choreographed the arias. We added rod puppet squirrels that scampered around the forest. We liked them so much we decided we'd find a place for them in our next show. When the script called for a forest fire, we tie-dyed silk in orange and yellow, attached the pieces to rods, and whipped the silk fires around the trees. We added some shadow puppet scenes for variety. We asked our Wisconsin friend Pam, the puppeteer who's done so many residencies with me, to direct the show over Zoom. When we were finished, the Opera filmed the show and sent it to all of the elementary schools in their district.

Next the Muscatine Art Center asked us to film some vignettes for their virtual Noon Year's Eve, using puppets that we made for them a few years earlier. The Art Center had several Chagalls in their collection, and we had built a stage and created puppets inspired by Chagall's work. We'd made a cello-playing goat, a red angel, a flying fish, a cat person in shades of brown and gold, humans with green, blue, or red skin, and many more. Stephanie wrote scenes taken from Chagall's life. We staged them, and the art center filmed.

And so, in late 2021, we're making it through the pandemic which, at this writing, is still raging. We're all vaccinated, so we have a bit more freedom. The littles are starting to get the vaccine, and the schools are beginning to open to us. Luckily, unlike many of my puppeteer friends, I've always enjoyed performing outdoors. We've done scores of outdoor shows, including our newest, yet another adaptation of *The Bremen Town Musicians* with live music by our friend Laura. It's large and tall enough to be a drive-in show, should that be necessary. True to our intent, we found a place for the squirrels. Now they lure Mistress Cat into a tree where she sings a mournful song, yammering about being stuck in the treetop. We're even doing fresh air shows for school field trips, regaining the pleasure of elementary school audiences.

Being the optimist I am—I've often been accused of being a Pollyanna—I try to find the silver lining. There are more than you might think: new audiences from all over the world, new creative challenges, and more time to reflect and enjoy nature. But the biggest silver lining has been bonding with Stephanie in new and unexpected ways.

The other day one of my longtime puppeteer friends saw Stephanie and me perform *The Bremen Town Musicians*. Her comment, after remarking how much fun we seemed to be having:

"I think Teri Jean sent Stephanie."

Afterword—The Wheel Turns

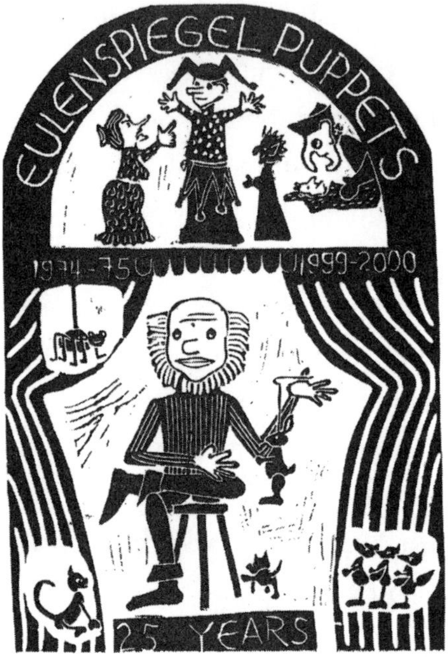

I've passed my double seven birthday. By the time you read this, I will be flirting with the big 8-0. I'm the same age my mother was when she made the first of two copper relief doors for the main entrances of Wartburg Seminary in Dubuque, Iowa. One illustrated Matthew 25:35 & 36 with 6 relief panels:

for I was hungry, and you gave me food; I was thirsty and you gave me drink; I was a stranger and you took me in; I was naked and you clothed me; I was sick and you visited me; I was in prison and you came to me.

She made the second one, two large angels when she was in her eighties. At age 96, when she died, she left an unfinished relief in her workshop. She told me her secret to a happy and productive old age: surround yourself with young people. She is my role model.

I began writing this book two years ago when we were still deep in the throes of the pandemic before the first vaccine was approved. Two years later, we're still not free and clear, but life seems much more normal. We're back in the schools. We're even hosting another regional puppetry festival, but attendance is down. People are still nervous about large group activities. Some lost so much work during the pandemic that they can't afford to attend.

We've discovered how much the community values us through their expressions of concern and unsolicited donations.

"We want you to survive…and thrive." several people said as they dropped off checks.

I felt my focus changing. Maybe it was time to lean into activities at home and put less emphasis on touring to faraway places, time to make sure this center survives me.

"Do you want to keep doing this after I croak?" I asked Stephanie.

"You're not planning on croaking anytime soon, are you?" she asked.

"No, but I will—someday—and you're thirty-some years younger than me."

"I do," she said, so I guess Owl Glass will be here after I'm gone.

In October, 2021, when we hired an Outreach Director, we chose Christopher Eck because his style and energy seemed to mesh with ours, but also because of his interest in bringing back the Young Puppeteers Festival, another way to strengthen our local presence. Almost a year later, our choice is confirmed daily as we work together to create puppet camps, new school projects, local events and soon a renewed Young Puppeteers Festival.

Things keep changing even as I write. Since I started this project, Ron has retired. I'm deciding which of the shows we did together need a second chance with another musician and which ones can retire into the virtual world. *Appleseed!*, the last show we created together shortly before the pandemic, is not ready to follow Ron into retirement. Johnny and the other apple heroes the story chronicles now perform to the stylings of young musician Alex Flesher.

The wheel turns.

Just days ago, during the regional puppetry festival, the audience filled the bleachers in Ron-de-Voo Park, our little downtown greenspace with a stage and seating. Stephanie took the microphone to begin our annual late-night puppet slam for teens and adults. I had no idea what was coming.

"Usually, when I start a show, I say 'Good evening, Ladies and Jellybeans, my name is Stephanie Schmephanie and I'll be your puppeteer this evening.' Tonight, I have something else in mind"

She went on to reveal that she, Chris, and others, including our recently deceased puppeteer friend from St. Louis, had petitioned the city to do something special in this little park. Stephanie knew I was part of the group that originally decided to turn a downtown trash hole into a lovely performing space. That I headed the committee hiring musicians to play there every Friday night each August. That I co-founded the Children's Festival and turned the stage into a destination for regional puppeteers. And that I insisted on scheduling a full performing season there—instead of indoors—during the pandemic. She thought the stage should belong to me, and she convinced enough locals to achieve her goal.

"And now, it's time for the unveiling," she said as she removed a cloth covering a plaque installed in the ground next to the stage.

"This stage is dedicated to Monica Leo for her commitment to the arts. 2022"

I was stunned, deeply moved, and embarrassed.

Schulz here: That figures. You puppeteers! "Don't look at me; look at my puppet!" I suppose you would have been comfier if they had put my name on the plaque instead of yours! Just say thank you, for pity's sake!"

I'm excited about a project I've wanted to do for decades. Buxton was a coal mining town in southern Iowa. For 25 years, it was a town like no other, 100% egalitarian, with as many Blacks as whites in mine management and professional life. The neighborhoods and all facilities were integrated. The town died when the mine played out. I never put this into a show because it seemed inappropriate for a 100% white puppet theater. Then I met African American historian Rachelle Chase, who moved to Iowa to study this town. I reconnected with musician Dartanyan Brown from Touring Arts Team days and learned that his grandma was a schoolgirl in Buxton. They signed on, we developed a show, and *Remembering Buxton* is touring around the state. It seems like the perfect hopeful story for our time.

I hope to have many more interesting projects before I put my puppets down for good.

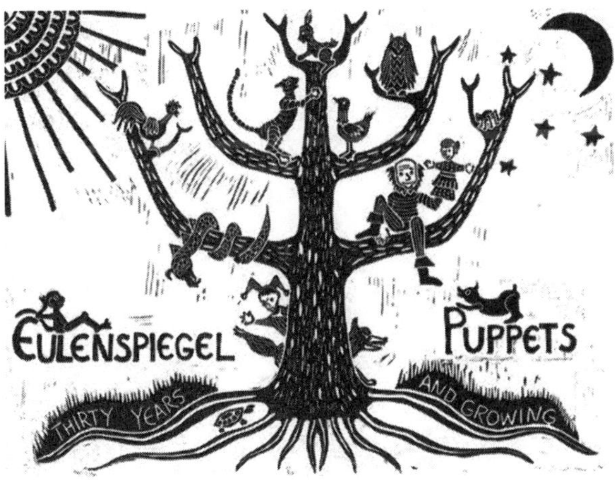

With heartfelt thanks to all who have traveled the
Eulenspiegel path with me, some briefly and
some for years, even decades:
In more-or-less chronological order:

Deanne Wortman
Jenean Arnold
Teri Jean Breitbach
Marilyn Levin
Sandra Quintero
Guy Drollinger
Joe Taschetta
Rip Russell
Ron Hillis
Peggy Fitzgerald
Macy Matarazzo
Michael Sokoloff
Isabel Malsch
Mallory Smith
Duffy DeFrance
Sue Drollinger
Chris Martin
Linley Heath
Johanne Groß
Cara McFerren
Lauren Haldeman
Mary Swander
Pam Corcoran
Eli Portugal
Justin Cornett
Angela Polowy
Buffy Quintero
Gretchen Little
Donna Janosik
Stephanie Vallez
Christopher Eck
Alex Flesher
Laura Kittrell
Bonnie Hamlin
Rachelle Chase
Dartanyan Brown

Special thanks to Mary Swander for guiding me along the memoir path and to my writing group: Jean Graham, Jane Yoder-Short, and Rockie Lyons Beaman. Thanks to Steve Semken and the Ice Cube Press for taking a chance on my story.

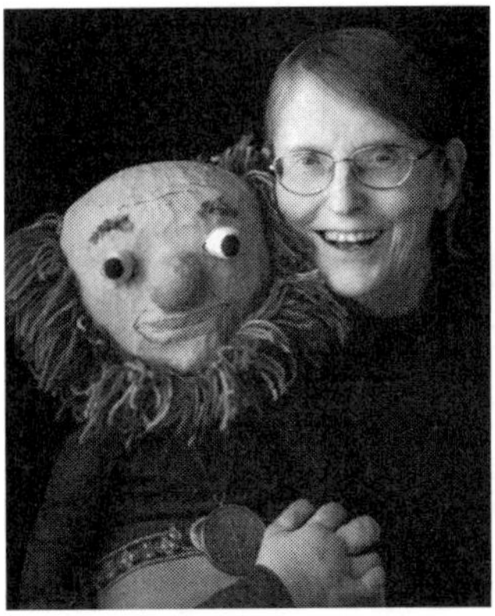

Monica Leo (Shown with co-author Schulz) is a first generation American, born to German refugees in the waning days of World War Two. After the war, her parents ordered a set of Kasperle hand puppets from a German craftswoman, and Monica was hooked. Since 1975, she has been creating and performing as founder and principal puppeteer of Eulenspiegel Puppet Theatre, which has been a featured performer at numerous national and regional Puppeteers of America festivals, as well as national and international festivals in Germany, the Czech Republic, Austria, and Japan. Eulenspiegel's home is Owl Glass Puppetry Center, a tiny center in the small town of West Liberty, Iowa.

Monica also creates block prints and writes the "Scene Between" column for *The Puppetry Journal*. She lives in a log cabin in the woods in rural Iowa City built by her late carpenter husband, John Jenks.

The Ice Cube Press began publishing in 1991 to focus on how to live with the natural world and to better understand how people can best live together in the communities they share and inhabit. Using the literary arts to explore life and experiences in the heartland of the United States we have been recognized by a number of well-known writers including: Bill Bradley, Gary Snyder, Gene Logsdon, Wes Jackson, Patricia Hampl, Greg Brown, Jim Harrison, Annie Dillard, Ken Burns, Roz Chast, Jane Hamilton, Daniel Menaker, Kathleen Norris, Janisse Ray, Craig Lesley, Alison Deming, Harriet Lerner, Richard Lynn Stegner, Richard Rhodes, Michael Pollan, David Abram, David Orr, Scott Russell Sanders, Barry Lopez and so many others. We've published a number of well-known authors including: Mary Swander, Jim Heynen, Mary Pipher, Bill Holm, Connie Mutel, John T. Price, Carol Bly, Marvin Bell, Debra Marquart, Ted Kooser, Stephanie Mills, Bill McKibben, Craig Lesley, Elizabeth McCracken, Derrick Jensen, Dean Bakopoulos, Rick Bass, Linda Hogan, Pam Houston, Paul Gruchow, Bill Moyers and on and on. Check out Ice Cube Press books on our web site, join our email list, Facebook group, or follow us on Twitter(X). Visit booksellers, museum shops, or any place you can find good books and support our truly honest-to-goodness independent publishing projects so you can discover why we continue striving to hear the other side.

Ice Cube Press, LLC (Est. 1991)
North Liberty, Iowa, Midwest, USA
Resting above the Silurian and Jordan aquifers
steve@icecubepress.com
Check us out on Twitter (X) and Facebook.
order directly at www.icecubepress.com

Celebrating Thirty-Three Years of Independent Publishing.
2023 Iowa Governor's Art Award | MIPA Gold Award 2023.

To Fenna Marie, MSW
those all-time
great puppet shows
you had in the doorway
and the life you live
now. It's all a grand performance!